CLIMBING OLYMPUS

Kevin J. Anderson is a prolific author. He has written the highly successful *Star Wars* novels, the *Young Jedi Knights* series and other illustrated *Star Wars* titles. He has also written fantasy novels, a host of short stories and articles, and is author of the bestselling X-Files novels *Ground Zero* and *Ruins*. To add to his credits, he has also been nominated for the Nebula Award and the Bram Stoker Award. He lives in the USA.

Voyager

KEVIN J. ANDERSON

Climbing Olympus

HarperCollins*Publishers*

Voyager
An Imprint of HarperCollins*Publishers*
77–85 Fulham Palace Road,
Hammersmith, London W6 8JB

The *Voyager* World Wide Web site address is
http://www.harpercollins.co.uk/voyager

A *Voyager* Paperback Original 1997
1 3 5 7 9 8 6 4 2

A portion of this novel appeared in *Full Spectrum IV*
as the short story 'Human, Martian – One, Two, three'.

A catalogue record for this book
is available from the British Library

ISBN 0 00 648305 4

Set in Century Old Style

Printed and bound in Great Britain by
Caledonian International Book Manufacturing Ltd, Glasgow

To
DOUG BEASON,
who has collaborated with me on many books
and *still* remains one of my best friends.
Imagine that . . .

Acknowledgements

I would like to thank Henry W. Stratmann, M.D., for his extremely thorough and helpful medical advice in designing the *adin* and *dua* adaptations, as well as suggestions on how the human body is affected by various changes in atmospheric pressure; if some of the medical details are incorrect, those errors are mine . . . but there would have been a great many more without Dr. Stratmann's help. I would also like to thank SSGT D.W. Etchison and Karen Anderson for their assistance with some of the Russian words, Frederik Pohl for *Man Plus*, my writer's workshop (Clare Bell, M. Coleman Easton, dan'l danehy-oakes, Michael Paul Meltzer, Michael Berch, Gary W. Shockley, Lori Ann White, and Avis Minger), Dave Wolverton, Daniel Keys Moran, and my Editor Betsy Mitchell for many helpful comments and suggestions. And particular thanks to my parents, my-in-laws, and especially to my wife Rebecca Moesta Anderson for their love, support, and encouragement in this and all my other books.

Bend your heart, proud man,
And bow your pride before all.
Bend your head, insignificant man,
And suffer on Earth before all.

PUSHKIN

When the heart is bleeding, only home does not
disappoint us.

RUSSIAN PEASANT SONG

It is easy to start a revolution in a country like this.
It is easier than picking up a pen.

VLADIMIR ILITCH LENIN

RACHEL DYCEK

UNDER A SALMON SKY, the rover vehicle crawled over the rise, looking down into the cracked canyons of Mars. Without a pause, the rover descended a tortuous path into the gorge, feeling its way with a thousand sea-urchin footpads.

The site of the old disaster lay like a broken scab: fallen rock, eroded fissures, and utter silence.

Alone in the vehicle, Commissioner Rachel Dycek held a cold breath as she looked through the windowport at the debris crumbled at the bottom of the toppled cliffside. The avalanche had been enormous, wiping out all thirty-one of the *dva* workers who had been tunneling into the canyon network of Noctis Labyrinthus, the "Labyrinth of Night."

Around Rachel, the wreckage still appeared fresh and jagged. Even after a full Earth year, the pain burned inside her. Another loss, the largest link in a long chain of disappointments, against which she had kept her face of stone. Russians were good at enduring, but inside she felt as fragile as stained glass.

The weathered rock walls of Noctis Labyrinthus formed barriers of reddish oxides, gray silicates, and black lava debris—all sliced a kilometer deep by ancient rivers. For millions of years, the entire planet had barely changed. But now, after six decades of terraforming activities had bombarded the planet with comets and seeded its atmosphere with innumerable strains of algae and free-floating plankton, Mars looked raw. The terraforming had awakened the planet like a slap in the face—and occasionally Mars lashed back, as it had with the avalanche.

The rover's engines hummed, and the telescoping sea-urchin feet underneath made popcorn-popping sounds as the pressurized vehicle scrambled effortlessly over the rough terrain. Letting the Artificial Intelligence navigator pick its best path, Rachel brought the rover *Percival* to a halt next to a stack of granite boulders. Back at Lowell Base, operations manager Bruce Vickery had reserved *Percival* for later in the day to check his remotely placed instruments, but Rachel had traveled only a hundred kilometers. She had hours yet before she needed to worry about getting back.

Alone in this desolate spot, Rachel felt as if she were entering a haunted house. She listened to the intense, peaceful emptiness. Then she began working her way into the protective environment suit. The slick fabric was cold. The chill never went away on Mars—but it slithered up her legs, hugged her waist and shoulders, and clung to the damp sweat of her hands as she worked her fingers into the tough gloves. It took her fifteen minutes, but Rachel was accustomed to suiting up by herself; she didn't like the interference of too many hands.

Technically, she was not supposed to be out in the rover by herself, but Rachel was still commissioner of Lowell Base—for the moment, anyway—and she could bend the rules. She had logged her intentions on the vehicle assignment terminal as "historical research." Duration of outside activity: half a sol (which was the correct term for a Martian day, though the fifty human colonists at the base simply called them "days"). And she had set out across the sprawling wilderness by herself, leaving Lowell Base behind.

Rachel sealed the suit and powered it up. A thin hiss echoed in her ear, and the stale metallic smell of manufactured air spilled into her nostrils. Pressurized, the suit puffed up, pushing the fabric of the suit away from her skin and making her feel less confined. The oxygen regenerator on her back burbled as its chemicals reacted to make air thick enough for her to breathe.

Lowell Base environment suits were lighter, more streamlined than the bulky monstrosities the original visitors to Mars had been forced to wear. After many decades of terraforming, Mars was more hospitable to human life, nearly as pleasant as the worst day she had lived through in Siberia.

Rachel clambered through *Percival*'s sphincter airlock and stepped out onto the powdery red dirt of Mars. With a crackle like wadded tissue paper, the cold wrapped around her body, and she turned up the suit's embedded heaters so that she could stand tall.

On the eve of her forced return to Earth, Rachel Dycek felt a profound sense of displacement. But she wanted to return to this place one last time, to see her shattered expectations, to see the buried dreams of Dmitri Pchanskii and his *dva* group who had given up everything for Mars, even their lives.

One Earth year ago today, a team of surgically augmented humans, the *dvas*, had been mining the labyrinth, using explosives to uncover channels of primordial ice. The blasting brought down a huge section of the canyon wall, burying everything beyond hope of recovery. . . .

Standing next to the rover, Rachel felt the weak but insistent wind push against her suit. Rust powder gusted into the air in tiny whirlwinds. She had been on Mars for a decade now, and she no longer felt light and springy on her feet. The red canyons, the extinct volcanoes, the growing tendrils of green in sheltered areas, no longer awed her. She had lost the energy for enthusiasm.

Rachel picked her way into the rubble, half expecting to hear some sound, some echo of the rocks crashing down into the gorge . . . the screams of dying *dvas*, pitched high in the thin air. All the tracks from the Lowell Base rescue missions and search parties had long ago been wiped away by storms and sifting microfine dust. Nothing left, just dreams.

In one wash of sloughing boulders that fell slowly in the low gravity, but with just as much mass and just as much inertia, thirty-one of Rachel's best *dvas* were lost—a sixth of their population. Rachel could not understand why her augmented human beings had been fated to suffer such disasters.

The *dvas*, an English bastardization of the Russian word for "two," were the second and most successful phase of humans surgically altered to live in the rigorous Martian environment. Performed under the bright lights of world scrutiny, the *dva* surgery had been much more successful than the great gamble of the *adin*, Rachel's secret initial phase.

The *dva* volunteers had been willing individuals, rather than subjects pulled from Siberian labor camps. The first three shipments of *dvas* were tough and dedicated workers, while the fourth group of fifty were true jewels, members of the intelligentsia who had volunteered for the augmentation surgery because they considered it their duty to the human race. A brilliant flash of glory, now smothered forever.

Dr. Dmitri Pchanskii himself, a talented Belorussian obstetrician and surgeon, had set an example as the leader of the fourth group of *dvas*. Watching his outspoken commitment, other medical professionals and scientists volunteered for the extreme surgery, with the justification that becoming a *dva* would be the best way to do research on an alien world. After the surgeries, they could be part of the environment, studying Mars hands-on, the same way field researchers studied Earth.

Firebrand legal representatives for the *dvas* had even demanded of the UN that their clients actually "own" the land they worked, not just receive lifelong leases. A Volga German lawyer named Rotlein had played on public sympathies—everyone admired the *dva* bravery, especially after learning of the horrors that had befallen the *adin* phase. Why not throw the *dvas* a bone? The *dvas* would probably not live long in such a harsh environment anyway. . . .

For a time, the *dva* project appeared to be a complete success. Over the years, the *dvas* had received

4

enormous, robotically piloted shipments containing the modules for Lowell Base and the four other human bases scattered across the surface of Mars. Before the first unmodified humans arrived to stay, the *dvas* completed all the prep work, like servants sent ahead to prepare the master's room. Three years after the last *dva* landing, Rachel and fifty others arrived at Lowell Base to prepare for the "Grand Opening" of a terraformed Mars.

But, when a project was as large as an entire planet, the work never ended. Pchanskii's team of *dvas* had been searching for subterranean water in Noctis Labyrinthus. But Pchanskii had been a surgeon on Earth, not a geologist or a construction engineer. He had not understood what he was doing when he blasted the fragile rocks.

When Lowell Base received no progress reports from them for several days, and with a large seasonal dust storm approaching, Rachel had dispatched a search team. She herself had rushed out on the rescue mission, as others watched the green-and-pink skies thicken with approaching waves of dust. Rachel had stared at the fallen rocks, the sheared-off cliffs, and the fine dust that refused to settle, whipped back into the air by precursor gusts of wind.

As much as a week could have gone by since the collapse; little wonder they found no survivors, no sign at all.

With grim irony, Pchanskii's avalanche had exposed a rich vein of water ice that looked like a steaming white gash on the rock. It created a thick, temporary fog in the canyons as the ice sublimed in the thin air. . . .

The weather satellites politely advised everyone to take shelter at the base and ride out the storm. The rescue team, unable to recover *dva* bodies or precious equipment from under tons and tons of rock, was forced back to the base. Later, after the abrasion from the month-long storm, there had been little point in even looking.

Pchanskii's group had been swallowed up by the tumbling walls of rock, but Rachel was left to face the avalanche of recriminations, and "I-told-you-so"s, and the sadly shaking heads. She had endured it, barely flinching, with no more than a tic in the right eye and a grim twitch at the corner of her wide mouth.

She could no longer deny that the entire *dva* project, her brainchild, was at an end, with only a few messy loose ends to tie up: 150 *dvas* still toiling on the surface of Mars, while spacesuited humans plowed ahead with their own work. In a few more decades, neither surgical augmentations nor environmental suits would be necessary to survive in the cold, brittle atmosphere. The remaining *dvas* were obsolete, the program a dead end, and they would live out their lives on Mars with no hope of returning to Earth.

Now, Rachel's decade as commissioner seemed like such a grand folly. She stared at the motionless rubble in the canyon and listened to the whispers of wind and the burbling of her air-regeneration system.

In the first launch opportunity from Earth after the *dva* disaster, the UN Space Agency had dispatched a new commissioner along with a dozen more mission members assigned to Lowell Base. Jesús Keefer, her replacement, would arrive tomorrow. The Mars transfer vehicle was already in orbit. She craned her neck, looked through her polarized faceplate up into the frigid sky that sometimes showed a few bright stars even during daytime when the dust or the algae clouds weren't too thick; but she saw no sign of the orbiter.

She stayed at Noctis Labyrinthus for a few useless and depressing hours. Finally, leaving the wreckage behind with the wreckage of her *dvas'* future, Rachel returned to the rover, brushing the clinging dust from her thermal suit.

She should get back to the base and put her things in order.

JESÚS KEEFER

THE MARS TRANSPORT SLID into high orbit as if with an exhausted sigh after the long marathon across interplanetary space. Then, in a leisurely manner over the next two days, the captain damped velocity to shrink and circularize the orbit in preparation for deploying the lander to the surface of Mars.

During the final weeks of the slow approach, Jesús Keefer ran thin fingers through his neat, dark hair and watched the planet's disk grow larger. Though the ground-based sensors indicated phenomenal improvement in the Martian environment, sixty years of aggressive terraforming had left little to be seen from this high up. It seemed disappointing, belittling the extensive efforts of mankind. But then, Mars was a big place.

Finally, Keefer distinguished a tinge of green through the on-board telescopes, a smear of murkiness in one of the deep canyons, which he insisted on showing to Tam Smith, the young agronomist, and Chetwynd, and Ogawa, and Shen, and any of the other passengers bound for Lowell Base. Everyone quickly learned to avoid him when his enthusiasm began to get out of control.

The terraforming process was working, by God, and it shored up his faith in the slow, long-term project. He cracked his knuckles and grinned like a kid in the small lounge. So much more exhilarating to see the awakening planet with his own eyes, rather than just viewing status reports and videobursts from the five UN bases on the surface.

Inside the cramped-but-tolerable craft that had been their home for four months, Keefer felt the tug of shifting forces as another short engine burn diverted the craft into parking orbit. Captain Rubens announced over the intercom that orbital insertion was successful. The Mars-bound people in the lounge cheered.

Though the view had changed little over the past few days, suddenly everybody hurried to the lounge viewport. Ogawa and Shen, Chetwynd, and Tam each took turns to gawk, silently jockeying to keep Commissioner Keefer last in line, since he had already spent more than his share of time at the observation scopes.

Keefer simply sat back in his webbed relaxation seat with an inward smile, feeling at peace.

Mars. At last.

He had been only twenty-eight when he had begun working with the United Nations Space Agency on the terraforming efforts. He had served with the ground support staff on Earth, watching the first manned landing in many years. The small multinational team of explorers had collected geological samples, taken data on how much hydrated water in the rocks was boiling out and how much permafrost was thawing and oozing into the soil to chart the progress of the terraforming efforts, already several decades under way. The mission specialists had endlessly imaged sun-exposed outcroppings and sheltered crannies, cataloging which species of the robotically introduced simple plants were gaining a foothold. The astronauts had returned to Earth to a genuine ticker-tape parade, leaving Mars to continue its slow and inexorable progress toward paradise.

Only four years after that, Dr. Dycek and her team from the Sovereign Republics had thrown everything into confusion with the surprise landing on Mars of the *adins*—monstrously altered human beings—long before any humans were expected to live on Mars. . . .

Tam Smith moved away from the viewport and gestured for him to look, her wispy blond hair crackling around her head with static electricity. "You're not fooling anybody with that bored act, Keef," she said with a smile. "Go ahead, take a look."

"Caught me," he answered and launched himself out of the web chair. At the viewport he peered down

8

through a wispy veil of thickening atmosphere, the faint milkiness of high cirrus clouds smeared out near the poles. The bloody-ochre surface carried a flush of olive color, the first heartbeats of new life. He realized he was grinning with glassy-eyed delight, and his enthusiasm was infectious. Ogawa and Shen were chuckling at him and whispering to each other.

What other project could be so grand? Keefer asked himself. This sculpting task could make men approach the level of gods. They were remaking an entire world! This had been his dream since his adolescent years.

Rubbing his black-brown eyes in the lounge's dry recirculated air, Keefer stretched out to touch the insulated wall of the ship. He pushed away from the port, drifting toward the center of the room. Ogawa and Shen claimed his space to ogle the planet once more.

History would eventually imbue the Mars project with the grandeur it deserved, although the apathy shown by Earth's general population frustrated Keefer. People had no patience for long-term projects. What was a hundred years or so in the grand scheme of things? The universe itself would blink its eyes in astonishment at how Sol's frozen fourth planet had suddenly exploded into life.

Long before Keefer had even been born, governmental huckstering had finally brought about a flags-and-footprint manned mission to Mars that managed to accomplish real science as well as take care of the political obligations for worldwide viewers, including the "For All Mankind" plaque.

But during the years of preparation and the actual landing, the world's space agencies carefully avoided the question of what to do next. Was Mars destined to be a dead end, a dusty trophy like the Moon? The red planet had enormous resources, but the sheer distance and the travel times involved made it unlikely that anything available there could make a difference to lives on Earth.

Seeing that the governments did not have their

hearts in exploiting Mars, multinational corporations scrambled to put together their own resource expeditions. Though Keefer had no love for the sheer-profit-motivated industrial mindset, he did credit the multinationals with finally forcing the UN Space Agency into action, to secure a beachhead on Mars before the companies could. In a bold move UNSA absorbed and adopted the other fledgeling programs, arm-wrestled all the competing work into a pool of combined resources, and secured the backing of the major governments. Riding the wave of support, UNSA struck out on a century-long program to make the fourth planet more like Earth, to change its hostile environment so that people could live there.

The terraforming process would be costly, but no more so than a handful of short-term missions to Mars. Terraforming involved merely a lot of time, a lot of tedious long-distance maneuvers, remote operations—and thinking on scales larger than anyone had ever tried before. . . .

Keefer found a coffee tube in the wall locker, pulled the zip-tab that made it heat itself, then sucked on the nozzle, careful not to burn the inside of his mouth. He frowned at the taste—he had accidentally removed a tube with cream-and-sugar flavoring. "Want this?" he asked Tam, who took it from him, brushing his dry fingertips with hers, but he was too preoccupied to notice her flirtations this time. Keefer rummaged in the wall locker again until he found a tube marked CREAM ONLY, and sipped idly.

Back at the viewport, shoulder to shoulder with the other four, Keefer saw how the orbit had carried them over Mars. Below stretched the gouge of Valles Marineris, the "grand canyon" of Mars, miles deep in places and wider than the entire United States. In the northern highlands, a giant whitewashed crater marked Encke Basin, the scar left by one of the comets that had been hurled into Mars as the first step in the terraforming process.

UNSA had undertaken a rendezvous mission to Encke as the comet whipped close to Earth on its 3.3-year orbit, detonating precisely positioned nuclear warheads that sent Encke straight to Mars, where it grazed the atmosphere, aerobraking to slow its descent. Thus it burned up and dumped its contents into Mars's atmosphere rather than ionizing all the gases into space. The comet strike brought with it cubic miles of free water, as well as enough energy of impact to warm the atmosphere. The shock wave and the heat imparted by the collision released an additional four times Encke's water vapor from the soil into the air.

The resulting Encke Sea had volatilized in only two years, but the changes in the Martian atmosphere were permanent. The upset in the climate and the brief greenhouse effect melted part of the ice caps, which increased the atmospheric pressure further, which melted more. . . .

The escalation had begun. Mars had been locked in an unsteady climatic equilibrium, waiting for a shove from ambitious humanity.

A year later two transports released samples of airborne algae—voracious for carbon dioxide—into the Martian atmosphere. The algae included a dozen different varieties genetically engineered to thrive on Martian conditions. They soaked up the weak sunlight, gathered minerals from the ever-present fine dust that whipped through the air, settled on exposed surfaces, and released bound oxygen. All this laid the groundwork for a terrestrial ecology. Two years later another cargo ship dumped more algae into the air, new strains. Monitors showed measurable improvements in the air concentrations.

That was the year Keefer had been born.

Six years after that, new algae and free-plankton strains were deployed, tweaked to optimize their metabolism in the changing environmental conditions, while the first species grew obsolete in an atmosphere becoming too rich for them.

Nineteen years after the first cometary impact, a second iceball crashed into Mars. The long-period comet Harlow-Burris, previously undiscovered, roared down into the solar system in an orbit that would take it astonishingly close to Mars on its trip through the ecliptic plane. A frantic mission was set up to give Harlow-Burris a nudge and change its course just enough to smack it into Mars, dumping more water, adding more heat, freeing more of the locked moisture and oxygen buried beneath the sands and hydrated within the rocks.

During Earth's worldwide recession, when Keefer himself began working as a student in planetary geology, most of the cost-intensive terraforming work ground to a halt, but the wheels of nature had already been set into motion. Algae strains continued to swarm over the planet, making the Martian atmosphere thicker in the lowlands, trapping more sunlight, reducing the rocks and the oxide soil.

When humans again set foot on Mars after an eighteen-year hiatus in manned missions, things had changed dramatically. Preparations for a permanent UNSA base were made. Living modules were sent by slow cargo ships, for automatic landing and robotic assembly. Supplies were delivered in cheap but slow trajectories, preparing for the day when people could establish a long-term presence.

As he continued his headlong drive for Mars Mars *Mars*, Keefer had tried to engender in his twenty-year-old son Allan an appreciation for the magnitude of the terraforming task. Keefer spent two months a year with Allan, who feigned interest whenever he talked to his father; Keefer felt sorry for Allan, because the boy had no burning goal. But Keefer vowed that when he finally set foot on the surface of Mars, waving his gloved hand at the cameras for newsnets back on Earth, Keefer would be waving at Allan and no one else.

The boy was entering college, where he would probably study space science because Keefer had opened all the right doors for him, planned out his courses, urged him to follow a good curriculum, pointed the way. Keefer had worked hard to ensure that his son's future was established, since his own new job as commissioner of Lowell Base would keep him away for years. Keefer promised himself he would pay the price just to make sure Allan had a clear trail of footsteps to follow. . . .

Now, hand over hand, he pushed his way to the orbiter's bridge. Captain Rubens sat back with all lights down except for the instrument panels, enjoying the best view available on the craft. The cherub-faced captain bore a wistful expression: he would not be going down to the surface with the rest of them.

Rubens swiveled around. He wore a bulky green sweatsuit and thick socks to insulate him from the ever-present chill on the spaceship. "Ah, Commissioner! I was going to go get you. I've contacted Lowell Base because I thought you might want to talk to Dr. Dycek, but she's unavailable at the moment. Think that means she's in the bathroom, or something?"

Keefer didn't know yet how he was going to deal with Dycek. He had never met the woman, but her work had certainly raised enough eyebrows and thrown a monkey wrench into UNSA's neatly planned terraforming schedule. Her surprise project had placed augmented human beings on Mars years before any other permanent presence. First the unruly *adins*, then the more cooperative *dvas* set up modular buildings and infrastructures that would have taken ordinary humans many years to complete. But though the 150 or so surviving *dvas* still provided a good pool of laborers, their special skills were no longer really needed, now that the five human bases had expanded their complement of inhabitants.

He nodded to Rubens. "No matter. I'll have plenty of time to talk to the commissioner once we get down. We've got a lot of transition details to work out, but you'll be sitting on Phobos for two weeks refueling."

"Yeah. Get some rest. Lander's leaving early tomorrow morning."

As a special treat, Captain Rubens allowed his dozen passengers to transmit brief messages back home. Keefer addressed a videoletter to Allan, admonishing him to work hard in school, making chitchat about how much he was looking forward to feeling real gravity again, not just the artificial tug from a spinning ship. He edited his message several times, vaguely dissatisfied that he could think of nothing important to say that he hadn't already said. As Terrence Chetwynd took his place at the communications station, Keefer pulled himself back to the lounge compartment.

Looking out the porthole, he could see the dark terminator sweeping around the planet, folding the long breach of Vallis Marineris into darkness. He recognized the giant swelling of Olympus Mons, the largest volcano in the entire solar system, rising to the upper fringes of the atmosphere.

Keefer picked out three smaller volcanoes clustered at the equator: Arsia Mons, Pavonis Mons, and Ascraeus Mons, each about seventeen kilometers higher than the surrounding plains, thrust out in a great swelling called the Tharsis Bulge. Lowell Base was centered between Pavonis Mons and the tangled badlands of Noctis Labyrinthus. The other UNSA bases were located at the eastern end of Valles Marineris, at the northern and southern poles, and in the lower part of the Hellas basin.

As the orbiter's local night approached, the twelve new arrivals went to get some rest for the last night in their cramped ship quarters. Unable to sleep, Keefer doublechecked all the preparations himself, then stewed with anxiety for another half a day. Tomorrow morning they would touch down on Mars.

In his mind he pictured the Mars he had read about as a child, the visions that had haunted his dreams after reading Ray Bradbury and Edgar Rice Burroughs. A shiver of anticipation fluttered down his back. The UNSA terraforming work was changing the real Mars into the Mars of fiction. And he was a part of it.

BORIS TIBAN

AN INHUMAN HAND ADDED finishing touches to the human face.

The sculpted visage stood two meters high, with pointed nose, Cossack beard, thick eyebrows, and a superior grin that scorned fear. Lighter rocks set into molded sockets gave the eyes a blank stare, looking down the slopes of Pavonis Mons. The black pupils would be painted on later.

The *adin* Boris Tiban squatted on the rough volcanic ground, ignoring discomfort as he watched his companion Stroganov work. The cold poked fingers through small rips in his worn jumpsuit, but could not penetrate his polymer-insulated skin.

His *adin* eyes were set deeply under a continuous frilled hood to shield them from the cold and the blowing dust. A transparent plastic membrane covered the eyeballs to prevent them from freezing solid. An additional membrane draped over the broad nostrils to help retain exhaled moisture. A set of auxiliary lungs mounted beneath the shoulder blades and surrounded by artificial diaphragm musculature made the *adins* look like grotesque hunchbacks. Their skin had a milky cast, nearly dead of feeling due to the long-chain polymers grafted onto the hide, like an insulating suit.

The sculptor cupped a lump of hot mud in one tough palm as he took a final glance at his creation. Touch-up dabs of mud on the towering bust froze into cement within a few moments in the harshness of the Martian high altitudes. Stroganov had to pry the ice-covered scraps from his numb fingers, plopping them back into the steaming bucket at his side.

"Another one finished," Stroganov said, his voice reedy in the thin air. "I apologize for the delay. You can

15

call the others now, Boris. Not that they haven't been watching from the caves. . . ."

Behind Stroganov, like guardians around the volcanic caves where the five surviving *adins* lived, stood glowering busts of other Russian rebels—Stepan Razin, Ivan Bolotnikov, Kondrati Bulavin, even Vladimir Ilitch Lenin himself.

Grumbling, Boris had argued against that sculpture of Lenin, since the man had fallen into disfavor with the backlash against communism and the resurgence of nationalism. But Stroganov argued quietly and patiently—in his teacher's way that always drove Boris to frustration—that Vladimir Ilitch, too, was a rebel in his time, and that Lenin had also been exiled to Siberia, though his sentence was vastly more pleasant than what the *adin* volunteers had experienced in the labor camps.

In the gathering twilight Boris used his titanium staff to haul himself to his feet beside Stroganov's sculptures, digging its hard point into the dirt and making a satisfying scar. Boris had torn the rod from UNSA's transmitting dish ten years before, when he and the other *adins* revolted against Earth, took whatever equipment they could salvage, and hiked to higher elevations where they could live comfortably and breathe the thin air for which they had been created.

Even here on the highest slopes of the enormous volcano Pavonis Mons, the air tasted thick and spoiled, a flavor of too much oxygen, ripe with airborne algae, tainted with toxic pollutants from *dva* mining and excavation settlements that sprang up like mushrooms in the lowlands. The air grew worse each year. Boris wanted to mutter a curse and spit—but he and all the *adins* had learned never to waste valuable moisture in pointless gestures or unheard words.

Brushing red dust from his arms, Boris turned toward the cave mouth to call the others. The shadows of Stroganov's sculpted heads grew longer, like the distorted silhouettes of history. Stroganov stood proudly beside his new creation, anxious to tell another story.

Night fell rapidly on the Pavonis caldera. Stars blazed down, more brilliant than the darkest Siberian night. Knowing where to look, Boris could make out the two tiny moons of Mars, Phobos and Deimos— Greek for "fear" and "dread." The moons were tiny rocks, fossilized potatoes in orbit. Phobos scurried across the sky three times in a single sol, while Deimos hung in nearly the same spot, day after day. Fear and Dread. Boris wondered how two such small pebbles could inspire such terror.

Cora Marisovna, Boris's almond-eyed lover, crouched in the darkness of the cave mouth, unwilling to come outside. Wiry and thin Nikolas, the youngest of their group, came out, hovering beside Nastasia, the *adin* woman he shared with Stroganov. Since Stroganov had been busy with his new project lately, Nikolas had taken extra turns with Nastasia, who never seemed to know where she was anyway.

She came out beside Nikolas, gasping in amazement at the new sculpture, and as she had done with each of the other faces before, pointed a blunt *adin* finger. "I knew him! I remember him!" Nikolas gave her a condescending smile. Boris kept his face expressionless.

There was no real love between Nastasia and Stroganov or Nikolas, because the person who lived within the mind of Nastasia changed from hour to hour. She was one of those who had suffered a defect in the *adin* augmentations; oxygen had been cut off to parts of her brain during the first few days, before she had somehow adapted and survived. All that remained of her personality were scattered fragments of memories, things she had imagined and things she had experienced, puzzle pieces that did not belong next to each other, but were forced by clumsy hands into a crude interlocking.

Nikolas helped Nastasia squat down beside him on the rocky soil. "Who is it this time, Boris?"

Boris shrugged. "Wait until Stroganov tells you. Somebody you've never heard of, no doubt."

Nikolas nodded. Of all the *adins*, Nikolas looked up to Boris Tiban the most, and Boris considered it his duty to adopt a protégé. Back on Earth, Nikolas had been in the Siberian prison camp for a stupid reason— he had stolen construction equipment for the black market, but got caught when he tried to sell it back to its original owner. Boris had helped the young man survive the rigors of the camp, when he would surely have died in the first year otherwise.

"I give you another hero," Stroganov said proudly, "someone we must not forget from our history." He stood beside the recently completed monument and raised his hands. The new sculpture looked darker and sharper than the others, unworn by abrasive dust. Next to the stylized human face, Stroganov's *adin* modifications made him look even more of a monstrosity.

Stroganov bent forward, as if to make certain his audience remained attentive. Nastasia could not focus her mind clearly enough, but she made a great show of it. Nikolas raised his watery blue eyes, though, and Cora Marisovna listened from the shadows.

"I give you Emelian Ivanovich Pugachev." Stroganov smiled.

At last, Boris thought, *someone we have heard of.*

The Sovereign Republics had seen many changes of boundaries and governments, but the people had a common history, common hostilities, occasionally even common cultures. They were tied together by strands much too strong to be severed by the winds of changing politics.

One of the strange consequences of the fall of the Soviet Union among ethnic Russians was that they looked at their Russian imperial history as a golden age, resurrecting tsarist heroes: Ivan the Terrible battling the boyars, Peter the Great and his eccentricities, Alexander I and his wars against Napoleon.

Boris Tiban was Azerbaijani, with a dash of Armenian and Georgian—but in his foster homes he had been forced to attend Russified schools that taught Tolstoy, Pushkin, Gogol, Turgenev, Dostoyevsky. All schoolchildren had heard of the great Pugachev Revolt.

Stroganov began to tell his story: "During the time of Tsarina Catherine II, whom old historians called Catherine the Great, Emelian Ivanovich united the Cossacks in a rebellion that stretched from the Urals to the Pacific. Pugachev forged serfs and enslaved ethnic groups into such a powerful army that the tsarina had to conclude an unsatisfactory peace with the Turks so she could turn her military against him.

"Pugachev gathered fifteen thousand supporters, claiming to be the true tsar whose death Catherine had falsely staged thirty years before. But when Catherine sent her full army against him, even Emelian Ivanovich could not survive. The tsarina's army captured him and brought him to Moscow in a cage. Pugachev was beheaded and quartered, and during the following months, peasants in the rebellious villages were hanged and tortured, their homes burned."

Stroganov sighed. "Pugachev was a brave man, but he struck at the wrong time. I think he would have done well on Mars."

"Yes," Nastasia said, "I remember him! I do." Nikolas shushed her.

Boris nodded grimly. "A good choice, Stroganov. Pugachev was one of Russia's greatest heroes."

Boris liked the great rebels. Even their missteps sent ripples through the tsarist governments and the mindset of the Russian people. Boris's own *adin* rebellion on Mars had caused as great a stir—for a time—though now it seemed Earth had forgotten all about his grand gesture.

Caught up in bickering and their own internal ethnic problems, the Sovereign Republics had remained side players in the terraforming of Mars. But all along they had had a surprise up their sleeves that would let them steal the show from the UN Space Agency, and at a relatively low cost.

Thirty *adins* were shipped to Mars in a cargo transport officially described as "unmanned," filled only with supplies for the eventual human colony. But when the ship landed and opened its doors to a world-wide audience, the transmission showed a human being—augmented, yes, but wearing no environment suit—setting foot on Mars. The *adins* were the show-pieces of the Sovereign Republics, displaying an imagination, bravery, and efficiency that no one else in the world expected of them. The uproar could be heard practically across interplanetary space.

Cut off from their Earthly masters, the *adins* had not meekly tamed a world and bowed to every command transmitted to them, though a few of the *adins* behaved like cowering serfs instead of pioneers. Sixteen years ago Boris Tiban had led his own bloody rebellion, like Pugachev. He had freed the *adins* to make their own lives on their own world. Now, though, only five of them remained.

The Martian atmosphere grew thicker and warmer. Hundreds of the second-phase *dvas* swarmed over the surface, trained dogs of the UNSA project. And now unmodified, unwanted normals had established a clumsy foothold with their permanent bases.

The *adins* were obsolete, no longer needed.

As night fell and the air grew even colder in the star-streaked darkness, Boris squeezed his fist until the reddish rock crumbled into powder, like freeze-dried blood. Taking one last look at the towering statues Stroganov had constructed, he turned and walked without a word into the caves.

Cora backed out of his way. She did not say a word to him. He glared at her, at how her body had betrayed both of them, and felt the long, dull rage eating at his stomach. Without the furnace of anger he kept stoked within him, Boris felt nothing at all.

I am obsolete, but I am not a museum piece! he thought. Statues and trophies gathered dust. But Boris Tiban could still act against his oppressors.

RACHEL DYCEK

By THE TIME RACHEL BROUGHT the long-distance rover back to Lowell Base, meandering aimlessly across the Martian landscape as she gathered her thoughts, the distant sun had already fallen behind the line of crags called the Spine.

Operations manager Bruce Vickery was there to meet her at the parking shelter, hands on stocky hips, suited up and ready to clamber into *Percival* as soon as Rachel opened the airlock. The speakerpatch in Vickery's helmet flattened his annoyance.

"Hey, Rachel, I needed to go out a lot earlier than this. You were scheduled to be back hours ago." Vickery turned his back on her and popped open the rover's storage compartment, slinging in a backpack of tools he had with him. It landed inside the bin with a hollow thunk. "It's going to be damn tough to calibrate those meteorology stations without the sun."

The strong tone in his usually even voice triggered her defensiveness, and she turned to him. The base had two long-distance rovers, after all. "Why couldn't you take *Schiaparelli*?"

"It's being serviced. Al-Somak is using it to meet the lander tomorrow, and he wants it bright and clean. I've been waiting here for you for hours. I wish you wouldn't do this to me, Rachel." Vickery sounded like an exasperated father trying to talk sense into his teenaged daughter. Rachel felt small, and hated herself for feeling that way.

"Take it then. It is all yours." Behind her, she heard Vickery climb through the sphincter airlock. The thousands of small telescoping legs reset themselves with a whisking noise, levering the body of the rover high enough off the ground to clear any obstacles on the terrain. Like an impatient bull, *Percival* snorted a thin whistle of cold steam as it cleared its exhausts.

Still sluggish from her self-indulgent afternoon, Rachel walked along the packed-dirt path to the outer module's entrance, then let herself through the main airlock into the changing area. She used one of the wall-mounted vacuum hoses to remove as much of the red dust as she could from her suit, then disconnected her helmet. The air smelled sour and metallic, with a musty, carbolic smell from the air-regenerating unit. She switched off the backpack and slipped it from her shoulders, then shucked her suit. Glowing resistance heaters shed small pools of warmth in the changing area, but they could not beat back the ever-present cold of Mars. The changing stool felt like ice against her bare legs as she tucked the suit components in the designated storage cubicle.

With a damp poly-sponge, Rachel rubbed down her body to remove the sweat and grit. The cold dampness made her skin tingle, like sitting in a sauna and then running across the snow in the camp in Siberia where she had secretly performed the *adin* surgeries.

As she dressed in a clean jumpsuit, Rachel checked her trim and compact body. Even under the one-third gravity, she had not degenerated to flab over ten years. At fifty she looked hard, annealed by the fire of human scorn and the cold of Mars.

Back on Earth, though, in the oppressive gravity of forced retirement, she would become a fossil soon enough.

Rachel made her way through the bulkhead door into the narrow corridor connecting the inflatable modules. As she passed into the central module that housed the main computers and communications facilities, Dr. Evrani, the meteorologist, burst in on her, waving his hands and simmering in anger. He was a little man, scrawny and hyperactive, as if his body were too small to contain the energy he generated. Even after five years of listening to his loopy Pakistani accent, Rachel still found him hard to follow. He reminded her of the Indian inquisitor that had dissected her on the world newsnets during the UN *adin* hearings, which might partially account for her dislike of Evrani.

"You were not here, Commissioner!" Evrani said, his pecan-brown eyes wide, as if Rachel had somehow forgotten about being gone all day. "I had to accept the transmission myself from Commissioner Keefer in the orbiter. How could you forget? Why were you gone at a time like this?"

"So what did he want?" She walked to her desk screen and activated it. Leaning over the clutter in her personal area, Rachel read the message herself even as Evrani summarized it.

"They have reached orbital insertion on schedule and all systems have checked out. They will deploy the lander at our local sunup—"

"—tomorrow morning," Rachel said, on top of his words. "Then everything is on schedule and routine? No problems?" She glared at him with cold gray eyes. "So what are you so upset about?"

Evrani shook his narrow, big-knuckled finger at her. "You should not go out of sight alone in a rover. We are on the buddy system. Those are the regulations."

Rachel scowled at him. "I will take your words under advisement, Dr. Evrani." In the back of her mind, she wondered how Evrani had ever passed all the human factors tests. Cooped up together under pressure on Lowell Base, the fifty people had broken into a bunch of insulated cliques, and Evrani had become the tattletale.

Tomorrow morning, Commissioner Jesús Keefer would land, and she had to prepare to be rotated home. After two weeks Captain Rubens would have refueled his interplanetary shuttle from the oxygen mining station on Phobos and prepared for the launch window to return to Earth. Rachel Dycek and five others would be rotated back home. Settling into her retirement, she would sit back in a comfortable dacha on Earth, maybe go on a speaking tour, maybe write her memoirs of the days of the *adin* project, or publish a final report on the success of the *dva* phase of human augmentation.

Though her work on Mars had been superseded by other terraforming concerns, Rachel did not want to go back home. Adapted humans had always been intended as a short-term phase in the overall scheme. But she was having trouble adjusting to that reality.

Erasing her screen, Rachel shut down the terminal. Feeling claustrophobic in the confined module, she envied the *dvas* out there in the open, breathing the air, feeling Martian breezes against polymer-insulated skin. "Excuse me, Dr. Evrani. I have a lot of preparations to make before tomorrow."

Rachel made her way to the tiny cramped cabin that had been her private quarters for a decade—"cozy," the habitation engineers had called it. No doubt they would have said the same thing about a coffin.

Rachel folded down her bunk and snapped it out from the wall with a tight clack to lock it into place, then adjusted the controls to soften the mattress. She lounged back on the thin, spongy layer and pulled a thermal blanket over herself to keep warm. As she closed her eyes, Rachel thought back, trying to count how much of her life she had wasted on augmentation projects.

For twenty-one years of her career she had been involved with the concept, initially as an assistant, then section leader, then overall head of the *adin* project while hiding in a secret installation built within the Neryungri labor camp. She had started the job when she was twenty-nine, rosy-cheeked and idealistic, with enough stamina to surpass her competitors and no politics to speak of—nothing to offend the changing groups in control of the Sovereign Republics. She had excelled in medical school, practiced surgery for two years, before her real work had begun. Separating from her husband Sergei after a lackluster marriage, Rachel had vanished into the labor camps at the far edge of the Earth.

As she worked her way up, she learned all phases

of the project, supervising specialists who took care of the specific details in each area—artificial lungs, mechanical secondary diaphragm muscles, long-chain polymer skin insulation, genetically modified hemoglobin molecules to process precious oxygen more efficiently. She studied autopsies on the failures to improve the process for next time.

In the cold isolation of Siberia, under the gray skies of incessant winter, she had fallen into a brief affair with one of the other doctors. But the intensity of Rachel's personality, her single-mindedness, had driven off close relationships all her life; the doctor had requested a transfer shortly afterward.

Throughout her career, Rachel marched straight ahead in a lockstep that allowed for no distraction, no deviation. Now she felt as if she had taken three steps beyond a precipice before realizing that the bridge was out. The *adins* and the *dvas* were her life: her substitute for what she had left behind along the way.

Rachel remembered the eleven months of intensive interviews with hardened prisoners who grasped at any sort of straw that might mitigate their sentences. She and her assistants searched for volunteers, conducted endless physiological and psychological tests, preliminary surgical inspections.

The sheer numbers of people were a blur, and she often forgot that they were people—not specimens. But she gave them hope, and they gave her a chance to make an impact for the Sovereign Republics, which sorely needed something to regain their lost prestige in the international community.

Many types of government had been tried since the fall of communism, and now the loose federation had many different flags, currencies, and languages. But the Sovereign Republics had been weaker many times before. The people viewed the seventy-five years of Communist control as a part of their history, a stumble in the progress of time, much the same as the Mongol invasions, the Polish invasions, the oppression of the

Teutonic knights.

The "united Earth" terraforming project had been an enormous drain on the world's treasury, siphoning off resources that—some said—might better be spent at home. Fifty years had passed, and still no humans smiled under the olive sky or romped through the rust-colored sands, as UNSA propaganda had promised. People were tired of waiting; the work seemed an unending quest, led by fools. With its own severe economic problems, the Sovereign Republics had declined to take an active role in making Mars fit for human inhabitants.

Officially, that is. . . .

In her quarters, Rachel cracked open her gray eyes and searched for the chronometer on the wall. Tomorrow morning Keefer's lander would be down, bringing another dozen workers for Lowell Base. Twelve hours from now, she would be shaking the hand of her replacement, welcoming him to Mars. She would make the transition in a politically smooth way, helping him to take over his new duties, helping him to take duties away from *her*. Rachel didn't know how she could manage to be cordial. But she would, somehow.

She looked on the wall, at the yellowed hardcopy news clipping she had sandwiched between layers of transparent polymer.

'Frankenstein' Doctor Exonerated of Charges by UN Panel: Second Phase to Continue

The gray-eyed Rachel in the photograph, looking exhausted but ecstatic, seemed no younger than she looked now. Perhaps the Martian environment had stopped her aging, or perhaps she had done all her aging at once during the hearings. Her cinnamon-brown hair had become streaked with metallic gray. Her nose was a bit too large for her face, her lips too full. Her eyebrows traced dark arches highlighting a flinty gaze. She had never managed to be photogenic.

"Frankenstein Doctor" the newsnets had called her. Vivid memories lurched to the front of her mind, like screams from the depths of a nightmare.

RACHEL DYCEK

THE UN HEARING CHAMBER in the new Geneva facility was huge. The walls echoed with every footstep, every door slam, every mumbled comment. With muttering whispers and general stirs the audience sounded like a gently snoring beast.

Newsnet camera lights shone like baking suns onto the victims on display, the witnesses about to be dissected. In the midst of it Rachel Dycek felt small and alone; her convictions had hidden from her, leaving only a rigid outside shell. Her attention spiraled down into two points: the livid expression on the Japanese delegate's face and the translator microphone speaking stiff and formal Russian in her ear.

"You have dodged these questions . . . for days, Dr. Dycek." The unintelligible words carried truckloads of strident anger; by contrast, the interpreter's voice sounded smooth and relaxed.

With the buzz of other conversations around the vast room, the asynchronous chatter of foreign languages, and the panicking voices in her head, Rachel had to squeeze her eyes shut just to pay attention to what the delegate was saying. The earphones made her breath thunder in her head.

Calm, calm, calm. Pay attention. Gather your thoughts. They want you to slip, so they can lunge in for the kill. Do not give them the opportunity.

"We ask again, in front of the whole world. You must answer us this time, Dr. Dycek. How can you . . . justify creating such distortions—no, such *perversions* of the human body? I am reminded of the English novel *Frankenstein* by Mary Shelley. Have you read it? Did you neglect . . . er, did you forget that these are *people* to whom you have done such a horrible thing?"

Rachel opened her eyes and sat up straighter, feeling anger come to her aid, like a staff propping her up. The man's line of questioning offended her, and she made that quite plain through her tone of voice. She flashed her granite eyes at him until he flinched.

With carefully chosen words she answered in English, not Russian; the legal counsel had told her that speaking English would gain points among the largest portion of the viewing audience, make her seem less of a foreigner, less alien.

"Yes, they are indeed people, Mr. Ambassador. People who now live and breathe and work on the surface of Mars. Perhaps you are the one who has forgotten the entire"—a buzz in her ear reminded her to slow down and allow the translator time to catch up—"the entire mission of the UN Mars Project. We have spent half a century throwing money at an inhospitable planet, to prepare it for just this event. For the day when human beings can survive on the surface of another world. And now the Sovereign Republics have succeeded in this—for the entire human race I might add, not just our own commonwealth—I expected celebrations instead of an inquisition."

Rachel took her seat, then watched the weather patterns of expression on the interrogating delegate's face as her answer to his question was translated from English to Japanese. Defiantly, Rachel took a long drink of ice water, avoiding any eye contact with the row of international interrogators crouching like old ravens at the front of the room. At the table beside her sat a Thermos pot of Swiss coffee and an empty mug, but despite the thick rich smell, she avoided pouring herself a cup. These hearings offered little in the way of piss breaks, and she needed to concentrate on the accusations being shot at her, without being distracted by a swollen bladder.

Sitting silently in plush chairs along the table on both sides of her, her army of legal counsel watched with keen eyes and blank expressions. They had put a safe distance between her and themselves, in case she had to take a fall.

A few of her colleagues waited in isolation rooms for their own turns in the interrogation chair, but at the moment everything depended on her. Rachel Dycek was under the microscope. She had been the head of the *adin* project, and she would be thrown into the roiling waters of inquisition, to "sink or swim" as the Americans said.

Scapegoat.

She had been vivisected on camera as the whole world watched. UN delegates pummeled her with question after question, hauling out details of her failed marriage to Sergei, of disciplinary records in primary school, quoting phrases from essays she had written during her undergraduate days in college.

The questioners from India and Japan were the most vehement, but Rachel saw jealousy in the eyes of the other delegates who would not have an opportunity to question her. The Sovereign Republics had succeeded in something that had been impossible for every other country on Earth. Just like the launch of Sputnik, the first satellite; or Yuri Gagarin, the first man in space; or Valentina Tereshkova, the first woman in space; or Alexei Leonov, the first man to walk in space. While other nations dickered for years about studies and assessments, Russians simply went ahead and did the task. Rachel had done the same with her *adin* project.

"Thank you, Madame Chairman," the Indian delegate—whom Rachel thought of as "Mr. Unpronounceable Name"—leaned forward and spoke into his microphone. The Japanese delegate, whose turn at interrogation had ended with his last question, sat back with a sour look on his face and keyed comments into his notebook. Someone coughed too close to an open microphone. Other delegates shuffled papers. Mr. Unpronounceable Name, however, seemed to rely entirely on his own memory. He spoke in English.

"Now then, Dr. Dycek, let us pursue this line of questioning further. I would like you to explain for us, in detail, the exact procedures you used to select your *adin* candidates. The world is concerned about possible human rights violations."

Rachel followed most of his words, though she double-checked them against the buzz of Russian translation in her ear. She took another deep breath. No hurry.

She used their own terminology, since the newsnets seemed set on sticking to the same words. One of the journalists who learned of Rachel's first and second phases of augmentation had dubbed them with the Russian words for "One" and "Two," *adin* and *dva*, using the *a* instead of the preferred *o* transliteration. The plurals should have been *odni* and *dvoi*, but that had been too much for the newsnets, who simply added the English *s* plural. She sighed. The more appropriate words for "Firsts" and "Seconds" should have been *perviye* and *vtoriye*—but she realized this would be a losing battle with the media, so she did not fight it. She had enough other battles to fight. So *adins* and *dvas* it was.

"The *adin* candidates were chosen from among prison volunteers in our facility at Neryungri. Every single person was fully briefed on the surgeries they would undergo. They were completely aware of the modifications that would be made to their bodies—and they knew they would never return to Earth. Every one of them knew all this. We have a release signature from each candidate."

The Indian's gaze bored into her. "But was this not a secret project? Classified government studies? Are you saying that you told every one of these people, these convicted *criminals*, of your country's most sensitive research?"

Rachel shrugged. "They were already imprisoned at the time."

The Indian delegate raised his eyebrows. "Am I to infer that once these 'volunteers' received a briefing from you, they were permanently removed from any sort of parole list? What if one of them were to be found innocent of his original crime? Would you turn him loose back into society, knowing he had knowledge of your precious secrets?"

Rachel slowed her thoughts to keep herself from spouting an answer before she had mapped out the proper words. She glanced sidelong at one of the legal counsel representatives; he nodded slightly.

"It is not my place to debate the ethics of the penal system in the Sovereign Republics. The question you ask is beyond the scope of any of my duties in the *adin* project. Perhaps you would do better to interrogate the warden of the Neryungri penal camp. I know only that all of the prospective *adins* came to our project of their own free will, fully knowing the consequences of their choice."

The Indian delegate drummed his fingers on the tabletop, causing his microphone to rumble. He spread his palms and smiled with an exaggeratedly perplexed expression. "But why would anyone want to volunteer for such a thing? To me, it sounds hideous."

Rachel pushed her own fingertips down hard on the tabletop in what she hoped was an invisible release of frustration. The panel had already asked these questions in varying ways. She had already answered them in preliminary hearings, in written statements, in public interviews. The annoying repetition made them look like fools, not her.

"Frankly, Mr. Ambassador, I fail to understand what is so difficult for you to comprehend. It has been a long-standing practice among many of the world's countries—yours included, I believe—to ask for volunteers among prisoners for medical experiments, to test dangerous new drugs, to conduct psychological studies. These people were all under life sentences in a rigorous work camp. I am certain they felt they had nothing to lose."

The Indian delegate's eyes widened as he latched on to her answer. "But if conditions in Neryungri were so miserable, as you say, how can we be certain you used proper medical procedures, proper precautions to ease the suffering of your patients—excuse me—I mean your 'test subjects'?"

Rachel saw the photographs spread out on the table in front of her, the UN investigative team's reports on the facilities. Each delegate had copies of everything. They already knew the answers. Yet still they asked. Again and again.

The research facility in Siberia had been a gleaming technological island compared to the squalid prison camp. The site had been quite a change even from the preliminary quarters in the concrete university buildings outside Moscow that had originally housed the project. Erected by the prisoners themselves, the Neryungri medical complex was new and clean, extravagant with heat and electricity. When the volunteers came inside for their interviews, more often than not the grandeur of the place struck them dumb.

"We had adequate facilities," Rachel answered. "In fact the UN investigative team concluded that they were 'state of the art and impressive'—that is an exact quote. Perhaps you have not read the summary report in front of you? Shall I give you the page number?"

She picked up her own copy to show him, to show the cameras. He obviously had an identical one right next to his elbow, but she pretended not to see it. "If for some reason you no longer have this information, Mr. Ambassador, I would be happy to procure you another copy." Her brittle smile could have sliced steel.

Mr. Unpronounceable Name looked away. "No, Dr. Dycek, that will not be necessary. But having one's ears and nose sliced off, a second set of lungs mounted on the back, the entire skin grafted with some sort of polymer . . . and then to be exiled from Mother Earth without any hope of returning . . ." He shook his head. "And you want us to believe they volunteered for this?"

Rachel laid her palm flat on the table in a deliberate gesture, half rising. "And they stood in line for it, sir! Russians have always been pioneers, explorers. We are accustomed to hardship. Nomads have survived on the hostile steppes for centuries, leading lives little better than what the *adins* now face on the planet Mars. Russians expanded into inhospitable Siberia at the time of Peter the Great. Russians were the first to send humans into space. Why is it so shocking that we should try to be the first unprotected humans to set foot on Mars?"

Pointedly ignoring his glare, she flipped through her own copy of the summary report, as if looking for more answers there. The pages felt slippery against her sweaty fingertips.

The *adins* had been created one step at a time, first the altered cosmetic appearances, the ears, the nostrils, since these were the least risky surgeries. At each step of the process, failures occurred—some fatal. But the volunteers knew the risks. They had signed the waivers and consent forms. She had given many of the preparatory briefings herself. Rachel had pulled no punches, but just by looking into their eyes, she could see how desperate they were. And she was giving them a way out of hell.

Four of the volunteers developed severe pneumonia or infections after the first round of facial adaptations; one died, and the other three were sent back to their former lives with a stipend and a dismissal that excused them from further labor, but they did have to remain in Neryungri. Though plastic surgeons tried to repair the damage done, those failures were never the same.

But with a large enough pool of volunteers, she had completed thirty *adin* subjects for the surface of Mars.

The adaptations were done under Earth-normal pressure: the skin polymerization, the addition of artificial lungs. Their digestive systems were seeded with harmless bacteria that would help them digest the strains of algae prevalent on the changing Mars; after these alterations, the *adin* volunteers were fed only algae grown in special tanks on Earth.

During the 120-day journey across interplanetary space, the air-pressure and temperature were gradually dropped on the cargo vessel to allow the *adins* to adapt. Their secondary lungs began to function. Two *adins* died en route.

The acclimatization process was gradual, and when the transport landed on Mars and the *adins* stepped out, they could breathe, they could stand upright on Mars, they could walk across the iron oxide sands unaided, turning their naked faces into the thin Martian wind.

Suddenly there were people living on another planet—and they were Russians. Siberians! As the world reeled in shock, the Sovereign Republics hailed Rachel Dycek as a national hero. She and her team came out of hiding in Siberia and raised their hands to accolades. It had been a dizzying few days, before the outcries from world authorities and demands for explanations grew too loud. Rachel had not been allowed to revel in her glory.

The Indian delegate continued his questions. "According to the transcripts from the first investigatory team, you claim to have sterilized all of the *adins*. Made them unable to have children." He looked up at her, as if to confirm his facts.

"Yes, that is true. All the males received vasectomies."

"Males? Do you mean the *men*?"

"Yes. The men."

"What about the women? The *females*?" His voice carried a hint of scorn.

"If all the . . . the men were sterilized, we saw no need to perform unnecessary surgery on the women. What would be the point? The failure rate of vasectomies is extremely low, and in a small group the expected success would be one hundred percent. Additional sterilization of the women by laparoscopic tubal ligation would have increased the risk of complications—by about three percent—but would have added very little to the overall assurance of sterility. We deemed it unnecessary."

"But wasn't the men's surgery unnecessary also?" the delegate pounced. "This seems appalling and cruel. I sincerely doubt that *adin* survival on the planet Mars would depend on whether or not the men were castrated!"

Rachel nearly shot to her feet, but one of the legal representatives next to her gripped her wrist and squeezed hard enough to deflect her outburst. She took a moment to calm herself.

"Mr. Ambassador, they received a painless, simple vasectomy, not *castration*. I would venture to say that a handful of people in this very room—and tens of millions in the viewing audience—have undergone a similar procedure. So please let us not use unprofessional and inflammatory terms."

Mr. Unpronounceable Name blinked with an offended expression, but Rachel continued before he could open his mouth again. "Perhaps I had better emphasize a simple point about the *adins* that you do not seem to understand. The augmented humans were never genetically altered. They were given enhanced abilities to survive the rigors of the Martian environment. They could not pass along those enhancements to their children.

"Thirty of the *adins*—men and women—were sent to Mars to live out the rest of their lives. We are not so naive as to think that they will never again indulge their sexual drives. Any children they might conceive would be normal human babies, unadapted to Mars, who would die instantly upon taking their first freezing, oxygen-starved breath. Do you consider it cruel to prevent that from happening, Mr. Ambassador? You have a strange conception of cruelty."

Rachel raised her face to the glaring lights, knowing that her expression was being transmitted from Geneva to newsnets around the world, displayed on television monitors and newspaper screens.

Riding her anger, she turned to the Costa Rican ambassador at the head of the inquisitors' table. "Madame Chairman, it has been two hours already, and I would like to speak with my counsel. If the Indian delegate has finished this line of questioning, may I request a short recess?"

In truth, she needed to go to the bathroom.

But while Rachel Dycek and her fellow team members went before the Geneva hearings day after day, delegates from the Sovereign Republics fought the real battle behind the closed doors of UNSA. They merely let Rachel give the world a show, like a dancing bear in a circus.

World interest in the Mars project had been flagging for years. The terraforming work had gone on longer than most people had been alive, and the average person could not comprehend the slow but steady progress of algae growth and increasing partial pressures of oxygen. The actual day when people could live on Mars was still dozens of years away. The world economy was suffering, and money spent on the project had become as easy a target as bloated defense spending had been in the late twentieth century. Stop the terraforming work, people said, and just imagine all the good things we could use those funds for!

But the unexpected appearance of Rachel Dycek's *adins* had shocked the world and catapulted Mars into the headlines again. Thirty human test subjects had begun eking out a living on the surface of Mars, setting up terraforming industries, installing automatic factories that would have waited years for the next manned mission. They ingested the algae and lichens they found in the lowlands, they recovered water from underground ice. The *adins* transmitted progress reports that the whole world watched.

Because of Rachel's *adins*, the Mars project again

36

had a kind of immediacy, a newfound legitimacy that the other nations had not been able to achieve for it.

And so, in the end Rachel Dycek and her team were vindicated, granted a rather grudging apology. They were allowed to move onto the second phase, the *dvas*, with research conducted in the open this time, with less-coercive calls for volunteers, with proper controls and techniques exercised.

But a year later, before the first *dvas* were completed, Boris Petrovich Tiban's rebellion of the *adins* on Mars had been a slap in the face, a demonstration of failure that set the newsnets hounding Rachel again. They accused her of insufficient psychological evaluations, poor choices from the camp volunteers. How could someone with a criminal record like Tiban's—?

Six years after that, UNSA had sent her to the austere habitation modules on Mars, and representatives of her government made it clear that she should not refuse the offer. At Lowell Base she would take charge of the two hundred *dvas* already toiling on the planet's surface, to keep an eye on them so that they did not revolt as the *adins* had done.

UNSA must have meant the assignment as a punishment, but Rachel thought of it as an escape, a way to come to another world she had helped shape. It was a place where she could be free from prying eyes, where she could emphasize her successes. She had spent the last ten years as commissioner of the base, performing to the best of her abilities.

But all the *adins* vanished years before she came to Mars. The *dvas* were no longer so important, especially after the disastrous avalanche in Noctis Labyrinthus had swallowed up their best and brightest. . . .

Rachel kept her eyes open, staring into the dimness of her cubicle in Lowell Base, looking at the curved walls of metal film. She felt confined, trapped, and unwilling to surrender. She closed her eyes, but there could be no hiding, not even the escape of sleep.

Jesús Keefer's lander would arrive in the morning.

BORIS TIBAN

THE TITANIUM STAFF WAS sharp and strong. Unyielding and deadly—like Boris himself. The smooth metal was so cold it would have stripped the skin off a human hand, but the plastic *adin* skin kept him from feeling anything. Crouching, Boris ground its tip into the loose volcanic soil, as if stabbing Mars. He pried up a heavy rock and knocked it aside.

The powder of the fine rusty soil puffed like wind-scattered flour. The high-altitude breezes on the long, smooth slopes of Pavonis Mons picked up the red particles and whipped them around his feet. The storm season would soon be here.

Through with staring at the ground, Boris stood up, brushing off his ragged jumpsuit. "We must go," he said to Nikolas.

Nikolas squatted near the rock. In his hand he held a scimitar that he had fashioned from a long strip of scrap metal taken from the original supply modules. He clanged its flat surface like a chime against the rough rock. Nikolas had honed and sharpened the edge repeatedly over the sixteen years of *adin* exile. For a moment it made Boris recall the anachronistic sickle and hammer of the old Soviet flag.

"Let us say goodbye to the women. Remember, we are doing this for Cora," Boris said. "Stroganov is staying here in the caves. You and I will be the ones to strike."

Nikolas nodded. "As it should be."

Hooded eyebrows and the flattened noses and ears muted the expressions on scarred *adin* faces, but after so many years the *adins* had learned to read each other's moods. When Nikolas grinned at Boris's invitation, he looked cadaverous, like a laughing skull. In the low gravity he bounded past Stroganov's frozen sculptures of Russian rebels to the mouth of the sheltering caverns. Boris followed him.

Inside the musty sheltered passages Nikolas lifted Nastasia from where she hunkered beside the volcanic steam vent. She dropped the wisps of wind-caught algae she had been boiling to remove the entrapped dust. "Let me kiss you, my passion!"

Nastasia shrieked in surprise, but then laughed as Nikolas wrapped his arms around her waist. "I shall return and make love to you all night long!" he said.

Boris turned his glance around in the dimness. Stroganov would be down by himself, deeper in the caves, exploring some of the labyrinthine lava tubes or polishing wall surfaces so that he could scratch his thoughts in stone. Stroganov was the only one who cared about making monuments and keeping a record of their toil. Boris intended to make his mark in a more immediate way.

Huddling away from the other *adins*, her only companions on an entire world, Cora Marisovna was by herself up at the caldera rim. Boris sighed and took long strides, squeezing his way through the winding upward passage until he saw Cora outside. He hesitated with a baffling rush of fear, just looking at her before she turned.

His woman, the *adin* he had claimed as his own. Boris had protected her during their first years on Mars; he had taken her away with him to a place where they could be comfortable and live out their remaining years as free people, not as serfs for the Earth governments. He did not know how to make her happy—and she did not know how to tell him, either.

Boris wanted to hold her tightly, crush her body against his, touching deadened skin to deadened skin. He needed to squeeze her so hard that it would hurt, inflicting his passion upon her in the only way their stolen nerves could feel. But the algae-tinted sky was like an open empty bowl above them, and the gentle winds around the caldera sighed with whispers of loneliness. He gathered his courage and shouted to her.

"Cora!" he called, trying to imagine the booming voice Pugachev might have used when rallying his rebels. "Wish me luck! Nikolas and I will take our revenge against the *dvas* for what has happened to you."

But Cora shied away from him, as she had been doing for weeks. She mumbled to herself as she picked at the rocks strewn on the crumbly ground. "The *dvas* did nothing to me, Boris. Do not make another of your grand gestures in my name."

He shrugged off her comment. Cora blamed him for her condition, but she refused to look at the entire picture. Everything on Mars was connected to everything else, and Boris Tiban and his surviving *adins* were at the bottom of the chain, as they always had been.

He tamped his staff down into the dirt impatiently. He breathed the air through his filtered nostrils, felt the bite of the cold on his sensitive inner mucous membranes. Cora was in one of *those* moods again, and Boris wondered how long it would last this time. He could not wait for her now; he had a mission to accomplish, a grand gesture to make.

"We shall return in a few days, Cora," he said. The wind snatched his words away. "I shall think of you."

He turned to leave her but, just as he ducked out of view in the downturning passage, he heard her say in a half whisper, "Be careful, Boris. Please."

Boris and Nikolas set off down the slope of Pavonis Mons in the early morning, before the frost faded from the shadowed rocks. They ran down the long slope, at times laughing and enjoying themselves, but never forgetting their main mission. In the low gravity they could run all day long. They were *adins*.

Overhead, a few glimmering streaks marked the

passage of meteorites through the atmosphere. Shooting stars had once been a rare sight in the skies on Earth, but the terraforming comet strikes had left a great deal of debris in nearby space for the battering ram of Mars to mop up on its journey around the sun.

Nikolas kept pace with Boris, breathing through his nose, working all four lungs to maintain the oxygen level in his blood. Boris put on an added burst of speed, and Nikolas ran right beside him like a loyal dog, flat-footed on the long and steady slope of Pavonis.

Back at the labor camp of Neryungri, Boris had been surprised when Nikolas turned out to be such a ready friend, eager and clinging, but much stronger than he had first appeared. Somehow, Nikolas had made it through the rigors of the *adin* selection process, just so he could remain with Boris.

Boris himself couldn't give a damn about making the *adin* selection. Whether in a Siberian labor camp, or sweating in the Baku oil fields, or turned into an inhuman on the surface of Mars, his life was shit and it would stay that way until he could make it something else, until he could wrest his due from the oppressors. And there were always oppressors.

Boris Tiban was the illegitimate son of some Azerbaijani government official who had abandoned his mother; in turn, Boris's mother promptly turned her young boy in for adoption when the money got too tight. By that time she had moved to the Armenian Republic, and the state placed him in a succession of orphanages, bouncing him like a soccer ball when he proved too intractable.

With the economy and social laws of the Sovereign Republics in constant flux, he went from reasonably comfortable conditions to austere barracks, from fresh meat to near starvation. He never felt happy, because he never knew how long anything would last.

At the age of fifteen he ran away from the foster home and wandered from Armenia, to Georgia, then back to Azerbaijan, finding work and trying to grab something worthwhile. Buffeted around so much in his life, Boris's standard response was to lash out first, before anyone could strike against him.

During his exile in Neryungri, he had viewed the testing for the *adin* project and the subsequent surgeries as another way for the system to slap him down against his will, to force him into doing something that would cause him pain and lead to someone else's benefit. He had volunteered, supposedly of his own free will, but what choice did he have?

The others treated Boris as a small man, an annoyance, an underling. But he had proved time and again that with unexpected brashness and no conscience he could make even powerful men quake in their boots, as he had done at the Baku oil fields and during the *adin* revolt when he had killed Vice Commander Dozintsev on worldwide Earth television. And now, after hiding for so many years, Boris Tiban would strike again. It would be his greatest act. . . .

Because of its smaller size, the horizon was foreshortened, and so sunset came rapidly. The sun set behind them, spilling the shadow of Pavonis Mons ahead of them. Darkness fell into a deep stained-glass violet with the air too thin to cloak the wealth of stars.

Breathing heavily through their noses, Boris and Nikolas stopped by a sheltered ledge of weathered rock, the collapsed walls of an ancient lava tube. "Down there," Boris said, pointing toward the flat ochre plain with his long metal staff. "Look."

Below, they could discern a metal pipeline leading away from the volcano, the small cluster of Quonset huts surrounded by cairns of rock. Distant substations run by *dvas* served as roasting plants for mineral samples to extract hydrated water molecules as well as freed oxygen and other volatiles. But this settlement was a pumping station at the intersection of two pipes. One line extended in the direction of the human base camp, while the other spread out to supply various *dva* mining clusters in the area. The water, kept liquid by volcanic heat in a reservoir deep under Pavonis Mons, could be carried all the way to Lowell Base in insulated pipes.

The work was done by *dvas*, the successors to the *adins*—but Boris looked on them as usurpers.

Through extreme measures, revolutionaries had succeeded in assassinating Tsar Alexander II in 1881, and the Bolsheviks had slaughtered Tsar Nicholas II and the entire Romanov family in 1918. He looked at the *dva* buildings and felt anger like an ulcer burning in him.

Boris Tiban held all the power in the world, because he had so little to lose.

"Let us rest here awhile, then keep moving," Boris said, tossing a loose stone over the precipice. It dropped too slowly, tumbling end over end, then struck a boulder below with a high *ping*.

"We shall strike in the middle of the night."

JESÚS KEEFER

ABOARD THE ORBITER, Keefer issued departure orders, studiously verifying the steps from the online checklists even though he had memorized them long ago. Eager to go, he felt like an enthusiastic child waiting to dash onto a playground, but he was also self-conscious about being in command. He preferred being a hands-off sort of boss, but he would have to make sure everyone else performed their appropriate tasks. The other eleven crew members bustled about, doing their jobs as they had been drilled, looking at Keefer's anxiety with bemusement.

In the main compartment of the orbiter he shook Captain Rubens's hand as the others climbed into the lander module. "I envy you, Keef," Rubens said. "This is my third back-and-forth, the last one the UN rad limits will allow, and then I'm grounded on Earth." He sighed, then clapped Keefer on the back. "I wish I could have set foot on Mars at least once."

Chetwynd popped into the doorway and slapped his palm twice against the frame of the airlock, "Let's go!" then slipped into the foremost seat of the cramped lander. He would pilot them down to the surface while Rubens and his copilot remained in orbit, "minding the store," as they called it.

Tam, Shen, and Ogawa crowded into their seats up front with Keefer. Ogawa giggled nervously, flicking his eyes from side to side, but Tam shushed him. Keefer ducked his head and followed them into the lander, where the sounds were muffled. The other eight buckled into the rear seats in the lander's passenger bay.

"Right on," Rubens said as he closed the hatch. "Smooth sailing. Come see me when you all get back to Earth in a few years."

"Get prepped, ladies and gentlemen," Chetwynd said to the complement of passengers, then remembered to add, "if you please."

Keefer was out of the loop at this point, more a mascot than a leader. The others knew their tasks, and he let them do their jobs. Keefer heaved a sympathetic sigh for Captain Rubens: he had spent four months in a cramped ship with the man and had not realized the captain's desire to set foot on Mars. But then, Keefer had been frequently told by Gina—his son Allan's mother—that he had a "clueless streak in him a mile wide." He just didn't notice when other people had hidden problems. Why couldn't they just come out and say so when something was bothering them? It exasperated him. Had everyone but him noticed Captain Rubens's deep desire? Probably.

Maybe Keefer could see to it that they named a Martian mountain after Captain Rubens or something.

With the chatter of operations going on around him, Keefer strapped himself into the descent chair, then closed his eyes, taking measured breaths of the stale, metallic air they had been breathing for the past four months.

With a sudden lurch, the reaction springs disconnected the lander from the slowly spinning main craft, and the velocity differential carried the two vessels apart. Keefer took shallow breaths of anticipation as they began to drop toward Mars.

The lander touched down with a gentle kiss of its pads on the packed rusty surface, concrete made from Martian sand and dust. With a noiseless whistle, Chetwynd lifted gloved hands from the control panels and let out a comical sigh of relief. "Okay, chaps, my work is all done."

Sitting in the lander's VIP seat, Keefer took over and spoke into the voice pickup. "Touchdown on schedule, on target, thank you very much. Lowell

Base, go ahead and send the rover vehicle for us."

While Chetwynd went through the twenty-minute-long shutdown and arrival procedure, scratching his bristly reddish hair with one hand, the other eleven people on board fitted each other into environment suits. The passengers double-checked every fastening and seal, though this gentler Mars would actually let them live a few minutes if their suits were breached.

Tam Smith helped Keefer mount his air-regenerator backpack and snap his helmet into place, and he did the same for her. "We're on Mars," he said with an astonished smile. "We're really here."

She laughed and flipped down his faceplate for him. "Better close your helmet, if you're going to keep grinning like a little kid."

"Hey, I'm the commissioner," he said through the speakerpatch, "I'm supposed to be enthusiastic about our work here. Just doing my job."

All prepped, he flexed his fingers in the thin gloves. Implanted heater wires kept the suit warm throughout, in preparation for the biting perpetual cold of Mars. The suit seemed so flimsy, so lightweight, so *comfortable* compared with the constant-pressure suits he had worn during some of the early training exercises. He wanted to run and jump and play on this new world he had helped make.

Maybe when nobody was looking. . . .

Glancing out the tiny viewport, trying to keep out of Chetwynd's way, Keefer could see how the red soil around the base had been churned and packed by the many rover tracks and construction activities. The loose, microfine debris had been blown away by landings and lift-offs from various vehicles. Humans had been true strangers on Mars little more than a decade ago, but now the fifty base inhabitants had turned the area into a pioneer town.

"Company coming," he said as he noticed the billows of red dust stirred up by the approaching rover. "Everybody get ready. Please remember all the precautions."

Ogawa and Shen nodded gravely. The others simply mumbled unintelligibly through their faceplates. "Thanks, Dad," Tam said.

After Chetwynd finished the shutdown procedures and mothballed the equipment, he donned his own environment suit. Then, with a silent puff of wind that made the slick suits balloon in the suddenly lowered pressure, he exhausted the lander's contained air before popping the hatch. The ship would remain vacant here on the pad for more than two weeks before Commissioner Dycek and the other old-timers climbed aboard for their return trip to Earth.

Below, a suited figure gestured them toward the waiting rover vehicle, which looked like a motor home that had run over a giant porcupine. The undertreads of articulated legs let the vehicle scuttle over rough terrain, adjusting to the uneven landscape like a souped-up sea urchin. The rover had plenty of computer equipment on board, a mobile encampment—much different from the stripped-down buggy the first Mars explorers had driven. Keefer doubted the big rovers were as much fun, though.

In pairs, the dozen passengers descended to the surface. Keefer waited as Chetwynd and Tam stood on the hydraulic lift platform that lowered them with agonizing slowness. When his turn came Keefer was tempted to jump down and raise some dust in the one-third gravity, but he supposed he had to set a good example for his people.

Like a regiment, they marched across the hard red concrete to the waiting rover, standing in line once more as they entered the vehicle through the sphincter airlock, working their way through the self-sealing membrane, again in pairs. Finally, when the entire group stood with barely contained excitement inside the pressurized rover, they clicked up their faceplates. Keefer smelled the bitter metallic tang of air contaminated with iron oxide dust, so strong that it made the back of his tongue taste flat.

47

Their driver turned around to show a chubby face of honey-brown skin and huge beetling eyebrows. His dark hair was streaked with wiry white strands, like lines in black scratchboard. "Welcome, my friends. I am Dr. Beludi al-Somak, one of the meteorologists at Lowell Base."

Before saying anything else, al-Somak turned the rover in a wide circle and trundled toward the black rocks of a steep ridge. The sea-urchin legs made the floor of the rover vibrate with an odd miniature-stampede sensation. Al-Somak headed for a cluster of dusty metal balloons snuggled up against the fractured ridge, in the lee of the prevailing winds.

"I hope you had a fine trip down," al-Somak said. "We will have a busy week as we give you tours and establish a new working routine. As always, there is too much work, and we are delighted to have fresh helpers. You each have colleagues here, coworkers to take you under their wing." He heaved a huge sigh. "Unfortunately I see by your dossiers that none of you has studied meteorology, so Dr. Evrani and I will have no rest. Pity."

Keefer leaned forward in the seat as the rover continued toward the modules. "Tell me, Dr. al-Somak, will Commissioner Dycek be waiting to greet us at the base? I tried to raise her several times from the orbiter, but I never managed to get through."

Al-Somak gave a troubled sigh. "I believe she will be there, but beyond that I cannot tell you. She is upset about your arrival, Commissioner Keefer. She does not wish to return to Earth, and you are here to take her place."

Keefer nodded, feeling his stomach knot. He had feared something like this might be the case. "Thank you for being so candid with me. I'm sorry to hear that, but I didn't make the decision. Dr. Dycek has been here for ten years. The regulations—"

Al-Somak raised a wide hand. "You do not need to make excuses to me, Commisioner Keefer. It is Rachel who needs to be convinced that you will not bury her work."

In truth, Keefer had little interest in Dycek's *dva* project. It had been shocking in its time, yes, but ultimately just a sidelight on the transformation of Mars. Keefer was an expert in extraterrestrial geology and terraforming processes. He had analyzed the paths of the long-term plan, tweaking, exploring possibilities as new data came available. The original scheme was based on some very broad assumptions, some of which proved too conservative, some too optimistic.

Keefer struggled to assemble a quick reply. "Well, perhaps we can straighten this out quickly."

Al-Somak blinked his deep black eyes. "I doubt it. Dr. Dycek has been convincing herself of it for too long."

Al-Somak brightened the tone of his voice as he changed the conversation, looking at some of the other passengers. "Ms. Smith," he said, turning to Tam with a solicitous smile, "you are scheduled to begin work in the greenhouse dome tomorrow. Several of you others have a tour set up with Dr. Vickery to see the solar arrays we have mounted up on the Spine, including you, Commissioner Keefer. No rest for anybody, I'm afraid."

Keefer, his mind still whirling from what al-Somak had told him about Dr. Dycek, tried to sound compassionate. "Shouldn't we try to get acclimated a little bit before jumping right into the routine? Give our team a chance to stretch our legs. We've been cooped up for four months on the flight over here—"

"The tour cannot wait, Commissioner," al-Somak said. "In fact, had you been a day or so later we would not have allowed you to land. Seasonal dust storms, spring and fall, you see. The weather satellites show a large storm approaching our latitude in the next day or so. The type of thing that makes a meteorologist go into absolute ecstasy." He smiled. "But I fear it would not be wise to have anybody wandering around in it."

Al-Somak keyed instructions to the rover's AI pilot program and brought them into a cavelike shelter hollowed out of the cliff, where refueling and recharging pumps stood waiting to connect to the long-range rovers and the putt-putt service vehicle.

Keefer noticed that al-Somak's lips were chapped from the dry air. Taking a tip from one of the other returning mission specialists, Keefer had brought along two small cases of lip balm—the type of thing everyone needed, but no one thought to requisition on the heavy interorbital transports. Distributing the packs of lip balm could be one way for him to win approval among the people he would have to supervise.

As they drove toward Lowell Base, Keefer recalled what he knew about the camp, feeling as if he knew every corner of it without ever having been there: the placement of the modules with the recreational facilities, exercise arenas, geological laboratories, meteorology shacks, sick bay, med labs, greenhouse tent, satellite uplink, and living quarters. During the tedium of the voyage to Mars, Keefer had spent time familiarizing himself with the workings of all five human bases on the planet.

The new arrivals resealed their suits as al-Somak fastened his helmet again and depressurized the rover. Emerging first from the rover's sphincter airlock, al-Somak led the group through a larger two-stage airlock into the Lowell Base changing area. The new arrivals knew the entire desuiting procedure without further coaching. The Egyptian meteorologist acted like a busybody, moving from person to person, pointing out small empty lockers for stowing equipment. The buzzing sounds of hand-held vacuums blended with excited conversation. Tam sneezed, and Ogawa couldn't stop coughing for several minutes.

"You will get used to the dust," al-Somak said, bowing his head as if in apology.

"Welcome to paradise," Keefer said, stretching high enough to rub his fingertips on the cold, smooth ceiling of the inflatable module. His skin crackled from the sudden, intense chill, and he felt light and tall and ready for a long physical workout. He wanted to jog ten kilometers.

Before they had finished dressing in warm all-purpose jumpsuits, the inner door opened and a slim woman stepped through. She had iron-gray hair and an opaque expression, as if an invisible polarized mask covered her face. She glanced at the group, then fixed her gaze on Keefer.

"Commissioner Dycek?" he asked, trying to smile warmly as he moved forward to extend a hand. He nearly lost his balance by overextending himself in the low gravity.

"Welcome to Mars, Mr. Keefer," Dycek said, brushing his hand in a brief, noncommittal grip. She gave him a false, pained smile, holding herself rigid. "Would you like to hand me my orders now?"

Keefer remained calm, finishing the task of stacking his suit components in a vacant cubicle. "No, but I would like to have a word with you in private, Commissioner Dycek."

She took him to an empty rec room and sealed the door behind them. Someone had left a videogame to play itself on the flatscreen. A Ping-Pong table had been pushed against the curved wall; one of the white balls—weighted, in a futile gesture to compensate for the lower gravity—had fallen to the floor. The smell of garlic and olive oil clung around the hot plate in the small snack area.

Keefer felt his stomach tighten with sour anticipation. His first day on a challenging assignment, and already he had a problem. He didn't want to be Dycek's adversary; he just wanted to be friendly, to make a smooth transition. But he had dealt with UNSA bureaucracy before, and no doubt they had given Dycek double-talk and deliberately vague reasons for her transfer. She had been left to stew for four months, knowing Keefer was on his way to take her place. What a way to run an important project!

"Please, I'm not your enemy," he said. "I'm sorry about—"

Dycek turned and crossed her arms over her chest. She was a good seven or eight years older than Keefer, and they had been hard years. Her face seemed bleached with weariness. Her bright, granite-gray eyes moved back and forth as if she were trapped. She tried unsuccessfully to strangle the bitterness in her voice.

"So what did they tell you about me, Mr. Keefer? Are they saying, 'thank you for devoting your entire life to the project, Dr. Dycek, but we no longer need your services?' Did you bring me a retirement pin? A watch, perhaps?"

Keefer had to move fast if he was going to keep up with her. Already it felt as if the confrontation was slipping away from him. Why did people have to look for so many hidden messages and secret agendas, instead of just taking things at face value? "Believe me, I'm not here to steal your glory, Dr. Dycek. The *adins* and the *dvas* were only a short-term project. You know that yourself, so why act surprised? I am your successor, yes, but you've been here ten years already—why should you be angry at being returned home?"

She stared at the changing geometric patterns of the videogame, but her eyes did not move as the colorful shapes continued their antics. With her back to him, she mumbled words that Keefer guessed she had said to herself many times before. "My work is obsolete. I am obsolete. Now I am forced to go home and listen to everyone else tell me so. That is the worst part."

He crossed his own arms, unconsciously imitating her gesture, but pried them apart again and let them hang at his sides. Open body language, he reminded himself. That had been in the management training. Keefer took a deep breath before answering.

"I did not request this assignment, but I am thankful for the opportunity—and I am thankful for the work you've already done here. In a few decades, Mars will be able to support unprotected humans as easily as it supports the *dvas* right now. You will be remembered as a prime mover in the Mars project. Nothing I do will change that. I am not here to rewrite history."

Privately, Keefer believed the *adin* and *dva* projects had essentially been political publicity stunts staged by the Sovereign Republics: They had gained some cheers and PR strokes, while contributing little of substance to the terraforming effort. But he did not say that out loud.

"When you sent the *adins* here, the whole world began to think of Mars again. Every newsnet on Earth carried weekly transmissions from Vice Commander Dozintsev. People watched it like a soap opera. Some of them even viewed Boris Tiban and his little rebellion as an amusing episode. Personally, it reminded me of the time the old *Skylab* workers went on strike!" He chuckled, but Dycek obviously saw nothing amusing in being reminded of the *adin* revolt. Keefer stopped laughing.

"Do—" Dycek began to speak, but her voice cracked, and she had to start her sentence over. "Do you have any specific long-range plans, now that you are in charge of Lowell Base, Mr. Keefer? Now that the *dva* phase is at its end? I can go back to Earth, but my *dvas* cannot. What do you intend to do with them?" She seemed overwhelmed with either dismay or rage.

Keefer could not fathom her response. It didn't make sense. "Why, I intend to do nothing with them. They can continue with the same tasks they've been performing for years. They are provided for. On paper at least, they own the land they have settled, for the duration of their lives. But they are all sterilized, and there will be no more *dvas* coming up from Earth." He drew a deep breath, keeping his gaze locked to hers. "Mars is a big place."

She looked at him strangely, then nodded. "Several of the *dvas* have asked me in all seriousness if they will be terminated, once I depart from Mars."

Keefer couldn't keep himself from rolling his eyes. "That's preposterous."

"You think so? I'm glad to hear you say it." She went to the rec room door and uncoupled it. "Now, if you'll excuse me, I have to go log all my *dva* activities. Even with the avalanche last year there are still 150 of them scattered around the area."

Keefer smiled at her again and unconsciously cracked his knuckles. "I know how you must feel, Commissioner Dycek, but this is purely professional. Really, it isn't anything personal."

She stood at the joint where the two modules were fused together and pushed the door hatch farther open. A breeze from the slight pressure differential ruffled her gray hair. "Maybe not for you."

BORIS TIBAN

FLAT *ADIN* FEET found purchase on the volcanic path under a star-saturated sky. The world around them was silent, stillborn, like a breath held in fear.

"Run!" Boris Tiban said at last in a hissing cough. Beside him, Nikolas put on an extra burst of speed, doggedly keeping up with him.

The thick air of these low altitudes pulled like shackles on Boris's legs. It weighed him down. It clogged his lungs like soup. But the bloodlust was on him. He wanted to be part of the wind, a storm striking the helpless *dva* puppets. The sooner he and Nikolas got down, and attacked, and saw the bright, wet blood of the *dvas* freeze on their hands, the sooner they could go back home in triumph. After striking out and proving that he was not after all a weak and insignificant man, Boris could sit satisfied in the *adin* caves, content for a time, his hooded eyes half-closed in euphoria, with the feeling of having done something. A feeling of power. If this action didn't make his mark, he would have to try something worse.

"Faster!" he gasped.

Boris swung the titanium staff as he ran, using it to lever his body forward. Nikolas stumbled, his breathing labored. He seemed dizzy and disoriented, trembling with the effort, but Boris would not let him slow the pace. They were *adins* and they were strong. They needed to sprint down, strike, and escape back to higher altitudes where it was safe. Where they could breathe.

For hours they scrambled down the steep slope in darkness, descending the sprawling apron of lava that had long ago oozed out of the shield volcano. Nikolas stumbled on a loose rock, but pushed ahead without a word. Before them, Boris could see milky wisps of steam from the pumping station, boiling into the thin air with a whispering, crackling noise that was muffled by distance. Tiny lights seeped through windows in the *dva* shelters.

The *dvas* were alone and insignificant. They had endured augmentation surgeries as well, but the *dvas* were not strong enough for Mars. Boris would make short work of them.

Phobos skittered across the sky like a bright artificial satellite; Deimos was a white dot indistinguishable from the other stars. The tiny sapphire of lost Earth glinted near the horizon, but Boris refused to look at it.

By midnight, the two *adins* had reached the level rock-strewn plain and sprinted toward the long thread of pipeline extending from the water mines deep inside Pavonis. Boris raised a clenched hand to signal a rest, and as he crouched, heaving burdened breaths into his four lungs, his heart hammered against his rib cage as if demanding to be let out. His head pounded. Knives stabbed behind his eyes from the pressure. How could anyone live in such air?

Nikolas made a high-pitched whimpering sound next to him, but he blinked his eyes at Boris and did not complain.

Resting would do no good, Boris decided. He let out an animal cry that converted the pain in his head into anger in his heart, like an alchemist changing lead into gold. He lurched back into motion, slashing with his titanium staff. "Time to strike. Are you ready?"

Imitating Boris, Nikolas pulled out his scimitar, as if that would help him keep his balance. A determined grin spread across his skull-like face.

Up ahead they saw the pumping station, nearer now, silhouetted by the silvery light of stars and limned by a glow of lights from the inside. Boris paused to stare. Posturing, he raised the spear in one hand and let out an ululating cry that sounded high-pitched and eerie in the empty, frigid night.

Nikolas looked at Boris as if he had gone insane. Boris forced his cheek muscles to form a smile on his uncooperative face. "That will put the shiver of fear down their spines," he said in a hoarse voice, then shrieked again like a wild man.

Never had any animal made a mournful nighttime cry on the surface of Mars. The miserable *dvas* huddling inside their shelter would hear it and feel true terror. They would have no idea what was about to happen to them—they must think all the *adins* were long dead.

A dappled yellow glow trickled from chinks in the Quonset hut adjacent to the pumping station. Sections of transparent plastic let the light escape but kept the heat inside. The hiss of a chemical-based generator came from behind the hut, near the pumping machinery. The structure appeared flimsy, set up as a shelter but not a *home* by any means.

What did the *dvas* even have to live for? Boris wondered.

He heard high-pitched, frightened voices coming from inside, no doubt stirred up by his howl. Nikolas snickered and ran closer to the shelter, scooping up a handful of small rocks. He tossed them onto the sloped metal roof so that they clanged and clattered all the way down. Then, with a howl of his own, he threw a large rock to smash out one of the window plates. Nikolas collapsed to his knees in a *whoosh* of exhaled air, as if the effort of lifting the boulder had strained him to the limit.

Boris did not hesitate for an instant. The *dvas* did not yet understand. It was time to strike.

His head pounding, he ran to the vee of thin metal pipelines that joined at the pumping station. He raised his staff and plunged the sharp point into the intersection, twisting it like a crowbar. The pipe seam split.

Rushing water burst through the crack and volatilized. The cold steam made a razor-sharp screaming noise as it squirted outward, spewing gouts of freezing ice water onto the ground. The sounds drowned out Boris's laugh.

Wielding his scimitar like a Cossack pirate, Nikolas crashed through the front door of the *dva* hut, spilling orange-yellow light across the darkened plain. Screams came from inside.

Water sprayed on Boris's deadened skin, flash-freezing into a sheath of ice. He flexed his arm and shattered the film, but he could feel cold seeping into his bones as Mars stole his body heat. He sloshed through the slushy muck to where the pumping conduits extended in the other direction. He plunged his staff in again and again, puncturing the pipe and leaving breaches for the flowing water to force its own way out, tearing at the thin metal.

Nikolas charged into the cramped quarters where five *dvas* lived communally like a pathetic peasant *mir* in Siberia, three women and two men. They had a small kitchen, cupboards, a tiny table that Nikolas overturned, spilling playing cards—real plastic playing cards!—on the floor.

With lesser surgeries, the *dvas* looked more like deformed humans and less like monsters, expanded chests and enlarged lungs with oxygen-efficiency modules, rather than hunchbacked from an extra set mounted between the shoulder blades. Their skin insulation was thinner, so their nerves could still feel, though the *dvas* had to bundle themselves up in thick, warm clothing against the cold of the Martian night.

In a frenzy Nikolas slashed with his scimitar and yowled, still blinking in the sudden stinging light. The largest male *dva* was already up, grabbing a chair to defend himself. But Nikolas cleaved the *dva* man's face with the honed edge of his blade.

In the low gravity, the dead *dva* man flew across the room. Blood sprayed in an arc across the walls, bubbling and steaming in the thin air.

The *dva* women screamed, two in terror and one in grief. Nikolas continued to flail with the sword and glared at the waiting victims. "Boris!" he shouted.

One of the women, her hands extended like claws, leaped on Nikolas, scratching at his hooded eyes. He staggered backward, tripped on the body of the *dva* man he had just killed, and fell down. Nikolas managed to turn his blade up and thrust it into the woman attacking him. She screamed as the tip plunged through her chest, then protruded from her back where a second set of lungs might have been . . . had she been *adin* instead of *dva*.

The other *dva* man, older and more bearlike than the first, kicked the fallen woman aside and wrenched the scimitar from Nikolas's hand. Covered in steaming blood, Nikolas grabbed for his makeshift, scrap-metal sword.

"Boris!" he shouted again.

The older *dva* man grabbed up the fallen table, raised it over his head in complete silence, and brought its heavy edge smashing down on Nikolas's skull. Again. And again. And again.

Covered with freezing mud, Boris felt the ice-covered staff freeze to his fists as he strode into the *dva* hut like a conqueror. He felt sluggish, urged on by adrenaline but held back by fatigue and weakness in the too-thick air.

As he hesitated at the broken door frame, letting his eyes adjust to the brightness, the two surviving *dva* women howled at him in fury. They snatched pieces of broken furniture and heavy tools from a workbench to defend themselves.

Boris reeled, feeling the wind kicked out of him as he saw Nikolas lying on the floor with rich red blood pooled beneath his crushed skull. Two dead *dvas* lay sprawled alongside him, blanketed in more blood. He stood motionless for an instant.

The big *dva* man heaved up the bloodied table and lurched toward Boris, but Boris snapped out of his daze and swung his titanium staff. Its arc caught the other man on the shoulder, cracking down and probably crushing bone. The *dva* man snarled, falling to one knee, and Boris kicked the side of his head with a flat, insulated foot. The *dva* man went down.

Then the two *dva* women rushed him. Boris stumbled back out into the darkness.

Outside, the burst pipe continued to howl as water and steam gushed through the ruptures. The air was thicker than ever before with cold steam, clogged with strangling vapor, making it impossible to breathe. Boris felt as if he were drowning in the dense mist. He could barely move, dragging his trembling legs one step at a time as he staggered toward the spraying water. His head pounded from the vise of pressure. Any second now his skull would crack like an eggshell.

Accustomed to the air and in their own element, the *dva* women went after him, wielding their sharp, crude weapons. Boris stumbled away.

The iron-oxide dirt at his feet turned to muck, freezing into slush as he ran. Though he could hear one *dva* woman yelling as she pursued him, he could make out nothing of the other behind him in the darkness. His eyes were still dazzled from the brilliant lights in the hut. The splash of illumination from the broken doorway did nothing but blind him.

Nikolas was dead. Boris could not comprehend it. *Now we are only four.*

Suddenly, silently, the second *dva* woman dove at the backs of his knees. Boris fell. She knocked him forward into the quagmire of icy mud under the broken pipe. The escaping water continued to scream just over their heads. She grabbed Boris's neck, digging her knees into the small of his back. Droplets of frozen steam sprayed around them, enveloping Boris with its paralyzing coldness, so frigid he could actually feel it through his polymerized skin.

Wasting no energy on words or a roar of defiance, Boris lurched back to his hands and knees, forcing his *adin* muscles to do as he commanded. Struggling, he tried to find a way to hit his attacker with the metal staff, but she clung to him from behind.

The other woman reached him now, still screaming, still flailing with a steel wrench in her hand. A sunburst of pain exploded in Boris's shoulder as she brought the sharp tool crashing down on his back, near the crease of skin that marked the implant of his second pair of lungs.

Boris heaved himself to his feet, clamping his lips shut and grunting. This was low gravity. He was strong. He could defeat these two *dvas*. Inside himself, he searched for the anger to give him strength, but it seemed to be fading away, running out like blood onto the ground.

The *dva* woman on his back tried to throttle him with her muscular forearm. Boris staggered backward, straining his leg muscles until they felt ready to rip, and slammed her into the jagged edge where he had broken the pipe. Precious water poured around her, around him, and finally the woman loosened her hold.

The other woman hurled her wrench at Boris, but it only nicked his calf as he turned and splashed away into the cold mud.

He used the titanium staff to regain his balance. The first *dva* woman, stunned and reeling from being hammered into the pipeline, lurched back out of the gushing water and came at him.

Boris whirled to see a figure standing in the doorway of the *dva* hut. For a moment, he thought it was Nikolas, still alive and coming to aid him—but the silhouette was too squat, too bearlike. This time it carried a long digging implement. The older *dva* man lumbered toward him with murder in his eyes.

In panic, Boris looked around, swung his staff in an empty whistling arc to ward off the *dvas*, and fled into the deep Martian night.

As he escaped, wheezing for breath and heading up to the blessed higher altitudes, the wailing water from the broken pipe sounded like a requiem for dead Nikolas.

RACHEL DYCEK

THE GATHERING STORM LOOKED huge on the weather-sat images—minor by Martian standards, but more enormous than anything Earth had ever cooked up. A tidal wave of suspended dust particles and free-floating plankton, it marched across the face of the planet like Mongol hordes conquering the Russian steppes.

Rachel punched up the climate models and ran through the usual prediction algorithms. Evrani's simulations always gave a slightly more conservative estimate than al-Somak's, and the two meteorologists spent a great deal of time bickering about it. But the result was clear enough, even at such an extreme distance. At such incredible velocities the storm would arrive in two days, three at the most.

Rachel stared at the swirling image. It seemed a hypnotic eye, beckoning her like the back-of-the-mind yearning to jump that lurks behind an agoraphobe's terror of heights. The storm was an inexorable force that would sweep all Earth politics—all of Rachel's past—aside. Tempting. Perhaps the storm would hang in the air for months, preventing the lander from taking off and returning her to orbit, leaving Captain Rubens stranded on Phobos and waiting for the next launch window. That way Rachel could remain an extra half year on Mars—but she doubted that would happen. Anyway, it would be only a delaying tactic, solving nothing.

The storm seasons came half a Martian year apart, when the north and south poles alternately thawed or froze out great hunks of the atmosphere, but the terraforming efforts had thrown the weather patterns into turmoil. The last time Rachel had seen such an all-encompassing storm on the weathersat images was just before Dmitri Pchanskii and his *dva* team had been buried under fallen rocks in Noctis Labyrinthus.

She wondered if this storm presaged another disaster.

Moving with a lethargy she identified as sadness at ending her work—not with a bang, but a whimper—Rachel looked around the inside of the inflatable module. She wanted desperately to stay here with her *dvas*, to continue her work and be left alone, but she was also tired. Tired of the problems, tired of the interpersonal details she had to manage as commissioner, tired of everything.

On Earth it would be worse. Even well-meaning people would hound her, ask her for speeches, challenge her decades of work with innocent yet biting questions. Here at Lowell Base she had withdrawn over the last four months, knowing that Keefer was on his way. She felt alone and isolated . . . but it would be worse to be with anyone right now. She had not been close to Bruce Vickery in years, and she had found no real companion among the other fifty people at the base. She could not count even the *dvas* among her friends.

This morning the inflatable modules crackled with an empty white noise. All the other personnel were hard at work in their various labs, keeping schedules to fulfill the core tasks the UNSA assigned them. The air felt cold and bright, heavy with the deep chill that never seemed to leave, no matter how hard the solar heaters worked. Rachel rubbed her arms to generate extra warmth in her soft sweater.

She checked the roster to see where everyone was, punching in a request for a summary grid and a sketchy map of Lowell Base, the Spine, and surrounding environs. Evrani and al-Somak had taken the putt-putt to deploy a wide net of climatological sensors in preparation for the coming storm. The two of them jabbered at each other in a machine-gun babble of heavily accented jargon. With storm season approaching, they acted like children on New Year's Day.

Bruce Vickery had taken Keefer and a handful of the new arrivals out in *Schiaparelli* to visit the solar-power collectors deployed on the Spine. A couple of the others began their orientation with the botanists and agronomists in the greenhouse dome.

The geology team had gone outside for a last sample-collecting expedition before the storm, which might keep them sequestered for weeks. Amelia Steinberg and her crew of maintenance engineers had suited up to double-check external seals on the modules. A handful of members who worked the off-shift slept in their quarters; a few used the recreational and exercise facilities.

Rachel Dycek, already phasing out her important duties, attended the communications center, staring at weathersat images and waiting for the radiophone to beep. *Phasing out*.

Useless. Unnecessary. You can't teach an old commissioner new tricks. When a person's work is over, what does she do? Rachel recalled old pensioners who had looked forward for decades to their retirement from the work force—and had then turned into pathetic wretches in rocking chairs, without the slightest idea of what to do now that they had no purpose in life.

Rachel looked around the empty module and saw nothing that interested her. She shuffled off to her quarters, refusing to glance out any of the windowports along the way. She was being too hard on herself, but she had no one to talk her out of her gloom, to pat her on the back, to cheer her up. Events had left her at a loss. All her life she had forged ahead with a drive, soaring toward orbit . . . but now the rockets had cut out and left her in free-fall, disoriented, with nothing to anchor her.

What was she to do now?

She would return to an alien home as a well-respected scientist and administrator. The public would give her false laurels. She would fill her days with celebrity banquets, lecture tours, writing memoirs, granting interviews. Charities would want her to endorse causes; corporations would want her to endorse products. Her face would appear on posters. Children would write letters to her. Talk shows would use her as a guest when movie stars and professional athletes canceled unexpectedly.

Tell us, Dr. Dycek, why do you think your projects were such dead ends?

The clipping on the wall of her quarters brought back the pointed reminders of what life could be like on Earth, how she would be treated.

"FRANKENSTEIN" DOCTOR EXONERATED OF CHARGES BY UN PANEL

Perhaps she would be better off exiled to Siberia, to live quietly in a place where others could not find her or bother her. She could probably request that.

She squeezed her eyes shut. Human memory retained the details of failure long after every success had been forgotten. Her accomplishments would be swept under the rug, the sweet triumphs relegated to footnotes in history books, until one day Rachel would just lie down, slit her wrists, and watch the bathwater turn as red as the sands of Mars. . . .

SECOND PHASE TO CONTINUE

With a burst of defiance that exhilarated her, she yanked the clipping from her wall. The protective polymer coating stopped her from ripping it to shreds, but she crumpled it as best she could and tossed it to the floor. A childish gesture, but it felt good for a moment. Only a moment.

This useless bemoaning of her circumstances was pathetic, she realized, but she could not stop it.

Rachel glanced around her quarters. Should she bother packing? The night before, after her discussion with Keefer, she had taken out some of her possessions and scattered them around the room, but left them in disarray.

She felt worse after sitting in her quarters, and she left them, wandering from one pressure door to the next, like a grandmother checking her family after everyone had gone to bed. But Rachel had never considered the Lowell Base personnel her family. The *dvas* were her children, and they were cut off from her by a barrier of air pressure and freezing cold.

She passed the rec room, hearing sounds of people attempting low-gravity Ping-Pong, laughing and trading good-natured insults. Someone else played an electronic game.

She kept walking. Her vision was focused into a narrow tunnel, muffled, with gray around the edges. Without realizing it, Rachel found herself back in the communications center. She slumped back in her chair and sighed. The air was cold enough that she could see a faint white wisp of her breath.

On a panel, she found an insistent red light flashing—an emergency circuit. She sat up quickly, her years of training and experience shunting the lethargy aside. She had no way of telling how long it had been activated; with her lack of attention earlier, it could have been on for hours. She muttered an insult to herself and squinted down at the indicator.

The signal came from one of the *dva* pumping stations. She ran the coordinates over in her mind, pinpointing its location. The *dvas* checked in regularly, but they rarely had anything to report. Something must have happened to them.

She touched the icon on the screen, linking up to their transmitter. "Yes? I receive you. What is the problem? Report!" With her other hand she punched up current status numbers for the pumping station and saw the severity of their problem. Water pressure had dropped disastrously in one of the pipelines, and the other had been shut off completely.

"*Dva* station, please respond! What has happened out there?"

She had to repeat the transmission three times

before anyone answered. No picture formed on the screen, only a burst of black-and-white static. "Hello?" Rachel said again. "I am not getting an image."

The voice that came back spoke Russian. "Emergency! Pumping station inoperable. Massive water spillage. Pipe breach. Please send help!"

"What is it? Why can't I get a picture?" she demanded. "This is Commissioner Dycek. Please tell me."

"Video circuits destroyed. Send investigating team." A short pause. "Better you see for yourself."

Rachel sat in silence, staring at the static skirling across the flat panel. She remained stony-faced. If something had happened to the *dvas*, she wanted to see it in person. She was the only one who cared enough to do a good job. This seemed to be more than just a few pieces of missing equipment or supply losses that had plagued the *dvas* since their beginning. With a leaden heart Rachel somehow knew this would be a disaster as great as the one that had destroyed the *dva* team at Noctis Labyrinthus.

On the eve of her departure for Earth, Mars would deal her one last great slap in the face.

"Acknowledged," she said. In the back of her throat, her voice started to tremble, but she stopped it. "I will come out to investigate this personally."

Suited up, Rachel let herself out of the Lowell Base airlock into the hollow shelter that protected the three vehicles. One long-distance rover, *Percival*, sat unclaimed for the day.

With a self-protective dread, Rachel did not want to leave any hint of the *dva* distress call until she had seen the situation for herself. Damage control. She debated going back inside to enter her destination and the purpose of her unscheduled excursion in the roster. If any of the other Lowell Base personnel had committed such a frivolous, unprofessional act, Rachel would have severely reprimanded them—but what more could they do to her anyway?

Rachel considered letting Keefer deal with the emergency situation. He was the new commissioner, wasn't he? But Rachel had to see what it was. They were her *dvas*.

Seated behind the AI piloting panel, she argued with the automatic pilot to switch off *Percival*'s locating beacon. Operations Manager Vickery would probably overreact, and Keefer would feel duty-bound—gung ho like a typical American—and charge out to drag Rachel back home. No thanks.

She wasn't supposed to go out by herself in the rover (as Evrani had told her in his last lecture), without filing a detailed description of her destination, how long she would be gone, and when rescue teams should be dispatched if she failed to return.

"Fuck it," she said, in perfect colloquial English. Her stomach felt cold and tight, as if someone with a spiked glove kept squeezing her stomach.

She eased *Percival* out of the cavelike garage and picked up speed as she moved across the packed area of pinkish concrete around Lowell Base. Passage marks from hundreds of daily excursions crisscrossed the dusty plain from the base, around the jagged Spine, out to the landing pad. The all-terrain legs of the rover could scramble over most obstacles, and Rachel instructed the AI pilot to pick the fastest course. According to her coordinates, the *dva* pumping station was about three hundred kilometers away, at the foot of Pavonis Mons—a five-hour journey at the rover's top speed.

Rachel circled the Spine, and when the sharp crags blocked her view of the inflatable modules, she headed out. With an odd, superstitious foreboding, she turned around to look out the side windows, and was disappointed to see that she could not take one last view of the base.

RACHEL DYCEK

ICE, THE COLOR OF spilled platinum on ochre dust, extended from the breached pipeline. Water jets had boiled into the thin atmosphere and frozen into steaming, lumpy stalactites and weird white pinnacles protruding from the pipe. Before long, the solid lake would erase itself again, frothing into the Martian sky.

As she brought *Percival* toward the pumping station, Rachel stared in horror and tried to assess the area of spilled ice. "Thousands of liters," she said to herself, "many thousands."

She thought again with dismay of all the misplaced spare parts, the lost equipment, the annoying long-distance UN mutterings of her own mismanagement and "thieving *dvas*." Had they begun engaging in sabotage as well—perhaps to protest her departure as commissioner?

No, she decided. *Dva* sabotage maybe, but not to protest her replacement.

Rachel felt a dull sinking sensation inside as she stared at the roiling, steaming fog of precious water. A disaster as bad as she had feared. Because it had happened at a pumping station supervised by the *dvas*, her *dvas*, someone would no doubt find a way to trace it back to her. Yes, Rachel had been right to keep quiet about it for now, until she could think of some way to salvage the situation.

Rachel turned a sharp eye from the clinging scabs of ice to the broken pipe itself. The thin-walled vessel was more than just breached—someone had torn it apart with a crowbar. Sabotage indeed. Were the various *dva* settlements feuding with each other? The *dvas* were composed of different ethnic groups from the Sovereign Republics, and such struggles had been common throughout history—but never here on Mars.

The rover eased to a halt outside the pumping shack. With a sigh of small pressure pumps, it settled to the ground, kicking up a halo of fine dust. Rachel suited up as the AI went through its automatic shutdown and standby procedures. She checked her suit's oxygen-regenerator system, then cycled through the rover's sphincter airlock.

Three *dvas* emerged from the insulated Quonset hut, their meager shelter constructed of prefabricated components. Rachel watched the *dvas* approach, recognizing none of them by name, though she placed the lead male and his ethnic group: Kazakh, from near the dried-up Aral Sea, which had been one of Earth's largest freshwater bodies until Joseph Stalin had obliterated it in the early twentieth century in his own disastrous attempts to rework the landscape to fit his whim. When the call went out for *dva* volunteers, many families from the Aral region had leaped at the chance to come to Mars, to make a new start. But even here on a new planet they clung to their ethnic groupings.

"Commissioner Dycek!" the leading *dva* male greeted her. Though he bellowed with expanded lungs, his voice sounded watery in the thin air, muffled through her helmet sound pickups.

He was a squat man with broad shoulders, wearing loose insulated overalls and padded gloves that made his fingers look like sausages. Steam swirled around his head as he breathed. The man's nose and ears were flattened to protect them from heat loss; the nostrils were wide sinks in the face to allow inhalation of greater volumes. Inside, the *dvas* had a labyrinth of sinuses to warm the frigid air before it entered the lungs. The enlarged lungs bore attached efficiency modules, tightly packaged membranes to snatch more oxygen molecules from the air.

The two *dva* females also wore padded silvery overalls. They clung beside the man like superstitious children. All three looked battered, as if they had tumbled in a heavy brawl. The male and one of the females sported bloodstained bandages. Rachel suddenly remembered there were supposed to be five *dvas* assigned to this station. Where were the other two?

The burly male did the talking. "We did not expect someone of such importance to investigate our mishap," he said. His accent was thick and exotic. "But we are glad it is you, Commissioner Dycek. Only you can understand how bad it truly is. You will understand."

Rachel turned her head inside the environment suit, trying to calculate the extent of the leakage. A heavy cost, naturally, but Lowell Base had plenty of surplus, as did the other bases. "What do you mean? How much water was lost?"

The *dva* man gestured to the metallic sheet of ice. "We managed to shut off the water up-line, and we will repair the damage here." With the flat of his hand he knocked away one of the hanging icicles. It shattered with a sound like breaking crystal as it struck the frozen ground. "Come with me, Commissioner. Let me show you what else."

Rachel's environment suit crinkled as she followed the *dva* man. She remained tight-lipped, afraid of what he might show her, of what last surprises Mars might spring on her. The air tasted sour and dusty from the chemical-regenerator pack.

Keeping together as if afraid to let each other out of sight, the three *dvas* led Rachel behind their hut. Part of the main door was battered in, and then shorn up from the inside. Bright scars showed where someone had forced an entry. One of the thick transparent window plates had been knocked loose.

Near the door, under a coating of reddish dust and tendrils of frost, two iron-hard *dva* corpses lay on the ground. Rachel bent down to look at the frozen crimson wounds, the splotched white skin. She had seen plenty of blood during her career as a surgeon, but the pure malice and violence here made the rancid taste of bile climb into her throat.

71

The dead male's skull had been cleaved through to the brain, and the woman had been impaled through the chest. A stained scrap-metal sword lay next to the bodies. With a brief shudder, she thought of a roving gang of bandits, creating murder and mayhem among the *dva* settlements. But that sounded ridiculous. What did the *dvas* have that someone else might want? And who would want it?

New ideas roared through her mind like the whirlwind of the approaching storm. A domestic squabble . . . two *dvas* killing each other over jealousy, or a card game, or one of the innumerable and stupid cabin-fever reasons she had seen so often in Neryungri? The Russian temper often led to drunken brawls that turned into manslaughter. But never before on Mars.

Yes, indeed, this would look far worse in her dossier than an accidental avalanche. UNSA would have a field day with her, and she would have to give all the explanations. "Tell me what happened," she said in a weary voice.

"Wait, that is not all. We left this other one by himself."

The *dva* man took her to the other side of the hut, while the women hovered over the bodies of their companions. "We did not want him tainting the soil beside our comrades."

Rachel's mind was already spinning. Another one? But only five *dvas* were stationed at this post. Who? An outside attacker?

The third body lay sprawled, arms akimbo, head cocked against a shoulder as if the *dvas* had hurled his body there in disgust, like so much garbage. Inside her helmet Rachel let out a gasp.

"*Adin*," the *dva* man said, stating the obvious.

"I . . . thought they were all dead. . . ." Rachel said, aghast, unable to cope with the flood of sudden realization. It was as if her whole world had shifted on its axis.

"Not all," the *dva* man answered, gesturing with his stubby gloved hand at the exaggerated adaptations of the *adin*. The *adin's* head was smashed, making him unrecognizable. The corpse wore a tattered, thin jumpsuit in the freezing air, with much of the skin exposed. The *adin* must have lived like this in the wild environment, unprotected.

"They came out of the darkness," the *dva* man said. "They made noises outside to frighten us, and as you know we *dvas* have no weapons. His comrade wrecked the pipeline. This *adin* smashed through the doorway of our dwelling and attacked us. He killed two of us before I could club him to death."

Rachel swallowed. "You said there was another one?"

"He got away," the *dva* man said. "The women injured him, but he escaped. We could not pursue him in the darkness. We had to hike up-line to shut off the water flow, otherwise it would have been worse."

Looking down at the dead *adin*, Rachel felt dizziness like black raven's wings fluttering around her temples.

"If he returns, though, we will be ready for him." The *dva* man's face showed a grim stoicism. From beside the hut, he pulled out a long digging implement and jabbed it into the ground. The frozen mud rang with the force of the blow.

Rachel turned back to the lake of ice and the broken pipeline that stretched from the water-rich volcanic rocks of the Tharsis highlands. The cone of Pavonis Mons rose high and symmetrical in the middle distance.

"But you think you can repair this yourselves?" she asked. Perhaps she would not need to give all the details to Lowell Base. She could doctor the numbers, file a routine leakage report.

The *dva* man hung his head as if in shame, then nodded. "We are self-sufficient here, Commissioner, but we will need extra supplies and equipment. Much was damaged. And there will be no more *dvas* to replace our fallen comrades. It will be difficult."

"You will have to make do." Rachel frowned, preoccupied. "I thought you already had a complete set of spare parts."

The *dva* man shrugged and spread his hands helplessly. "Components do not last long in this environment, Commissioner. We have so many hardships."

"I will see what I can do, but you need to make your repairs with haste," Rachel said. The skies to the north looked thicker than normal, clogged. "Our weathersat shows a class four dust storm on its way. It should arrive late tomorrow."

The *dva* women looked at her with sharp, deep-set eyes, but kept their silence, as if they held Rachel in awe. The *dva* man shrugged and took a step backward. "We already know about the storm, Commissioner. We can smell it in the air."

Rachel nodded behind her faceplate and hesitated. "One last question. This *adin* who escaped—where did he go? Do you have any idea where I might find him?"

The *dva* man lowered his eyes, then turned to extend his arm, spreading a gloved hand toward the gently sloping symmetrical cone of Pavonis Mons that rode the foreshortened horizon. "We think he may have been the Man of the Mountain. There have been sightings, rumors, for many years. We *dvas* see many things, Commissioner. If you wish to find the *adins*, look there."

Rachel turned back to her rover, her mind buzzing with fear and uncertainty. Did she really want to find the *adins*, if they still survived? They had caused more damage to her career and pain than any of her other failures. But Rachel Dycek wanted to face them, to demand answers . . . and to learn what they had been doing for the last fifteen years.

The *dva* man followed her, touching her suited arm. She felt the pressure of his strong grip through the tough, insulated fabric. His eyes were shadowed under their sheltering brows, deeply concerned.

"About your successor, Commissioner. . ." he said.

"He does understand what we are doing here? The *dvas* will not be sent back to Earth?"

Rachel felt a stab inside as she stared at the *dva* man and his two women, looking forlorn beside their ruined pipeline, their damaged shelter, their dead comrades. "No, you do not have to worry about that. Mars is your home now. You own this land, remember? It is in the UNSA agreement for all *dva* volunteers. You will stay here for the rest of your lives. Continue to do your best."

"We will, Commissioner."

Rachel clambered back through the airlock membrane of the rover. Her eyes stung with disappointed tears. Just what *would* Keefer do with her *dvas*? If he proved too unfeeling, maybe they would rebel just as the *adins* had.

She flipped up her faceplate and took long breaths of the cold air inside the vehicle. After sitting motionless behind the controls of the rover for a long moment, she noticed the *dvas* staring at her, waiting for her to depart. "Power on, *Percival*," she said. "Prepare to depart."

Rachel drove off toward the volcanic highlands and the mighty rise of Pavonis, leaving the *dvas* behind with their spilled ice and their dead.

CORA MARISOVNA

SHE WAITED AT the cave mouth, watching the desolate face of Mars below. She waited for *him*. Cora felt as if she died every time Boris went away. He had been gone for so long.

Barely able to move anymore, Cora Marisovna took her monotonous meals just inside the sheltering passage. Her joints swollen, her muscles creaking, she waited for the inevitable.

Always keeping himself busy, Stroganov went about the unending tasks that only he seemed to care about. The other *adins* had settled into an angry or apathetic listlessness, but Stroganov continued to find work, to find goals, to leave his mark in a way that Cora secretly suspected would last far longer than any grand gesture Boris made. And Stroganov's sculptures and text chronicles were far less dangerous than Boris's attacks.

Nastasia paced back and forth, chattering, sometimes speaking to Cora, sometimes to the bare rocks. Cora wished that she could find her own fantasy world to live in, as Nastasia had, a place where she could live happily ever after with her prince and a family of laughing children.

Inside, the *adin* caves were comfortable, the air warm and breathable, if tainted with sulfurous exhaust from the slumbering shield volcano. The dim light hid the traces of green lichen that crawled over the rocks. The distant sun had risen, spilling pale light along the cracked slopes. The interior of the lava tubes sparkled as frost exhaled into steam with the day's warmth.

Though she could not feel the cold wind against her *adin* skin, Cora took comfort in knowing she was in some kind of shelter—though it held little comfort without Boris Tiban.

She had begun her vigil at the cave mouth as soon as Boris left with Nikolas the day before. Outside, Stroganov's tall stone faces stared like palace guards, scowling visages of famous Russian heroes. Cora wondered how her Boris Tiban would stack up against them in the march of history. Would anyone sing folk songs about the first great Martian rebel?

Cora thought of how long it had been since she had tried to sing. Had she ever sung on Mars? It would be a frivolous waste of moisture and air.

Boris had heard her lovely voice only a few times in the rich atmosphere of Earth, in Neryungri in the spring before the surgeries. Cora's voice had been deep and musical, not the shrill tones caused by thin air. By its very nature, Mars ruined everything.

Cora had also been beautiful as a girl. As a human. But she refused to leave the caves now, especially now.

In the grotto, out of sight but not earshot, Stroganov and Nastasia were making love—he, somber and silent; she, calling him by various names from her imaginary world. Stroganov seemed pleased to be confused with historical figures, especially when she cried out the name of one of his sculpted heroes. In the echoing upper chamber Stroganov gasped loudly and then he was finished, as always. He got up to return to the lower tunnels, back to his work. Nastasia lay by herself, cooing.

Cora continued her vigil. Phobos passed overhead again, trailing a few dim shooting stars. The shadows changed positions on the rocks.

Barely noticeable, a tiny figure appeared on the slope below, toiling upward. Cora leaned forward, trying to see better. It was an *adin*, moving at a steady pace—an *adin* alone. He plodded without enthusiasm, as if defeated.

She felt a stab go through her abdomen and she winced. Her muscles clenched, distracting her—but the physical pain was nothing. What if Boris had been killed? She was terribly afraid of him when he was with her, afraid for him when he was gone. Cora knew the lengths to which Boris would go, the desperate actions he had taken in his life, the foolhardy risks. Cora didn't understand why.

Or what if Nikolas had died? Young Nikolas, who looked up to his leader with selfless adoration, had volunteered for the *adin* surgeries the moment he learned that Boris had been selected for the program. Boris had been angry with him, annoyed that Nikolas would voluntarily play the government's game, but Nikolas would not relent. He had his mind set on going to Mars with the rest of the *adins*, with Boris Tiban.

What if Nikolas had been the one killed? Or lost, or captured? It would be a devastating tragedy for the surviving *adins*, but Cora found herself praying for the lesser of two disasters. She could not bear to lose Boris.

"Someone is coming!" she shouted down into the cavern, then drew a deep hitching breath. "He is alone!"

By the time Stroganov had worked his way back to the entrance, still holding the metal stylus he used to etch his words into the polished rock wall, Cora could squint through her frilled eyeguards and make out the body outline of the approaching *adin*. Yes, it was Boris, the man she had held, around whom she had wrapped her arms and legs in the frigid sands or on iron-hard lava rock.

Boris had returned from his raid, leaving Nikolas behind.

Stroganov brushed past Cora, ignoring her, and hurried out of the cave. "Oh, no," he muttered. Nastasia clung to his arm.

The long morning shadows streamed out behind the tall, thin statues of old Russian rebels, making a forest of dimness. Stroganov hesitated, staring at the solitary *adin* trudging up the slope. He waited, standing like a dead tree.

Feeling awkward and bloated, Cora pulled herself to her feet and went to the pool of sunlight at the cave's edge, but she stopped short of going outside. She felt herself trembling, not wanting to learn what had happened.

"Where is Nikolas?" Stroganov shouted as soon as Boris came near enough.

Boris did not answer until he had come all the way up to their shelter. He looked at Stroganov and Nastasia, glanced toward Cora before she could flinch back into the darkness, then stared beseechingly at the tall, glowering heads of the historical rebels, like a penitent praying before an icon.

"Dead," he finally said. "Nikolas is dead. The *dvas* killed him." He leaned against his pointed metal staff for a moment, as if in defeat, then winced before striding toward the cave mouth.

Stroganov hunched suddenly, as if he had received a blow to the stomach. He leaned against the weather-worn sculpture of Lenin for support. "Oh, Boris!" Stroganov said. His words sounded too human and too sympathetic coming from the tight, insulated lips, the flattened face.

Boris mumbled so quietly that Cora could barely hear him. "We destroyed one of the water pumping stations. Now they know that the *adins* are still around, and perhaps they will tremble in their beds, fearing where we will strike next. They must know we will avenge Nikolas."

At first, Nastasia did not seem to know who Boris was talking about, but then she fell forward to the crumbled lava, wailing in grief. She picked up a fistful of the sharp volcanic debris and rubbed it on her face, scoring the plasticized skin. She pounded her fist in the dirt, making small craters. Boris and Stroganov just watched her, unable to help, accustomed to her unpredictable reactions.

Boris turned toward the cave, paused to look at Cora uncertainly, but she flinched, feeling the fear of him return. He plodded toward her, as if a great weight bore him down, despite the low gravity. Carrying his titanium staff, Boris looked very regal, like a tsar in his own right.

Fighting her fear, Cora stepped out to meet him, swaying as she walked. "I am glad you came back, Boris. I was worried." He embraced her, and he actually seemed to be trembling.

She remembered how this angry man had taken control of the other *adins*, how he had led them in his dreams for their future on Mars, just like the Cossack rebel Pugachev. Though the *adins* had seen more death than any of them had ever imagined, the loss of Nikolas had dealt him a deep wound. With Nikolas dead, only four *adins* remained of the initial thirty. Twenty-six dead in sixteen years. It had once been a grand dream for them to be *adins*, following their great hero Boris, but now . . .

Boris stood rigid, in silence, for a long moment. The stubby ends of his fingers pressed against Cora's back. "I can barely feel you against me, Cora," he whispered into the protected ear holes. "I'm like a man in a rubber monster suit from one of those ridiculous American films about Martians."

Cora shook her head against his chest. *No*, she thought, *we are all human inside. Human!* The changes to Cora's body were vivid reminders of that. Boris must never forget it.

Thirty *adins* had survived the transformational surgery in Siberia—fewer than half of the candidates, though the camp doctors had not been forthcoming with the actual numbers of their failures. The uncertainty and the rumors among the hurting and recovering patients made the fear seem greater.

A young woman, Cora had been terrified, but she remained quiet through every step of the process, trying not to be noticed by anyone else who could hurt her. Taking the medications they gave her, willingly performing all the test routines, inhaling the anesthetic, refusing to complain when she felt the agony of healing incisions and dissolving internal stitches over and over and over again. From the time of her childhood, any thought of argument had been squashed out of her. The best thing was usually to nod and do as she was told. She remembered trying to sleep in the dim recovery ward, listening to the others whimper, her head filled with a thousand questions she was too afraid to ask.

As with many of the native Siberian children in the villages around Neryungri, Cora was ethnically mixed, mostly Siberian with an obvious trace of Mongol and a dash of gypsy blood. She had dark beautiful eyes, long glistening Asiatic hair, and a wiry body that might have looked delicate at first glance but had been tuned and strengthened by a life of hardship. At least, that was how she *remembered* she looked.

Cora had been raised by her mother and grandmother near the labor camp after her father died in a construction accident. Sometimes her mother took Cora on bricklaying projects in cold so intense that the mortar froze faster than the workers could lay bricks. At other times, her grandmother made her sit and do embroidery in a poorly ventilated room, with fumes from kerosene heaters that made her dark eyes burn. Once, her grandmother had commented on how beautiful and shiny Cora's eyes were.

By the time Cora turned twenty, her mother and grandmother were in desperate financial straits, losing ground each year. With the repeated economic upheavals and devalued currency in the Sovereign Republics, no one had money to buy the pretty embroidered things the women produced at home. The population in the camp itself was growing smaller.

Then the big scientific facility had appeared. The *adin* project needed healthy young female subjects. The call for volunteers extended beyond the camp boundaries to the Neryungri village proper.

Cora had not known the purpose behind the original questionnaires or medical screening. Unschooled, she had not known anything about planets or orbits or terraforming. Mars was simply a name, a bright orange light in the sky her mother had shown her once.

When the representatives from Moscow came from door to door in the village, Cora filled out the forms her mother and grandmother gave her. After the doctors ran several tests and asked probing questions, someone else from the project came and offered Cora's mother twenty thousand New Rubles for her daughter's participation. There had been no real choice in the matter for her. Never any choice.

Cora had not even asked what the doctors were doing until after the first surgery started, and she woke up, looking in the mirror to see her disfigured nose, her ears, her eyebrows. She had not screamed, or wailed, or struck out at the doctors as some of the other subjects had. She had endured. That was her first lesson in learning how to be an *adin*.

Thirty *adins* had been smuggled off to the aging launch complex at Starry Town for the cargo shuttle that would boost them into orbit for rendezvous with a Japanese-made cargo carrier to Mars. Because of the secrecy, they had to use the old facilities at Baikonur instead of newer establishments in the western Sovereign Republics. Head down, Cora had gone where the people in charge told her to, kept quiet unless she was asked a direct question. She waited for it all to end. But it never ended, only changed.

The months she spent crowded in zero gravity on the substandard cargo transport had been an uninterrupted nightmare, with nothing to do except wait and listen to the other *adins* talk of the wide-open spaces across the surface of Mars, vaster than the whole of Siberia. Cora longed to be free, to stretch her legs and run as she had once done through the birch forests.

But other *adins* claimed that conditions on Mars would be worse than anything they had yet experienced. The few *adin* officers kept themselves isolated from the Neryungri convicts. As weeks passed, the air pressure inside the space vessel dropped lower and lower, the temperature turned colder. The passengers were adapting for the environment of Mars.

Cora Marisovna had been one of the last to emerge from the lander, watching other *adins* as they milled about on the barren sands of a new world. Some frolicked in the low gravity—Boris Tiban had been one of them. Others stood dazed. A few clutched their throats and retched.

They had been told to expect as many as seven of them to die because of failures to adapt, imperfect surgical augmentations, and unforeseen circumstances. But it was worse than that. Ten *adins*, fully a third of their number, perished within the initial week, unable to breathe, unable to metabolize, unable to see. One of the first had been the leader of the mission, Commander Gotenko, who succumbed before camp was even set up.

Vice Commander Vadim Dozintsev took over, whipping the other *adins* into a familiar work-camp routine to establish living quarters—not comfortable pressurized habitats like the eventual human inhabitants would enjoy, but crude open-air shelters. Month after month, they had worked together in selfless exertion to make Mars a better place. For *themselves*.

Many of the *adins* resented having to make the planet more comfortable for humans who had not gone through the painful *adin* surgeries. Others argued against continuing an outdated UNSA plan that had been developed without knowledge of the *adins*. The presence of augmented humans should change all schedules and estimates. But Vice Commander Dozintsev insisted, and used draconian measures to squelch any complaints.

The work went on for a year, with daily and then weekly informational updates beamed back to Earth. Earth wanted to watch an adventure, the quaint struggle for survival. Before the surgeries, though, all of the *adins* had been completely cut off from their homes. They had no family, no friends, no one to whom they wanted to wave greetings.

When the inflatable components of UNSA's modular base arrived on the surface of Mars, delivered by robot ships, Vice Commander Dozintsev ordered the work details to assemble parts of the initial human outpost several years ahead of schedule. The assembly would be ridiculously easy for the powerful and adapted *adins*.

But the *adins* had grave misgivings about building a pressurized and heated paradise for humans who had not even arrived. Boris Tiban rebelled. He refused to make the slightest effort to help other humans enjoy Mars. He defied Dozintsev's orders to assemble the base components, destroying one irreplaceable component in his anger. Many of the *adins* grumbled along with him, and Dozintsev tried to force him back into line, to discipline him—but Boris was stronger, and defeated the vice commander in a low-gravity brawl that left Dozintsev battered and Boris in the leader's role. The other *adins* stood beside him, expecting their lot to change . . . but Boris did not make changes in small increments.

In the last official *adin* transmission to Earth, Boris Tiban had hauled the bloodied vice commander in front of the cameras. With a forty-minute round-trip transmission lag, the *adins* could be gone from the station before the Earth monitors could even respond. Boris had liked that, using the delayed messages to taunt and frustrate Earthbound observers. Neither UNSA nor the Sovereign Republics could do a damned thing about it.

As the others watched, not knowing what this angry rebel intended, Boris snapped Vadim Dozintsev's neck over his knee. Before any of the *adins* could cry out or argue with him, it was too late.

"There, your puppet is executed!" Boris said, grinning into the camera. "Now the workers have taken matters into their own hands. We will make our own home on Mars. You are not welcome here." He then disconnected the transmitting array, snapping the metal spire from the center of the dish and keeping it as his royal staff.

A few others fought against him; two died. But the *adins* really had no other choice, and no one else wanted to battle for the leadership of their small band. Nikolas had been Boris's staunchest supporter and helped rally the surviving *adins* after Dozintsev's execution.

Abandoning what he called the decadent and comfortable modules, Boris had taken his group away from the civilized areas of Mars, away from the prepackaged examples of technology that humans needed to live outside, away from the graves of the fallen *adins*. They needed none of these things. The *adins* scavenged all the equipment, supplies, and technological items they could carry. Boris took only his long staff, a symbol of his victory over the old masters, and he led the *adins* to the higher altitudes of Pavonis Mons, to a more suitable climate, where they could live in peace.

The *adins* had been the first true Martians, feeling the soil with their bare feet, breathing the razor-thin air directly into their enhanced lungs. They had set out to conquer a world, and they had succeeded, too well. Now, none of them could breathe the dense air below. The terraforming process was stealing the world they had worked so hard to create.

In less than three Martian years, the first *dvas* arrived. They had been planned to replace the *adins* all along.

JESÚS KEEFER

DOZENS OF REMOTE experimental substations lay scattered across the top of the Spine, like a collection of mad-scientist apparatus exposed to the greenish sky.

Jesús Keefer and his companions craned forward to peer out *Schiaparelli*'s wide front windowport as Bruce Vickery, their tour guide, brought the rover to a halt. Moving at about fifteen miles per hour even with the vehicle's terrain-gripping mobile legs, Vickery had spent part of the morning toiling along the rugged slope. The crumbling rock looked as if it barely held together in the low gravity.

Finally they reached the top, emerging from the morning shadows into the bright wash of light, where the shielded mound of Lowell Base's small power reactor steamed and hissed in the frigid air. To Keefer, the reactor mound looked like a snoring dragon, and his faint gasp echoed inside his helmet. "Would you look at that!"

"Okay, everybody out," Vickery said, clapping his gloved hands with a muffled sound. He was blustery and personable, and Keefer liked the operations manager immediately upon meeting him. "Check your suits, just like in all the bleeping training videos. Once we get lined up, I've got a surprise for everybody. It'll give meaning to your lives."

Vickery grinned at them from behind the controls, his blue eyes sparkling. He had reddish hair, a sandy and freckled complexion, and a beard that looked grayer than it should have been. Wide face and ruddy skin gave him an appearance that reminded Keefer of a stereotypical roughneck. Vickery was also the base's undefeated Ping-Pong champion. During the drive up the winding access road both Ogawa and Shen had challenged him to a game later that day in the recreation module.

On reaching their destination Vickery directed the AI to shut the vehicle down, then fastened his own helmet. The fizzing sounds of all the O_2 regenerator systems made Keefer feel as if they were trapped inside a giant bottle of mineral water.

Keefer and Chetwynd passed shoulder-to-shoulder through the sphincter airlock, following Vickery. The other riders waited for their turns to disembark. Encased in his suit, Keefer could not feel the soft Martian wind, though far off he saw red-orange dust devils skirling over the monotonous boulder-strewn flatlands. A bland, scoured Mars that seemed to flaunt itself in the face of the terraforming efforts. The algae and lichens had fixed some of the dust, cutting down erosion, but the effect had so far been minuscule.

Outside on the high peaks Keefer stood next to the rover and gawked up at the sky smeared with olive clouds. The rover made tocking noises as it settled into idle mode, retracting its sea-urchin legs. Chetwynd bent down to peer at exposed rocks, running a gloved finger over tendrils of lichen on the sunward surfaces. "A veritable oasis here, I might say."

Bruce Vickery marched out to the scattered experimental stations, nets of thermocouples stretched from shadow to sunlight, anemometers, hygrometers, and a varied array of automated atmospheric analysis stations. Keefer followed him, amazed and delighted to see the Lowell Base data-collection array that had been featured in so many online space publications.

Standing at the cliff edge looking toward the sun, Keefer raised a gloved hand to his faceplate, then remembered to adjust the polarization to drown out the unwanted glare as he scanned the breathtaking landscape. The crags blocked his view of the full plains of Mars, but he could see incredible distances. The clear thin air did nothing to distort vision. The horizon was foreshortened, swallowing up the beginning jumble of Valles Marineris in the east, but he could see the distant swellings of three parallel volcanoes brushing the horizon to the west, Ascraeus, Pavonis, and Arsia Mons. He had studied the satellite photos and the gazetteer for so many years, waiting and dreaming, that it seemed unreal now to see the actual landmarks.

Amazing! he muttered. One day, he vowed, Allan would see it for himself. If only the boy worked hard on his studies, took the right courses, completed the right apprenticeship programs. Keefer would make sure he had every opportunity. It was the least he could do, to make up for being away from him for so many years.

Vickery opened *Schiaparelli*'s back storage bay, swinging the flexible aluminum hatch up to display a stack of nested plastic domes. He waved his hands to get everybody's attention. "Okay, stand together for a minute while I talk." His deep voice came out fuzzy through the speakerpatch.

"Turns out this is going to be more than a sightseeing trip. I brought you guys up here because I need some help battening the hatches, so to speak. I intended to do most of this work yesterday, but our illustrious Commissioner Dycek wandered off with the rover until late in the day, so I only got the lower tiers done. Now you're going to bail me out before the dust clouds come."

Keefer stepped forward, eager to do something hands-on rather than just take tours and review summary reports. "Okay. What do you need us to do, Bruce?"

Vickery gestured to the scattered experiment stations. "Those collectors need to be protected from the storm with shieldcaps mounted on top of them. I'm not going to let those reflective surfaces get sandblasted."

He went over to the nearest station, a small ultralight anemometer whirling in the thin breeze. "Just watch me and figure it out for yourselves. You're smart people." Vickery popped out a lower brace, then disengaged the apparatus. "Okay, now for step two." Returning to the rover, Vickery removed one of the translucent plastic shieldcaps and mounted it in position, snapping the metal edges onto holder pins around the meteorological instrument.

"I've had plenty of practice at this, but you all might want to work in pairs." He moved to the next collector in the array and repeated his performance. "We've got a hundred of these puppies to stow—and if any of you bangs up a single one of them, I'll make you walk back to Earth to get me a replacement. Got it?"

Keefer and Chetwynd raised eyebrows at each other behind their faceplates, silently agreeing to be partners. Keefer took a crank from *Schiaparelli*'s storage bay and Chetwynd tucked a stack of flimsy shieldcaps under his arm before hiking to one section of collectors.

Keefer thought of the first manned expedition, when the crew had roughed it in inflated tents, worse than the most unpleasant camping trip on Earth. Now, as he thought of the cluster of modules below, the greenhouse, the meteorological sensors up here, even the water pipelines and the ice mining, he felt renewed awe at the progress humanity had made. They had a planet in the palm of their hands and they were caressing it into life.

It was early afternoon by the time they finished the work. Vickery strode around the shielded apparatus like a burly crew boss, checking to make sure nothing would come loose in the high winds. "Good work," he said. "Sincerely. Now, let's go back to base and goof around. You guys deserve a little relaxation."

His words met with no complaint.

While his companions gathered in the recreation module, Keefer went instead to the single privacy booth in the communications center. He collected his thoughts, wanting to get his videoletter right the first time, since he hated the tedium of editing.

On board the Moon-Mars spacecraft, while the others used the exercise equipment or Captain Rubens told tall tales, Keefer often kept an electronic journal, which he uplinked and transmitted to his son's e-mail address. He had no idea whether Allan read his father's ramblings, but Keefer kept transmitting them anyway.

Now, Keefer sat straight in the booth and checked himself in the small courtesy mirror to the side, out of camera range. Sound baffles covered the ceiling and floor like geometrically perfect stalactites made of blue foam. He had already shaved. He straightened his thick dark hair, tried on various expressions, then turned to the image area. He cracked his knuckles in a last nervous gesture and then stepped on the ACTIVATE button with his right foot.

"Hi, Allan! Or should I say, 'Greetings, Earthling, I speak to you from the planet Mars'?" Keefer smiled. In the milky opaque image area, he pictured Allan's face, looking at him with rapt attention.

Allan was Keefer's son by a former lover, Gina. Although Gina and he had gone their separate ways back when Allan was only a baby, Keefer had followed his son closely, paying generous child support and helping Allan go to the best schools. He was confident the boy would one day surpass him by leaps and bounds.

"I really wish you could be here, Allan, and someday you will be. I know it." He gave a wistful smile. "It's been a long time since you and I had a real back-and-forth conversation. There's so much I want to tell you, but right now the transmission lag is about fourteen minutes. We'll have to be content with a videoletter."

Relaxing, he chattered about the day's expedition up the side of the Spine and working with the solar panels. He talked about the people on the base, his impressions. With glazed eyes and a distant expression Keefer spoke of the colors in the skies, the lichens on the rocks, the frost in the morning . . . all direct results of the UNSA terraforming work.

Which led to a discussion about Allan's future, his schooling, his work in college. "Yes, I know there will be some courses you won't like, but don't let it be a stumbling block. Trust me, it's worth it. Always keep the end in sight. I know you can do it."

He folded his hands behind his head, then noticed the red light blinking. "Uh-oh, time's up. I can't wait to see you again, but you'll be almost thirty by then. Man, that's hard to believe. I'll send another message as soon as I can, and I'll try to get authorization for you to send your own videoletter reply. Bye."

He clicked the button a second time with his foot and got to his feet with a sigh. Then he encoded it with appropriate passwords and transmitted the videoletter in a datapackage to the communications satellite.

Weary and wrung out, he decided against further socializing in the rec area and found his way to his quarters. He had not had much time to unwind since they reached Mars orbit. Though cramped by Earth standards, his room seemed spacious compared to his cabin on the Moon-Mars craft.

A new module had been added to Lowell Base in the last year. Robotically landed, the module had remained in its packaging for weeks until it was attached and inflated. Despite UNSA's request that the base personnel connect it themselves as an exercise, Rachel Dycek had ignored the orders and insisted that her *dvas* do the work. The augmented humans had completed the task in half the projected time, though a few items of equipment had turned up missing shortly afterward. Stories about sticky-fingered *dvas* were getting to be a joke, and Keefer promised to look into it. He suspected Dycek had a blind spot where her own project was concerned.

Yawning, he snapped out his bunk from the wall and locked down the braces. Moving slowly, feeling his muscles unknot, Keefer stripped out of his jumpsuit, turned up the space heater, and sponged off with an everdamp pad. He pulled on another insulated garment, moving quickly in the inescapable chill.

Finally, he lay back on the bunk, closing his eyes and hissing out a long, relaxed breath. He smelled clean, he felt at peace. *He was on Mars*. Outside, separated from him by only a thin wall of metallized plastic, the air of another planet tickled the modules.

Of course, the contentment could not last more than a few moments. It was the way of things.

Quick footsteps, then an insistent tapping on the wall near his quarters. "Commissioner Keefer! Excuse me. We have a problem. Are you in there? Commissioner Keefer?"

He got up to greet Dr. Evrani, a small, active Pakistani who seemed a constant blur of motion—fidgeting, shuffling feet, darting eyes, palms brushing his thinning hair back.

"Yes? What is it?"

"It is no surprise, that is what it is! Some people cannot be bothered with the simplest responsibilities, no matter how important they may be." Evrani scowled and shook his head, looking at Keefer as if he were a coconspirator.

Keefer leaned against the door. "Who are you talking about?"

"Commissioner Dycek, of course! We left her in charge of the communications center this morning. But now she's gone. She has taken one of the long-distance rovers without even signing it out! No destination marked." Evrani made a disgusted sound. "She constantly is doing things like this. I am glad you are replacing her, sir."

Keefer felt a coil of tension wind up inside him again. He recalled Dycek's resigned attitude, her veiled hostility. He had no idea how to assess what she might have done. Had he missed something obvious, again? He decided to ignore Evrani's pandering attitude. "Any idea where she might have gone?"

Evrani held up one brown finger. "Ah, it gets worse. We cannot raise her or trace her. She has switched off *Percival*'s locator beacon. Deliberately! Can you imagine such irresponsibility? There are fifty people at this base, and she is not the only one who is needing to use the rover—"

"Sixty-two," Keefer said. "This base now has sixty-two people."

"Yes, yes." Evrani jerked his shoulders with more enthusiasm than Keefer had ever seen in a shrug. "I checked in Commissioner Dycek's quarters—she doesn't lock them, you know. There's something you might be wanting to see. You are in charge here, after all. We cannot let this sort of thing keep happening."

Scowling, Keefer slipped into a warm sweatsuit and slippers and followed Evrani through the pressure bulkheads. The meteorologist led him into the older habitation module where the first group of inhabitants had settled. This module had a much more lived-in feel to it. As a passing thought, Keefer wondered if he might like to move his quarters here, if any of the rooms emptied with the rotation of personnel.

Evrani led him to Dycek's quarters and jabbed a finger inside. "Look. I knocked, but got no answer. I opened the door, but she is not here."

A few belongings lay on the floor and on her tiny desk, scattered about as if Dycek had aimlessly considered packing but given up in disgust. Something lay crumpled on the bunk.

Keefer picked it up: a hardcopy newspaper clipping, sandwiched in plastic. He unfurled it to skim a few paragraphs about the UN hearings Dycek had faced, inflammatory descriptions of her *adin* work, and skeptical postulations about what the *dvas* would be like.

Apparently, Dycek had saved the clipping as a keepsake, displaying it on the wall of her quarters—but why had she now torn it down and wrung the clipping in her hands until it lay twisted and unrecognizable on her bunk?

And then she had left the base without signing out, when nobody could see her, giving no indication of where she intended to go. She had deliberately made it impossible for the satellites to track her. Was she fleeing? Or did she have some innocuous, legitimate reason?

Keefer felt uneasiness crawl down his spine. Just

how unsettled had she been, really? Had she cracked somehow in the isolation, the close quarters? It didn't make sense to him, but similar incidents were common enough in long-term Antarctica research stations. Keefer had read about them. Had he missed something important in his conversation with her the previous evening?

The work Rachel Dycek had done with the *adin* project was controversial in its time, and she had suffered terribly for it. Keefer felt sorry for the way the newsnet wolves had attacked her. The *adin* rebellion, the avalanche in Noctis Labyrinthus, and now Keefer coming to kick her out of a job—had Dycek seen this as the last straw?

"You don't think she's doing something . . . something dangerous, do you?" He peered into Evrani's curious pecan-brown eyes. The meteorologist seemed to be enjoying the situation.

"With Commissioner Dycek, one can never tell. Time and again, she—"

Keefer looked at the clipping of the UN hearings again. *A trial by fire*, he thought. What if Dycek had been damaged in ways that no one had realized?

"Let's go to the communications center," he said. "Are you sure she didn't leave any message?"

Trotting ahead, Evrani took him through the rec module where Vickery and Shen were laughing and playing Ping-Pong while several others watched; they passed the mess room and entered the unimpressive nerve center of the base. No one else was there.

"Look for yourself," Evrani said. "She has made no regular log entries since early this morning, and it is full dark outside now. The rovers have spotlights on them and terrain guidance systems, but we never take them out during the nighttime. There's no need. She has never been out after dark by herself before. Something is definitely unusual here. I don't like it."

Keefer snooped around, but he did not know the controls well enough to see anything that Evrani might have missed. "No record of any messages coming in?"

"The person on duty is responsible for keeping records,

94

and Commissioner Dycek rarely bothered to do it."

Keefer scowled, trying to think of what Dycek might be doing. His mind kept insisting that Dycek must have a clear, logical reason for leaving without any hint as to where she was going, but his heart continued to suggest otherwise.

Had some emergency demanded her immediate attention? That must be the answer. But why hadn't she told anyone? And she had intentionally left the destination blank, intentionally shut off the locator. That was no accident.

"How long can she stay outside? How far can she go?" Keefer asked.

Evrani gave another of his spastic shrugs. "Enough air and food supplies for expeditions up to a week. *Percival* is safety-rated for four hundred kilometers."

Keefer felt his heart sink to his stomach as the maze of possibilities opened before him. "And you know about safety factors—she can probably drive twice that if she really wants to. What's to stop her?"

Evrani rubbed his palms together and strode over to one of the larger screens, tapping on the icon-based access board. "This is."

The image changed, fading out to be replaced by a detailed weathersat picture of the northern hemisphere of Mars. "Dr. al-Somak and I have watched this system very carefully. It is the largest storm to appear in this hemisphere in a year. Our terraforming activities play havoc with the climate, you know. Beludi and I are very excited at the possibilities of what we might learn from this. Viking Base is already in brown-out conditions, and they are collecting data."

He rubbed a thin finger on the image, showing the location of Lowell Base near the Martian equator. "The storm should reach our latitude late tomorrow."

Keefer stared at the gigantic cloud sweeping toward them, like a sledgehammer ready to smack anyone foolish enough to venture outside in it.

Someone like Rachel Dycek.

RACHEL DYCEK

THE GREAT VOLCANO Of Pavonis Mons looked like a noble beacon as the storm approached from the north. Through *Percival*'s trapezoidal windowports Rachel could look out at the Martian sky and see bright stars even during the daytime. In the distance the lurking haze from the wall of windborne microfine dust swept into an impenetrable murk.

The uphill slope of Pavonis was shallow, taking forever to rise from the Tharsis Plain. The shield volcano had oozed thick lava and slowly built its cone in the low gravity over thousands of years, sliding out in a gentle slope, flat and inexorable until it pushed clear of the lower atmosphere.

Scrambling ahead on its numerous legs, gliding over all obstacles, *Percival* made steady progress, kilometer after kilometer. Rachel hunched forward, letting the AI pilot do the driving. Somewhere up there, the *adins* were hiding.

At the turn of the twentieth century, Percival Lowell had seen canals on Mars through his telescopes in the mountains of Arizona in the United States. He made a public sensation with his depictions of a dying race, a civilization winding down to extinction. Now, perhaps, the *adins* were like that mythical dying people, hiding in the high altitudes. Rachel needed to talk to them, before it was too late.

The monotonous reddish landscape sprawled on all sides. She felt small and insignificant, unable to believe the arrogance with which the UN Space Agency attempted to change the face of a world, how she herself had tried to alter the human race.

That phase of the project is over, UNSA had said. After all her work she found herself at an impasse, perplexed as well as depressed. Regardless of how stimulating and glorious the work had seemed at first, it was still a dead end. Everyone could see that now. Rachel had never bothered to prepare herself for this day.

A long time ago she had had a choice: to feed the flames of possibility or to live her life in the comfort of obscurity. Sergei had wanted no fame, no glory, no triumph for the Sovereign Republics—just a simple, satisfying, and unchallenging life. Now, at the end of her career, she had spent four months waiting for Jesús Keefer and wondering if she had made the wrong decision.

But if the *adins* had somehow survived after so many years, perhaps it wasn't so empty after all.

The apartment Rachel and Sergei shared was small and compact, cramped but no worse than anyone else's in the district, since everyone had the same model. The suburbs of Moscow had been battling housing shortages for a hundred years, still with no visible progress. Living conditions had changed little in decades.

Prefab buildings went up in ever-widening rings around Moscow. The number of workers taking the monorail to the inner city and the office buildings surrounding the old Kremlin doubled every five years. But demand for housing continued to exceed supply as if through some bizarre government plot, and nothing seemed to help.

Rachel and Sergei had resolved not to have children, ostensibly to keep a greater share of space for themselves; but the truth was that neither of them had any emotional energy left for little boys or girls.

She remembered a grayish spring day, warm enough to thaw the ice on the sidewalks but with a stiff breeze to chill anyone who went outside. Sergei finished his online newspaper, flipped through the stations on the satellite TV before switching it off in disgust, and as a last resort attempted to talk to Rachel.

She sat at the kitchen table that doubled as her private desk between meals. On her tabletop computer, plugged into the wall socket to maintain its battery charge, she toyed with biochemical models, trying to find optimal oxygen-absorption configurations for the membranes in artificial lung tissue, given the parameters of the new modified hemoglobin-Y molecules. In a university lab, her team had made the new alveoli as efficient as possible—but different statistical methods of packing them into the lung membrane could increase their oxygen-transfer capability by as much as thirty percent.

Since the *adin* project was supposedly secret, Rachel could bring only the most innocuous research home to pore over on Sunday afternoons, though she had occasionally taken a few obscure but classified computer codes home when deadlines got too tight and security seemed lax enough.

Sergei never knew the difference; he never even showed an interest.

"That work you are doing is too risky, Rachel," he said without any sort of preamble. "It makes me uneasy."

She looked up at him, and made the response. "You don't know anything about my work."

It didn't matter to him. It never did. Already, she knew what he was going to say; she just didn't know what tack he would take this time.

"Rachel, I have spoken to my friend Barakov. He says they still need someone to work at the new geriatric medical center. Your qualifications are exactly what they need. With a recommendation from him you could get the job, certainly." Sergei's voice held little enthusiasm, since they had had the fight so many times. Barakov made the same offer every month.

Rachel frowned at him, but took the time to store the file on her computer before responding. She couldn't think of any clever new research twists right now anyway, and Sergei would not relent until they had

had The Fight. It seemed to satisfy him somehow.

"What if I like my current job, Sergei? Why should I want to leave?" Though she could not tell him about it, she had just been promoted to the position of section leader, with a corresponding increase in pay. She had outlasted many of her initial colleagues in the project, and through her own forced schedules, the *adin* work surpassed all of its expected milestones. Already, her superiors talked about moving the work out to a new, secret installation somewhere in Siberia, which Rachel herself would administer.

"This government research! How can you trust the government? You never know where tomorrow's funding is going to come from. What if someone challenges your results? What if there is an accident in your facility? Perhaps the Americans or the French have their own 'man plus' project and will place somebody on Mars long before you ever get finished—and then where will you be? No one in the Republics will continue your funding! I will be stuck supporting us both."

She crossed her arms over her chest, knowing she was closing herself off from him. She was amazed at how much he knew about her project, but if she overreacted, it would confirm any doubts he might still have. "The work is too important to drop simply for political reasons, Sergei."

Sergei cocked an eyebrow and covered his mouth to muffle a small belch. "Oh? And what is wrong with political reasons? Remember our own space plans! The Soviet cosmonaut program was trying to get the first man on the Moon—but when the American Apollo spacecraft got there first, what happened to us? Nothing! Apollo-Soyuz? A public relations show! Our program vanished like the wind, with the Red Army taking all the spare parts, and later selling them to the Americans just to keep *their* space program afloat. I don't like gambling with ideas—your job has no guarantee like mine does. Why not become a regular doctor? Think of the people you could help!"

Sergei worked as a minor functionary on the new Moscow stock exchange, one of the few occupations—along with farmers and doctors—that were indeed protected by the government, which considered a conversion to capitalism of paramount importance, though they were still talking about it a hundred years after they had started. Russian society was somehow not equipped to adjust to rapid changes.

"Frankly, I am willing to take the risk," she said. "It's important to me."

"But *I* am taking the risk, too! Think of how we will have to live if you lose your employment. If your project fails in disgrace." As if to emphasize his point, Sergei stood up and took a two-man bottle of vodka out of the freezer. He yanked the cap off as if he were brawling with it and poured himself a glass. His fingers left dark spots on the coating of frost that blanketed the outside of the bottle. The oily clear liquid swam on the bottom of the glass as he swished it, needing no ice cubes. This time, surprisingly, Sergei had not started the fight with a drink already in hand. "We could lose our apartment, our lifestyle."

Rachel looked around their dismal quarters and fought to keep herself from laughing at the imagined tragedy. "Sergei, you have nothing to live for as it is. You don't like your job, you don't like your home, you don't like our marriage. Why should you care if I feel passion for what I'm working on? Are you jealous?"

Sergei sat with his back to her in the chair and took a gulp from his glass. He blinked his pale eyes at her, as if he did not see her at all. "I don't like it, that's why. We have little enough as it is. I won't risk losing it. Experiments fail sometimes. Then where will you be? Where will I be?"

Looking at him—the wide face, the rheumy eyes, the stomach below the barrel chest already turning into a potbelly—Rachel saw a complete stranger. "It will not happen."

"You can't know that, Rachel!"

"I know things because I keep my eyes open." She flipped down the screen on her tabletop computer and disconnected the portable module that contained her data. Even the anger such arguments usually ignited was no longer a part of her. "You don't know because you refuse to pay attention."

Carefully, she patched up the chinks in her emotional wall and turned to Sergei with an unreadable face. "I am going into the facility. I'll get more work done there."

Sergei shrugged and stared back at her with an identically unreadable expression. He poured himself another glass as she pulled a warm shawl over her shoulders and stepped out the door.

Percival continued to toil up the lava slope of Pavonis Mons, its multiple legs like a stampede of arachnids across the terrain. Black lumps of ejecta thrust out like monoliths from the dust, scoured and polished into contorted shapes by furious winds during the seasonal storms, though sheltered patches were muted with the dull greens of clinging life. On the sunward side of some of the rocks she noticed grayish smears of lichen, even a tendril of frost. It made her heart ache. Even the little details signified monumental changes on a planetwide scale.

Siberia had primeval forests of pine and birch, thicker than a brick wall. Up in the permafrost latitudes there were mossy bogs, herds of reindeer, flowers in spring, clouds of mosquitoes as dense as a thunderhead. Even the desolate wasteland of Antarctica had its bright colors, fish swarming in the waters, penguin rookeries, seals.

But here on Mars, a dot of lichen was still a remarkable occurrence.

In that moment Rachel actually caught herself feeling homesick for Earth. But even in Mars's one-third gravity, her body felt old and weak. Returning to

Earth, and the extra weight it would make her carry, would be hell for her—on top of everything else.

If she did not find the *adins*, perhaps it would be enough just to go to the highest point in the area, seventeen kilometers above the Tharsis Plain. On general principles she had considered making the trek to Olympus Mons, the true highest peak in the solar system—but the chugging *Percival* could never carry her that far. The top of Pavonis Mons would be high enough for Rachel to watch the storm roll in . . . and envelop her.

Make sure you finish up at the top, she had always said. And her life's work was indeed finished. Pavonis Mons stood above much of the atmosphere, nearly two times the height of Mount Everest on Earth. Yes, high enough.

Was that what she planned? She flinched away from the thought each time it came to her, but it grew stronger.

On the edge of the forty-kilometer-wide caldera, Rachel Dycek would stand in her laboring environment suit and look out across her new world. She could see the howling red-brown wall seeping closer across the northern sky as airborne dust marched toward the southern hemisphere.

The rover itself might survive the punishment—those vehicles had been designed to be tough. Someone might eventually find the battered and pitted *Percival* at the top of the volcano, like a salute to Rachel's surrender.

But the sandstorm would obliterate all traces of *her*.

CORA MARISOVNA

Steam escaping from a cracked vent filled the chamber deep inside the lava tube with a low snoring sound. Tough, fibrous algae clung to the walls in a thick carpet, smoothing the jagged coarseness of the rock.

Cora Marisovna and Boris Tiban reached the natural sauna by climbing through a winding maze toward the slumbering heart of Pavonis Mons. A buildup of slick frost covered the sloping walls where frigid outside air had halted the steam, forcing it back against the rock.

Cora had difficulty maneuvering her ungainly body down the steep slope, but she wanted to follow Boris. He reached back with one large and powerful hand to help her, gripping her own with a negligent disregard that made her wonder if he really noticed that she followed him. Though she could not feel the texture of his skin against her own plasticized layers, Boris held on with a crushing strength that made her bones ache—but Cora did not dare pull away.

Boris sat in the sour-smelling, briny steam in sullen silence, wallowing in his anger and his regrets. He brooded inside, not feeling the warmth, his head bowed. Though he would never admit it, Boris needed her right now. Cora could tell.

After waiting an appropriate time, she came up behind him without a word and began rubbing his shoulders, his back. With his thickened *adin* skin Boris could not enjoy the heavy heat of the volcanic air any more than he could feel the biting Martian cold, but he could feel her massage, squeezing, kneading. She dug in hard with her fingertips, trying to loosen the wire-tight muscles that were roped like a noose around his neck.

She liked to watch herself caress him, transported to an artificial distance by her lost sense of touch. When she pushed down she could feel his skin rough and rubbery, inhuman. Yet she felt a love for Boris Tiban, an awe that this great rebel would select her as his lover, even from the beginning.

"It will be all right, Boris," she said, leaning close to where his ears would have been. Around them, the gurgling hiss of escaping gas made the air smell of brimstone. Mars had been seismically quiet decades earlier, but the two enormous comet strikes caused the planet to snort in its sleep.

Boris sucked in a deep breath of the acrid air and hunkered closer to the floor. Cora knelt beside him. He started to moan, but bit it off quickly.

"For Nikolas it will not be all right," he said. "I should have defended him. Together we could have killed the *dvas*." Boris continued to stare at the broken vent where thin tendrils of steam sighed into the chamber. He refused to raise his misshapen head and look at Cora. "Now the humans and the *dvas* will hunt us down."

"Then you must protect us, Boris." Cora continued to massage his shoulders. "You always have."

It had taken her a long time to grow accustomed to the abomination of his body, the lumpy alien appearance, the functional adaptations. But now, after ten hard years, Cora Marisovna loved him for what he was. The loss of Nikolas made her wonder what she would ever do without Boris.

As an attractive young woman in Siberia, she had been noticed by the handsome men, but her choices had been limited around Neryungri, especially with her mother and grandmother watching like falcons. On Mars, though, everything had changed.

The first time she and Boris had made love, just after his execution of the vice commander, Boris had taken her under the dull sun, inside a sheltering ring of lava rock that reminded her of a primitive temple.

The other *adins* were out chipping lichens off outcroppings, digging downward to free chunks of permafrost to use for cooking water.

Boris led her away from everyone else. Knowing what was about to happen, Cora could do no more than gaze at him with dazzled, hooded eyes. With his monstrous visage Boris Tiban seemed worse than the foulest criminals from the labor camp. She had just watched him snap the vice commander's neck over his knee. But awed as she was by his presence, she could not help herself. The *adins* were few, and Boris was their leader.

Cora lay back in the cold, red dust but did not feel the sharp rocks against her padded back, cushioned by the auxiliary set of lungs that made it impossible for her to stretch out flat. When Boris held her and caressed her and settled his body on top of her with quick breaths that whistled out of his nose slits, she could enjoy little of his touch. Too much skin sensitivity had been blocked.

Realizing what she was doing, Cora felt terror and despair. In front of her Boris looked like a caricature with ears and nose removed, thick brow ridges, a swollen hunchback. No doubt she looked as hideous to him, even after a year without seeing a normal human face.

But she drove all such thoughts deeper inside herself.

As Boris touched her, kissed her, Cora closed her eyes, picturing a proud Cossack pirate taking her as his prize, as his queen, as they escaped down the river. She let herself smile at the fantasy, and opened herself to him.

Cora's external skin may have been deadened, but the nerves within had not been changed at all. She felt him enter, large and hard, slipping deep inside and touching all her sleeping nerves, jolting them back awake. The sudden rush of furnace-hot sensitivity made her squirm, and someone made a small noise in the back of her throat. Thin wind whistled around the rocks, but she could hear Boris's breathing, faster and faster, as he thrust repeatedly into her.

They moved and grabbed at each other for a long time as they reveled in the feeling, the reminder of living sensations inside them meaning more than the orgasm itself. Their lovemaking left an indentation in the dust that looked afterward as if a great struggle had occurred.

The *adins* had no need to be concerned about contraception. The project doctors had made sure their experimental subjects were sterile before dumping them on this planet. Sex was one of the few pleasures they could still enjoy, and Boris encouraged the survivors to enjoy each other in a celebration of their victory against the slave masters from Earth.

Over the years, Cora and Boris had made love often. What did they have to lose? she thought bitterly.

Her thoughts returned to the present as Boris reached up and clasped her hand against his shoulder, forcing her to stop the massage. She waited for him to say something. Finally, he muttered, "Just let me be alone. I am thinking about Nikolas."

Feeling cast aside, Cora left him in the steam, the stench, and his guilt.

Cora spent most of her days in the shadows of the lava tubes, partly out of shyness, partly out of the revulsion she felt toward her changing body. She was not hiding from the *adins*. They could see what had happened to her, though none of them would speak aloud the dread she saw in their sheltered eyes whenever she met their gaze.

Thirteen years ago in Neryungri, her almond eyes had been modified for the wan Martian sunlight. They had been sparkling eyes, like polished ebony, slanted with a trace of her Mongol heritage. Her Martian eyes, though, were set deep within sheltering cheekbones and brow ridges, covered with a thick mesh of lashes.

She remembered her grandmother braiding her hair and singing to her, marveling at what a beautiful little girl Cora was. She had spent hours doing embroidery in a dim room beside the old woman, receiving sharp whacks on the knuckles if she missed a stitch or chose the wrong color of thread.

Seeing Cora now, her grandmother would no doubt run away shrieking, making the three-fingered sign of the Orthodox cross.

Cora looked up as Nastasia danced into the main grotto from her wanderings in the bowl of the Pavonis caldera. Already, she seemed to have forgotten about dead Nikolas.

Nastasia ran over to Cora, holding one hand behind her back. "See what I have found! A great treasure. The stories were true! I went down in the caldera, and look! This was right on the side of one of the rocks."

She held out a delicate green growth, serrated and curled like an oyster shell; lines of purple and orange striated the grayish-green of the main part. It was an unusual type of lichen, one Cora had never seen before—but the terraforming strains were prone to interbreeding and mixing, adapting to whatever conditions they found.

"That is beautiful, Nastasia," she said.

"It is the fern flower! I found it, so it is mine. You remember what happens to the maiden who finds the fern flower!"

Indeed, Cora did remember the stories about the fern flowers supposedly growing hidden out in the fields. During Siberian summers when she was a little girl, Cora had gone out with the other children during the Festival of the Birch, hunting the tiny mythical plants that would bring magic to anyone who found them.

"Maybe it will bring something special for us," Cora said, nodding. "We need as much magic as we can find."

Nastasia stared down at the lichen growth she had picked. "Maybe it will bring Nicholas back to us."

Cora touched her on the shoulder. "Yes, we will miss him. Nikolas was a great friend."

"He was a great tsar!" Nastasia raised her voice. "He was my father—but the Bolsheviks murdered him! They murdered all of my family. Only I escaped. I ran through the countryside, telling all the peasants that I was Anastasia Romanov, daughter of the tsar. Some of them hid me, but most did not believe. I got away. I am hiding from them here on Mars. The Bolsheviks must never be able to find me!" She stared down at her fern flower with a forlorn expression on her face. "Maybe I can use the magic to keep us safe."

"Don't worry," Cora said. "Nobody will ever find us up here. The *adins* are safe."

Nastasia stared at her treasure for a few moments—then she popped it into her mouth and ate it. Forgetting Cora, she wandered back through the cave opening into the late-afternoon sunshine.

Outside, Stroganov had already begun work on another sculpture of someone else. The old Siberian schoolteacher continued to find energy and refused to give in to apathy and despair. Cora could hear him planning and mumbling to himself. She envied his stoic outlook on life.

Deeper in the grotto, she made her way up the sloping passageway to where sunlight warmed the rocks on the caldera rim. The wind picked up as she stepped outside. A storm would be coming soon. The *adins* would have to huddle in the caves for days, bickering with each other, eating the bit of food they had managed to set aside, perhaps even cracking into one of the few packages of UNSA supplies Boris had hoarded from the first days on Mars.

The cramps in her abdomen struck again, making her hiss in pain. She waited for it to subside, and wondered how long it would be until the next spasm. After bracing herself momentarily against the rock wall, Cora forced herself to keep moving.

Outside, with the shadows lengthening at the end

of day, she used her fingers to peel the dusty strands of algae that had clung to the flapping skimmer-screens set up to capture airborne tendrils that drifted around the mountain peak. The *adins* would cook the algae down, leach out the dirt, and make it into dense, edible wafers.

Placing the collected algae in front of her on a sunny rock, Cora slumped against the rough wall, breathing heavily. She sorted the strands. Her thick fingers worked quickly, as if doing needlework for her grandmother, but her mind wandered far from her activities.

In the tunnels below, Boris continued to sit by himself, simmering with an anger he had not begun to slake. He would not let her comfort him. It had been so long since the last time they had made love. Was he afraid of her now?

She felt tears spring to the corners of her eyes as she thought of that last time, and the months of growing dread that had followed.

Brushing the algae aside, Cora patted her swollen belly and felt the infant kick within her—the last great practical joke of all.

STROGANOV

STORM SEASONS HAD NOT BEEN KIND to the stone visage of Ivan Bolotnikov. The lashing winds and scouring dust weathered away many details on the sculptured face, and smears of hungry lichens made the old Russian warrior look as if he had a skin disease.

Stroganov stood among his sculptures with another bucket of sulfurous mud and ash drawn from the steaming pit deep within the volcano. Subvocalizing the words of a bar song, he made repairs where they seemed most necessary before the next storm came.

Bolotnikov was the first monument Stroganov had constructed up on the mountain, just after Boris Tiban led them to their new home. The *adins* had felt quite proud of themselves back then, sixteen hard years and many deaths ago. They marched up the side of the volcano, cocky after having successfully thumbed their noses at Earth—but the place had looked so bleak and forbidding. It had needed guardian angels. Boris's rebels were setting up a kingdom on top of the mountain, and Stroganov wanted to give them a few patron saints.

Bolotnikov had been Stroganov's favorite of the historical heroes he had taught in Russian schools. The man's rugged eyebrows were worn down to the level of the forehead, and the squared-off beard was chipped away. But that could be easily fixed.

Dipping his fingers into the still-hot mud, barely feeling the heat, Stroganov hauled out enough goop to reconstruct the brow ridges. The mud's consistency thickened as its meager water content froze, but he slopped it into place, nudging the hardening cement into the right contours. After it solidified completely he would use a shard of volcanic glass to scratch and chisel hairlines. It was a temporary improvement at best, since the first storm winds would buff away all fine detail, but Stroganov took pride in his work. These were great historical figures from his homeland, and they deserved to be done right, no matter how transient the monuments were, or how few people would actually gaze upon them.

Closing his eyes as he felt the petrified features, Stroganov worked from how he imagined Ivan Bolotnikov must have looked, since he could not recall ever having seen an illustration of the man. His mind brought forth a vivid imaginary portrait of Bolotnikov, who had lived in the early 1600s, gathering his rebellion during the years of turmoil following the death of the usurper Boris Godunov, when Russia had no true tsar but only a series of incompetent pretenders.

Bolotnikov was a Don Cossack, captured in his youth by Tatars and forced to serve as a galley slave for the Turks. Pondering, Stroganov blinked his heavy eyes and reached up to add a long scar to the sculpture's right cheek—the result, he imagined, of a brawl when Bolotnikov attempted to escape the Turks, killing the galley master, until another treacherous slave smashed him on the side of the head with a loose oar, thus creating the scar. Yes, that made a good story. It had never taken place, of course, but it should have. None of the other *adins* would realize the embellishment. They believed everything Stroganov told them in his tales. He had been a schoolteacher, after all, and he should know these things.

Bolotnikov had gathered a great revolutionary army of runaway slaves, displaced Cossacks, and serfs. He distributed inflammatory leaflets—the first time printed propaganda had ever been used in Russia. "Kill the boyars," they said, "kill the merchants and all commercial people and seize their goods." He besieged Moscow, defeating the forces of the puppet tsar.

Stroganov usually ended his story there, without telling of the inevitable dissension in the rebel army between Cossacks who wanted to free all the peasants, and gentry who wanted them kept in service. The strife weakened Bolotnikov enough to bring about his defeat. Much later, though, during the Soviet years in the twentieth century, Ivan Bolotnikov had been glorified as a popular hero, one of the few acceptable folk legends that promulgated proper Communist party ideals.

In the bleak afternoon he looked at his other monuments outside the cave mouth. So many rebels, so many dreams in the history of the Sovereign Republics. Stepan Razin, whom Pushkin had called "the one poetic figure in Russian history"; Bulavin, even Lenin. And all of the revolts had failed in similar ways. Even Lenin's Communist revolution lasted only a few generations before it, too, crumbled.

Stroganov knew that Boris Tiban pictured himself as one of those great heroes, the first Russian rebel on the planet Mars. But Boris was a pale shadow of these others. Stroganov recognized that easily, yet Boris seemed to have convinced himself. Though he had led the *adins* in their rebellion against UNSA, Boris was no charismatic, brilliant general like Bolotnikov or Pugachev. Boris had a tendency to lash out at anything just to ease his feelings of helplessness. He did not understand that the simple ability to destroy did not make a man powerful.

Boris made no secret that he wished Stroganov would erect a sculpture of him, to stand with the other proud rebels. Each time he began a new work, Stroganov felt the silent pressure, hints that Boris thought were subtle. And each time Stroganov chose someone else.

Now he had to make another decision. Gorbachev or Yeltsin? Peter the Great? Stroganov had already found the best vacant spot to erect a new face. He had already laid down a sturdy base, erected a tall cairn of rocks mortared together into a solid structure that would provide a framework. After storm season, Stroganov would apply mud to form the features of a face.

He smiled as he put down the now-cold bucket of touch-up mud. He would have to melt it again down by the steam vents just so he could clean out the debris. Scraping his coated hand against a rough boulder to rub off the ash, he went over to the site he had chosen for the new sculpture. Kicking loose rock aside with his hardened foot, Stroganov etched out an approximate outline for the base of rocks.

He would indeed create an *adin* sculpture this time, making no secret of the distortions of the face, the features altered by the augmentation surgeries; and that would keep Boris happy.

But the sculpture would bear the face of Nikolas, not Boris.

Since setting foot on Mars, Elia Stroganov had chosen never again to use his first name. His family name was sufficient, he thought, and a proud family name it was.

The Stroganovs had been a wealthy merchant family, dispatched in 1581 by Ivan the Terrible with a small mercenary army of Cossacks to move across the Urals, across the steppes into Siberia. Within two years, the Stroganovs founded a great commercial empire on salt and Siberian furs, defeating even the Mongol Khan Kuchum. The Stroganovs' wealth and power grew so great that during the Time of Troubles they made a large loan to the Moscow treasury. Centuries later, Count Paul Stroganov was deputy minister of the interior and close adviser to Tsar Alexander I, who defeated Napoleon in his invasion of Moscow.

The *adin* Stroganov had fixated upon the importance of his family name, telling anyone who would listen, dismayed that most people remembered the surname only for a sour-cream-and-beef dish one family member had created.

In Siberia, in the city of Novosibirsk, Stroganov taught in the Akademgorodok, the center for scientific research built as a suburb by the old Soviet Union.

Despite the famed scientists and engineers trained in the Akademgorodok, Novosibirsk was primarily an industrial city, manufacturing steel and heavy equipment that was then exported down the Ob River.

In his classes Stroganov deified the old Russian rebels, emphasizing history and culture to the detriment of the physical sciences curriculum. But most of Stroganov's students were the children of factory workers who had no interest in the broad social implications of long-ago failures. Stroganov was reprimanded repeatedly; he backed down only until the education committee members changed, then he started all over again.

One night he got into a drunken brawl, arguing with another teacher over whether people like Stepan Razin or Pugachev were heroes or villains. In the reckless fight, Stroganov knocked one of his colleagues over a chair. The awkward fall snapped the man's spine and left him paralyzed for the rest of his life.

Stroganov was sent to the Neryungri penal camp. It was a bitter irony to be exiled deeper into Siberia, which his ancestors had conquered.

Stroganov had volunteered for *adin* testing after he realized that it was his duty as a Stroganov to be among the pioneers and explorers on Mars, one of the *adins*, one of the first. But the landscape of Mars was bleaker than any part of Siberia his ancestors had ever seen.

Now, his arms laden with enormous rocks he could never have lifted in Earth's gravity, Stroganov began to pile up the base for his bust of Nikolas. To the north the air held the murky haze of an impending storm. The sun had already gone behind the caldera, spreading long shadows. Overhead, stars swarmed through the deepening sky.

As he dropped the rocks in a pile, they clacked together like children's building blocks. Kneeling in the reddish dirt, he began to arrange them, placing the largest on the bottom and scooping out depressions to mount them. He could already visualize what the sculpture would look like: Nikolas with his head tilted upward, gazing at the sky with hooded *adin* eyes— either looking to the stars, or back toward Earth. Stroganov considered, shaping the lines until the picture of the monument stood large and sharp in his mind. He wouldn't use any real mud or mortar until tomorrow, unless the storm came first.

Stroganov stopped, then turned to listen. He heard an approaching mechanical noise, tinny in the thin air. The stillness of the falling night was so absolute that even a faint far-away sound caught his attention. The glowering stone faces blocked his view of the lower slope—but he clearly heard a sound he had not encountered in a long while.

Leaving the rocks and his cold bucket in place, Stroganov walked through his towering sculptures. Emerging from the shadow of the last stone face, he looked down the slope and saw an orangish-red cloud of dust raised by an approaching vehicle. An UNSA rover scrambling up the rock-spattered path—one of the vehicles from Lowell Base.

"Boris!" Stroganov shouted. His breath spurted cold steam into the air. He stumbled back toward the cave, still miscalculating his running footsteps even after so many years in the low gravity. He caught himself just in time to keep from fetching up against the edge of the cave opening.

Already the other *adins* had heard it. Boris Tiban ran out of the grotto where he had been brooding, his body glistening with diamonds of frozen vapor. He held the pointed titanium staff in his hand like a spear, a warrior ready to defend his home against invaders.

"They are coming to get us," Boris said. "At last."

RACHEL DYCEK

PERCIVAL'S AI PILOTING SYSTEM helped Rachel choose the best uphill course. The screens automatically downlinked weathersat data, as well as updates from the five human bases, two of which were already inundated by the storm.

Once again, *Percival* asked her if she wanted to turn the locator beacon back on to reestablish contact with Lowell Base. Once again, Rachel assured it that, no, she did not. She was glad it did not ask her what she intended to do; Rachel was not yet ready to articulate it, even to herself.

The rover's guidance mechanisms scoped out the obstacles ahead, seeking a shallower gradient for the climb, warning her of possible precipices or loose soil. Like multiple teeth, the articulated legs chewed the dust and swallowed up the distance.

Rachel sat in silence, staring out the viewport and munching a bland snack of sugar wafers from the supply bin. She didn't quite want tea badly enough to swing back to the galley and heat herself a cup. Perhaps later. She listened to the rumble of the methane engines, the slow vibration of the vehicle's flurry of legs.

As the afternoon dimmed with the rapidly setting sun, she kept her eyes scanning for any trace of the *adins*. The broad path up the conical volcano seemed to be leading her upward like a giant funnel. Hints of lichen and algae on the rocks grew scarcer, and a thin embroidery of frost appeared in the shadows of sharp outcroppings. But she saw no sign of any primitive encampment.

Rachel opted to follow a gaping chasm like a slice out of the shield volcano's outer shell. The chasm was one of the only landmarks she found on the vast uphill plain. She rode as close to the edge as *Percival*'s safety algorithms would allow.

The chasm suggested days long past when liquid water had spilled downhill from melting ice on the mountaintop. Or perhaps the enormous volcano had split its seams from below in a last spasm. Rachel didn't know. Geology was not her area of expertise.

Jesús Keefer was a geologist, though.

Gauges showed the outside air pressure dropping as she ascended the mountain. The wind speed picked up, bringing gusts that carried enough muscle to rattle the rover's double hull. Behind her reeled a curving swath of chewed dust and sand marking the path of her rover. The tracks would be erased when the storm hit—certainly before anyone thought to come looking for her. She wondered if anyone back at the base had yet noticed that she was gone.

As the crown of Pavonis Mons cut off the horizon in front of her, a pragmatic part of Rachel's mind pondered what exactly she intended to do to herself when she got to the top. Park the rover on the caldera's edge and embrace the storm when it arrived, strain for a glory she could never reach?

Nonsense. She was a biomedical researcher, thoroughly familiar with the effects of the Martian environment on the human body. The dust storm would claw at her environment suit until the faceplate or the fabric was breached. If she happened to be lucky, the wind might hurl her to the rocks at the bottom of the eight-kilometer-deep caldera. More likely, her suit would simply rupture, leaving her to breathe air as sharp as knives and cold as ice, her mouth and nose clogged with rust. Her lungs would be flayed from the inside out; she would cough freezing blood.

And thanks to all the progress of the UNSA terraforming, she could live through it all for five minutes, perhaps longer.

No, suicide on Mars was a childish, cinematic

fantasy. She had known it all along, despite her anger at being replaced as commissioner. There would be nothing noble about her surrender.

She had never looked far enough ahead. She had thought the low point of all this work was enduring the UN hearings over the *adins*—but that had only been practice. Everything should have improved once the governments exonerated her of wrongdoing and allowed her to continue with her work. The perpetual optimist.

"You always think everything will work out happily, Rachel," Sergei had told her once, with his back turned, as he stared into the shadows of their apartment. "You are too much of a dreamer—and dreams do not usually happen. You will never learn anything else until you learn that."

Her priority now was to find the *adins*, to learn what had happened to her dreams.

Ahead, Rachel saw the concave mountain peak, dotted with the hollow pores of what looked like ancient volcanic steam vents, lava tubes, and jagged teeth of black rock rotten with cavities from blowing dust. Sunset shadows oozed like dark oil spilling down the slope.

As *Percival* approached, one cluster of the towering columns looked different: curiously shaped, but of a uniform size, arranged in rows. Gathered in the brittle enhanced contrasts of sunset they appeared to be . . . faces. Human faces carved out of volcanic rock.

An eerie chill ran down her back as she drove closer and switched on the piercing blue-white spotlights. The monuments were indeed sculptures—tall stone heads like the angular prehistoric faces found on Easter Island. This was impossible! Superstitious awe made her mouth feel dry. Each visage was different, most of them sporting beards, sharp noses, wide-open eyes that stared at her as she approached. She had found what she sought.

She slowed *Percival* and leaned forward until her

neck and shoulders ached. A cold sweat prickled her body like the tingle of a faint electric shock, making her jumpsuit feel clammy. If she stopped here she knew what she would discover.

Just then, burly misshapen figures stepped away from the rocks, emerging from the shadows. They moved quickly, taking cover again, growing bolder and peeping out to stare at her. Human figures—no, not quite human. The breath caught in her throat. In the fading light she recognized them.

Adins.

Though the *adins* had been assumed dead years ago, Rachel knew better than any other person how versatile and enduring her creations were. The hope had remained with her always, died down to a flicker after ten years, but still there. Twenty or so *adins* had vanished after the rebellion. The *adins* had gone into hiding for all these years, but the two renegades who had attacked the *dva* pumping station had not been alone. This appeared to be an entire settlement!

Rachel saw two of them at first, hiding beside the sculptured faces, and then a third *adin* stepped out of the darkness of the lava tube. This one carried a long metal staff.

Boris Tiban himself. How could she not recognize him even after so many years? Her chapped lips curved in a smile.

She brought the rover to a halt and just sat there staring out the windowport for a few moments. "I have so much to ask you," she whispered.

Percival's AI pilot asked if her query had been directed to the rover's systems; she left it wondering as she scrambled to put her environment suit on.

Rachel's heart thudded with amazement, anticipation, and more than a little fear. She wanted to leap out of the rover and embrace them, to show her joy at finding them alive. She wanted to know how the *adins* had fared, what they had done in the intervening fifteen years, why they had broken off contact with Earth.

Her second impulse was to turn *Percival* around and flee back downslope. What would the *adins* do if they caught her? Murder her, as they had with the *dvas* at the pumping station? She remembered watching videoclips of Boris Tiban's execution of Vice Commander Dozintsev on worldwide newsnets. The *adins* were capable of savage acts, and she had no reason to believe they would spare her.

No matter.

Rachel parked the vehicle, and initiated the automatic shutdown procedure. The bulky rover settled to the ground, retracting its motile legs.

What might they do to her, indeed? Rachel had nothing to lose and, in an ironic way, this would bring closure to her work.

She sealed the protective plates over *Percival*'s windowports, then stood up. The recompressed air in her suit tasted cold and metallic, flattened by her own anxiety. She cycled through the sphincter airlock of the rover and turned back to key the locking combination.

Rachel had to find out for herself, even if no one else would know. She was probably the only one who cared about the *adins* anyway, though it would leave Keefer with another mystery on his books. Something else to explain to UNSA.

With a terrified sense of wonder she stepped forward to meet the *adins*.

JESÚS KEEFER

THE MESS ROOM IN the outer ring module was the only space large enough to hold all sixty-two Lowell Base inhabitants at the same time, and even so it was crowded. Keefer blinked his eyes and looked uncomfortably at all the faces. This was not how he had envisioned his first few days on Mars. What a way to welcome a new commissioner!

With the exception of Dr. Evrani, none of them knew what the emergency was. Bruce Vickery kept looking at Keefer with just a hint of frustration, probably upset because he hadn't been consulted before Keefer called the general assembly. Making a calming gesture with his hand, he hoped the operations manager would settle down once Keefer had a chance to speak.

Keefer stood at one end of the room and cracked his knuckles, looking toward the module entrance as he waited for the remaining two members of the off-shift to arrive. The last was Amelia Steinberg, a short, muscular structural engineer who made sure the inflatable modules maintained their integrity and all systems continued to function. She was always wrapped up in her own duties and didn't seem to care what was going on with the rest of the base.

Steinberg elbowed her way to the coffee dispenser and poured herself a cup with an unself-conscious arrogance that told Keefer she did not disrespect authority; she simply ignored it. She had wavy mouse-brown hair that might have made her look attractive had it not been for the angular features of her face—square jaw, square nose, square cheeks, and square teeth. She took a sip of her coffee, set the cup on a bare spot on one of the tables, and plodded over to the food unit.

Before Keefer could speak, the other off-shift people stood up to serve themselves, following Steinberg's example. They looked groggy after being roused several hours early from their regular sleep period. Conversation began to rise, but Keefer remained silent and watched Steinberg, trying not to show too much annoyance. She shuffled four trays as she looked at labels describing their contents. Selecting one, she put the others back, leaned against the food unit door to close it, and popped her tray into the microwave.

"Should we keep waiting, Ms. Steinberg?" Keefer said. "All sixty of us are eager to assist you."

"I'm listening," Steinberg said without bothering to look at him. "You rang the dinner bell, so start talking."

Keefer frowned, then sighed. "All right," he said, placing his hands behind him on the curved fiber-composite structural wall, "we've got a problem. Commissioner Dycek is missing. She took one of the rovers and drove off without a recorded destination. She's been gone since early this morning, and she hasn't reported in. She intentionally switched off her locator beacon, so we are not able to locate *Percival*."

Vickery groaned.

"You got me out of bed for that?" Steinberg said, yanking her tray out of the microwave. She lifted the paper lid and frowned at the steaming breakfast she saw. "Maybe she'll drive off the edge of a cliff and do us all a favor."

"But she must not drive over a cliff!" Evrani stood up, flapping his hands. "We need the rover! Do you know how long it would take for us to get a replacement from UNSA?"

Keefer saw that the mood of the people in the room supported Steinberg's attitude. He expected some shock or concern, but only the new arrivals appeared worried. Dycek seemed to have alienated not just Keefer but everyone else on the base as well.

"She's probably out on a picnic with some of her *dvas*," Steinberg said. "Everybody knows she's helping them steal us blind."

"All right, enough!" Keefer shouted, genuinely angry now. "Every person is a valuable member of this base. Commissioner Dycek may be in danger. She has done something foolish, and I don't condone it for a minute—but that doesn't mean we shouldn't be concerned."

The rest of the people fidgeted. After an uncomfortable moment, Vickery scowled. "The man's right. I don't particularly care for some of you clowns either, but I'd go out and rescue *you* if you got into some sort of fix." A few people chuckled.

Keefer clapped his hands to get their attention again. "We don't know why Commissioner Dycek went. She could have a legitimate reason."

Steinberg laughed and started eating her breakfast.

"Okay, however unlikely that may be," Keefer amended. "But our first concern is to find her and bring her—*and* the rover—back to base. Does anybody have an idea where she might have gone? Did anyone see her leave? That rover can take her a good distance, and she's already been gone for something like eighteen hours. She could have covered a hell of a lot of territory in that time, and we don't have the manpower to mount a search."

"Fucking right we don't!" Steinberg said, raising her plastic spork in the air. "Look, that storm is coming tomorrow. I've got my whole team scheduled to spend the day going over every module seal and all of the external equipment, slapping down some extra protection to make sure it can take the punishment. I don't have time to waste chasing Chicken Little because the sky is falling on her project."

"You know, Rachel signed the rover out day before yesterday, too, come to think of it," Vickery interrupted. "Took her bleeping sweet time with it. I have no idea where she went, though."

Evrani raised his hand, like a schoolchild. "I know! I checked the logs. She traveled to Noctis Labyrinthus, where the big avalanche occurred last year. She goes there quite often—like someone visiting a cemetery. I have been keeping track of her movements. She was miserable about all those dead *dvas*."

"Another one of Dycek's 'angst appreciation' trips," Steinberg snorted. "Oh, boy, I hope she captured it all on videodisc."

Keefer frowned. He thought of the crumpled newspaper clipping on her bunk and the belongings scattered around her quarters. His gut feeling pointed to an unpleasant possibility. "We have . . . reason to believe that Commissioner Dycek may not be in a completely stable state of mind."

"Bingo!" Steinberg said. A few of the others snickered.

"She will probably come back in the morning," Beludi al-Somak said. "You will see."

Keefer began to reply, but then an explosion of noise cut off his words. Alarms shrieked through the wall intercoms. Everyone scrambled at once. Keefer looked around in confusion.

"Oh, shit!" Steinberg and her two companions leaped to their feet with so much force in the low gravity that they nearly banged their heads on the ceiling. She flung her food tray in the air and swatted her full coffee cup aside as she shot toward the doorway.

Bruce Vickery reached the wall screen in a single leap, ramming his fingers down on the buttons. A schematic of Lowell Base blossomed on the screen with a flashing red light in one area. "Greenhouse dome!" he shouted over the racket. "Just a second, I'll tell you how bad it is."

"Fuck that!" said Steinberg as she vanished through the door, shouting over her shoulder, "We'll find out as soon as we get there."

As Vickery pushed his way out of the mess room, Keefer ran after him, trying to make his legs work in some approximation of a useful run. Some of the people panicked; others kept close to the wall to give the others free access. The babble of conversation, the shouted advice and warnings, the alarms, the smooth and too-identical corridors of the base, filled Keefer with confusion. "Hey, what's going on?" he called.

Vickery didn't even turn toward him as he did an awkward gallop down the corridor. "Puncture in the greenhouse dome. Massive pressure drop."

The alarms kept screaming, each sound worse than fingernails grating on a chalkboard. The base was deserted, since nearly everyone was still in the mess hall. Keefer seemed to be running through an eerie abandoned ship.

Vickery popped through several modules, taking unexpected shortcuts. Pressure doors had closed automatically, compartmentalizing the base, and Vickery was forced to punch in overrides, wasting precious time. Amelia Steinberg had vanished ahead of them, moving faster in an emergency than Keefer would have believed possible.

The pressure door to the greenhouse module had automatically sealed itself and the AI housekeepers refused to let anyone inside. Steinberg and her teammates were already there, pummeling the controls. "Brute force can defeat computer intelligence any day of the week," Steinberg said as she used a prybar to break the seal. "Open your mouths!" she called. "Pressure drop."

It took three of them to unseat the door and yank it open. Keefer's ears popped as air gushed through the module corridor into the greenhouse.

Inside, the flapping transparent dome sounded like a war zone. A small gash at the top and left of the dome was like a funnel through which air poured with the velocity of a gunshot, screaming and ripping the tear wider.

Crude resistance heaters glowed red, casting furnace heat into small areas in a vain attempt to stave off the deep freeze. Atmosphere pumps roared as they worked to compensate for the breach, dumping Martian air back into the inflatable dome, but the translucent walls had already begun to sag.

In the darkened interior Keefer saw rows of test plants whipping back and forth in the upward hurricane. A whirlwind of loose potting soil spattered into the domed space. Corn tassels, wheat stalks, pine seedlings, all seemed to cry out as their air bled away.

"Oh, gawd!" Vickery said, craning his head toward the ceiling.

The other two techs grabbed self-sealing patches from stations by the wall. Loose scraps flew about in crazy circles, whipped by the breeze. Keefer stumbled into the center of the chaos, not sure what he could do to help.

The flexible walls of the modules were multiple-ply transparent polymer with radiation dampers, thick enough and tough enough to withstand most impacts. But not all. The puncture had occurred in the most inconvenient place for a major rip, nine feet off the ground. Steinberg wheezed, hauling in great breaths as her wavy hair flailed like seaweed tendrils about her head. "We'll need the scaffold! It's too high."

"Screw that!" Vickery said. "Hold your breath, Amelia. I'll lift you up there."

Steinberg snatched three of the wide mylar patches from one of the techs. Vickery stooped down, grabbed her by the calves of her legs. "Knees stiff! You can stand on my shoulders."

"Just do it, dammit!" Steinberg yelled.

In the one-third gravity, Vickery—with his barrel chest and heavy arms—had no trouble lifting the short, wiry woman straight up, placing her feet squarely on his shoulders like an acrobat.

Steinberg caught her balance and reached up with the opaque patches, but the airflow yanked at the self-sealing pieces in her hand. The first patch bent, stuck partly to the interior of the dome with the vicious adhesive, while the rest of the fabric was sucked through the rip, to flap in the icy breeze outside.

She took a second patch and slapped it up, covering most of the hole. A puckered indent showed where the low pressure on the outside still sucked at it. Wobbling, then regaining her balance on Vickery's shoulders, Steinberg took the third patch and covered the remainder of the hole.

Mercifully, the shrieking noise stopped, leaving only the rush of the emergency atmosphere pumps and the heater fans. Keefer shivered, looking for a thin film of frost on his own skin where the sweat had frozen. His ears ached.

With a grunt, Vickery wrestled Steinberg back down to the ground. "I'm awake now," she said, shaking her head. "No more coffee."

The emergency pumps continued roaring as they pulled in streams of cold air. "Shut those pumps off and use the subsidiary tanks!" Vickery shouted to one of the two techs inside the door. "That outside air's going to freeze the bleeping plants!"

While one of the techs turned on green emergency tanks to let warmed CO_2 into the dome, Amelia Steinberg went to the wall controls and convinced the AI housekeeper to switch the emergency pumps to support-and-replenish mode, shunting the outside air through secondary steps in the chain so that it passed through heaters and filters before entering the dome. Keefer could smell the rusty richness of the outside atmosphere.

"That'll do it," she said. "Pressure should be back to normal in a few hours. Then they can come in and survey the damage. For now, let's go somewhere we can breathe! I'm getting dizzy from all this. The plants can have it!"

Steinberg pushed open the door and retreated back to the corridor. A handful of the other base inhabitants had gathered like spectators, including Tam Smith, who looked as worried about the plants as she was about Keefer. After Vickery followed the last man out, he sealed the door behind him and slumped to the floor.

Steinberg looked down at her stained coveralls. "Christ! I dumped hot coffee in my lap and I didn't even notice."

"Adrenaline's good stuff, ain't it?" Vickery said.

Keefer thought of the wreckage inside the greenhouse dome. Tam would have an interesting introduction to her first days of work as an agronomist on Mars. "Okay, so now can somebody tell me what the hell happened?" he said. "What caused that?"

Vickery shrugged. "Probably a meteorite. We've seen a lot of activity left over from the comet strikes. And the air's not thick enough to stop the medium-sized rocks yet. The little stones get through—it probably vaporized on impact. We just happened to be in the middle of the targeting cross."

Keefer blinked his eyes. "The walls aren't thick enough? Shouldn't there be more protection?"

"Commissioner, this isn't a fortress here. The walls aren't much more than aluminum foil. You're living inside a balloon. It's a risk we all accepted before coming up here. You, too."

"Natural hazards," Steinberg said. "You just have to put up with them." She knitted her brows. "Now, some zoned-out doctor stealing a rover and taking off on a joyride is something else altogether. We shouldn't have to tolerate that kind of crap."

Vickery's face looked ruddy and more flushed now. He lifted his eyebrows. "I believe the alarms interrupted you from making an important commissioner-type announcement back in the mess hall? Something about Rachel?"

Keefer took a moment to recall his speech. "Yes. I was about to say that if Commissioner Dycek isn't back by morning, I want somebody—" In his mind he saw Vickery working with the solar panels, Vickery lifting Steinberg so they could seal the puncture in the dome. "—I want *you*, Bruce, to go out with me to look for her."

BORIS TIBAN

WHEN THE UNSA ROVER ground to a halt and sat hissing exhaust from its methane engines, Boris expected a squad of armed security guards to emerge—like the ones in the Siberian prison camp. The swarm of legs on the vehicle's underbelly made it look like some strange undersea creature, and its white metallic hull looked out of place among the rust reds, textured blacks and browns with highlights of encroaching green. The rover made too much noise, lumbering ahead as if it assumed everything else would get out of its way: unmistakably a human artifact.

Nothing happened for a long moment, second after slow-motion second ticking into the cold silence. Boris tensed, knotting his muscles, squeezing the titanium rod, knowing that if the humans did not emerge to confront them soon, he would lose his patience and rush howling at the rover, jabbing with the titanium staff like an aborigine with a stone-tipped spear.

"Are they taunting us?" he asked in a growling whisper.

When the outer airlock finally opened, Boris flinched backward, gesturing wildly for Cora to stay out of sight and out of danger. He hoped that Stroganov and Nastasia would dive for cover behind the stone faces if the humans started shooting. But Boris stepped forward proudly to meet them, his feet crunching on the broken soil.

To his surprise, only one person emerged from the sphincter airlock, backing out so that the oxygen regenerator pack sighed in the thin air first. The human stepped free and turned around to stare at Boris, moving slowly and with obvious hesitation. Behind the faceplate, he could see it was a woman, scrawny even in her environmental suit. Inside the suit she looked fragile and pathetic, like eggshells strung together with spiderwebs. Unarmed and alone.

A fool.

Boris felt the tension drain out of him, leaving him with a rejuvenated sense of bravado. He stifled a laugh and jammed his staff into the ground. "Stroganov! Help me," he bellowed, though the thin air snatched the fierceness from his words.

The two *adin* men marched forward while the woman just stood unmoving and stared at them, as if in complete surrender. They grabbed her arms, lifting her off the ground in the low gravity. Her reflective suit felt slick and unnatural in Boris's numb grip. It was made of some kind of tough, metallized plastic that strained against the internal pressure she required to stay alive. The human woman said nothing, just gazed at them through the visor with an expression of wonder and awe on her narrow face. Her silence made Boris uneasy. Stroganov wore a perplexed expression.

The two *adins* carried their prize easily. "You are our prisoner," Boris said, pushing his lips close to her faceplate to watch her cringe. "We will talk inside."

"I can walk by myself," she said. The voice from the speakerpatch was husky, but did not tremble with fright.

"Nevertheless, we will assist you. You are on our mountain, and we must be gracious hosts to the first visitor we've ever received on Mars."

Oddly, the woman let them manhandle her to the cave without a struggle. Seeing that he could easily take charge of the captive, Boris turned offhandedly to Stroganov. "Make sure Nastasia comes inside," he said.

Boris set the suited human down in the dimness of the lava tube and scrutinized her. Control lights inside her helmet illuminated her face. Boris saw granite-colored eyes and angular features, red-brown hair laced with iron-gray, wide mouth, generous nose. He discerned no expression of fear, though, which he found disconcerting. More unsettling was the fact that she looked hauntingly familiar to him. After all this time, how could he remember any humans at all?

He had spent the last sixteen years seeing nothing but scarred, monstrous *adin* faces, and he had learned to read their new expressions in the harsh Martian environment, learned to decipher subtle emotions on visages that bore no customary noses or ears, with radically modified eyes, milky skin. He would not allow himself to think the stupidly narrow-minded remark that all humans looked alike—but the woman was a shock to his senses, with her facial features and expressions so extreme that they seemed a caricature.

The woman straightened herself and looked around the grotto, ignoring him and studying how the *adins* lived. Boris felt momentarily ashamed and embarrassed at their squalid, primitive living area. He could read her thoughts, as if they were words in Stroganov's wall-journal, characters etched in Cyrillic letters onto smooth black volcanic glass. *Is this all the* adins *have done for themselves? Is this all they have made of the world on which they once were kings?*

Stroganov came back inside the cave, ducking his head and leading Nastasia, who ignored the suited human and went deeper into the cave. She mumbled something about looking for another fern flower, then toiled away into the dim passages.

Stroganov returned to Boris, eager to ask his questions of the human woman. "Why did you come here?" He looked from the helmet visor back to Boris. "Who is she?"

"I have not asked her yet," Boris snapped. The teacher should know his place by now. Boris drew a deep, deep breath, puffing out his chest and the auxiliary lungs on his back. He felt the icy air ache in the corners of his lungs.

"I recognize you," the woman said, turning to Boris and interrupting his posturing. Her words filtered out from the speakerpatch below the faceplate, in crisp textbook Russian straight from Moscow schooling, with no Siberian accent. "You are Boris Tiban. Boris . . . Petrovich, isn't it?"

"I never knew my father, so don't call me Petrovich," he said, then bent closer. "How do you recognize me?" With strong *adin* arms, Boris forced her to sit on one of the boulders inside the grotto, just to show he was in control. Cora often sat there, staring into the distance of her mind, thinking whatever inexpressible thoughts had haunted her since she had learned of the baby. Now, only a little light trickled inside from the dying day.

"Ah, you must have watched our transmissions to Earth. The cosmic adventure sponsored by Vice Commander Dozintsev and his masters at UNSA? Were you entertained by our struggle for survival on this world, while you and the rest of Earth sat warm and cozy on yours?"

Holding his rigid staff in front of him, he preened like a bird. He held his head high and spoke in a distant voice. "How often do they replay my last transmission to Earth, just before I executed Dozintsev? I wonder." He rang the metal rod on the lava floor for emphasis.

She did not respond at once. She was a quiet one, not easily intimidated. "No, Boris Tiban." Her wide lips smiled, a disturbing and superior smile that he wanted to tear from her face. He peered closer.

"I remember you from my selection procedures," she answered. "All the interviews, all the forms. Given time, I can probably recall details about every one of these *adins* here."

She paused and poked one finger down on the opposite slippery glove, as if counting. "Let me see . . . you were sent to Neryungri for several years prior to the *adin* surgeries, correct? You had been a worker at the Baku oil fields in Azerbaijan. Your record showed that you got into many brawls, you came to work drunk more often than not. You had an accident that started a fire in one of the refinery complexes. The resulting explosion killed two people and ruined a week's oil production."

Stroganov stepped away, looking from Boris to the human in amazement. Boris felt a cold shiver crawl up his spine even through the thick polymer-insulated skin. Flickers of memory brought Boris fuzzy glimpses of this woman, dressed in a white uniform, bustling down cold tile halls, talking to him and recording his answers on an electronic lap-pad.

"How do you know all this?"

The woman responded with a short laugh. She seemed genuinely amused. "I selected the final *adin* candidates myself. I performed some of the surgery. I *made* you, Boris Tiban. You and your little group survived here because of the augmentations I gave you." She turned around, flexing her arm inside the crinkling suit. The glistening fabric sounded like old leather.

"I don't remember these others as well as I know you, though, Boris. You were always such a trouble-maker. I did supervise the *dva* development, but spent most of my time justifying the work to UN investigative boards. Then I came to Mars to be commissioner of Lowell Base—the foundations of which you *adins* graciously built for us. Thank you, Boris Petrovich."

"The *adins* rebelled before any of that work could be done!" Boris growled. "And I told you I have no father. He abandoned me before I was born."

She was provoking him, taunting him. Perhaps she did not know him as well as she thought. Boris felt the fury boil within him. It came back to him now. "Doctor . . . Dycek—is that your name?"

She made no verbal answer, but the gleam in her gray eyes and the faint smile told him what he needed to know.

Stroganov gaped at her, then at him; yes, he remembered her, too—the deceptive warmth and light inside the Neryungri research hospital, the smell of chemicals, the slice of pain, the dullness of medication, the promises of freedom . . . the long and wasting exile on Mars.

"It is dangerous to taunt me, Dr. Dycek." Boris brought his metal staff up. "I should just smash open your helmet. For what you did to me, and to all of us!"

Even that didn't bother her. "Do what you will." She stood up and wandered deeper into the grotto like a curious explorer. The voice from her speakerpatch followed, transmitted clearly even through the suit. "My work on Mars is done, and I am to be packed up and shipped home to Earth."

Crouching on a blocky lump of worn, pitted rock, Stroganov nodded, his lips curling in a small smile. "So now you know how it feels to be obsolete yourself. What a beautiful Russian irony."

Dycek touched things, looked at the places in their tunnels where Stroganov and Nastasia made love, where Nikolas had slept. She stared at the meager stash of hoarded supplies and equipment they had taken from the original UNSA encampment. It made Boris furious.

"We thought the *adins* were dead," she said. "It had been so long, and we found no evidence of you anywhere. Even the *dvas* had never encountered you, though they have some sort of folktale about a man of the mountains."

That pleased Boris, and he turned away to keep her from seeing his satisfaction, though this human doctor probably could not read expressions on an *adin* face.

"In fact, Boris, if you had not attacked that pumping station, we would never have had a clue. Your secret would have been safe forever." She turned her back to him, as if shielding herself with the boxlike oxygen regenerator that spilled its chemical fumes into their grotto. With clumsy gloved fingers, Dycek picked up a battered box of sealed high-protein rations that Boris had never allowed the *adins* to eat. She turned it over to read the scuffed label.

Losing control, Boris leaped in front of her and held up his staff as a barricade. With his other hand he slapped the package out of her grip. "Stop! Those are ours." Boris stared into her narrowed eyes that were distorted by the transparent faceplate of the helmet. She placed her hands on her hips, waiting for him to say something else, but the words volatilized from his throat, and he clamped his thick lips shut. She had made him helpless in the face of his outrage.

"Tell me why you are so angry," she continued, sounding puzzled. "We set you free of your labor camp. You signed all the papers. You knew what you were getting into, and you leaped at the chance. You and your clinging friend . . . Nikolas? Was that the body I saw at the pumping station? Yes, I remember him now."

She brushed past Boris, peering at the walls of the grotto. For a moment, he was relieved that Stroganov had chosen to scratch his rambling journal record on the deeper walls, away from her prying eyes. "We gave you a world to tame and the freedom to do it. Better to rule in hell than to serve in heaven, is that not correct? What more could you want?"

All the clever words tumbled in Boris's throat, clambering over each other to come out. Where was the tough, charismatic leader who had conquered Mars? He had made his speeches over and over to the *adins*— but now that he had the proper target audience before him, he was acting like an idiot. Boris clenched his armored hand so tightly that he actually felt the nails against his thickened palm.

His anger finally burst out, and Boris shouted in a way that overrode his training for shallow breathing and conservation of exhaled moisture. "You created us for Mars—and then you took Mars away! We no longer belong down there!"

He gestured out beyond the cave walls. In his mind he held a picture of the growing lichen, the tracings of frost on the lava rock, the thickening air in the lowlands. Dr. Dycek frowned at him. He saw a weary patience in her gray eyes, which made him even angrier. She did not understand anything at all about what the terraforming work had done to the *adins*.

"We watch our world slipping away day by day with each new *dva* establishment, with each water-recovery station, with every normal human setting foot on our planet! And you ask me why we are so angry?"

"Why is she here?" Stroganov asked him, pestering. "Find out why she is here."

Boris looked down at Dr. Dycek. He shifted the titanium staff to his other hand. "Yes, why? Did you come to hunt us down? You should have brought some bodyguards with you if you meant to wipe us out once and for all! We will fight like wolves and sell our lives dearly." He forced a laugh.

Dr. Dycek sat down again. "No, Boris. I just wanted to see if I could find the *adins* before I was sent back to Earth. No one else knows I have come."

A bright new idea shot through his head like a cannon going off in a May Day parade. The *dva* pumping station had been nothing, even the death of Nikolas had not been a great enough sacrifice. "Then the time has come to send the humans a message they cannot ignore, to let them know we do not want them on Mars." He leaned closer to her again, forcing her back. "I will kill you and show them that the *adins* can still survive better than humans. We will dump your body just outside their inflatable base. They will get the message."

Dr. Dycek just looked up at him and sighed. "Why bloody your hands? No need to add another murder to your conscience."

Boris laughed at that. He felt easier now, more in control. "Another murder would make little difference to my conscience, Dr. Dycek." He chose not to hear her other words, since the bright vision shone so clearly in his mind. He could feel powerful with a simple act, let it wash away his helplessness. He hefted the metal staff over his head, ready to swing it down upon the curved faceplate.

"It is the way with all creatures," he said. "Those who cannot adapt to their environment must die. So here, breathe the clear, cold air of Mars—just as we do every day. It will be a grand gesture in the name of the *adins*!"

Dr. Dycek tilted her head up, as if actually welcoming it. As well she should, he thought, after what she had done to them.

"Boris, stop it!" It was Cora's voice, clear and strong.

She made her way out of the shadows from the back of the cave, moving with ponderous steps because of her obviously pregnant body. "Must you always make a spectacle of everything? That is how we lost Nikolas."

"It was justified!" Boris said defensively. But the tense moment crumbled around him. By invoking Nikolas's name, she had thrown a net around him, reminding all the *adins* of Boris's recent failure.

Dr. Dycek's attention flicked away from him as soon as Cora stepped into the light. Cora panted, then winced at internal pain. As if the outburst had expended her, she sat down, gripping her abdomen.

"She's pregnant!" Dr. Dycek said, with the first true emotion Boris had heard out of her. "How? That is impossible!"

For a moment, Boris found her comment so ludicrous he could not answer. "*How?*" Stroganov asked with a chuckle. "Does a doctor not know how a woman gets pregnant? A remarkable example of education in the Sovereign Republics!"

"Perhaps your sterilization procedures were not one hundred percent effective," Boris said, impaling her with the words as a substitute for his staff.

Dr. Dycek's entire attitude altered, and she gave her full attention to Cora instead of Boris. "But your baby will die if it is born up here. It cannot breathe. It will have none of your adaptations. Just a normal human child."

"We already know that!" Boris shouted. "Why do you think—"

"This changes everything," Dr. Dycek said, ignoring him again. Again! "An *adin* having a child. The first human born on Mars!" Flustered at first, then overwhelmed with awe, her voice rose with command as if they were her slaves—just as she had spoken in the training and therapy sessions before they left Earth.

"We will have to take you in the rover vehicle back down to Lowell Base," she said to Cora. "I can pressurize the cabin slowly so you will acclimate. That should take care of the low-altitude difficulties you might suffer. I will remain in my environment suit."

Boris felt his control of the other *adins* slipping like red dust through his fingertips. And the hatred rose up in him, white hot. Stroganov nodded, also looking at the suited figure with a new enthusiasm.

"Do you hear what she is saying?" Boris said. "You cannot live down there, in the heavy air!"

Dr. Dycek scowled at him. "Of course she can, Boris. You all can. You just need to take the time to adapt."

"No, that's impossible," Boris insisted. But he felt like an actor whose part has already been played, but refuses to leave the stage. Dr. Dycek was obviously much more interested in Cora and her cursed child.

Cora stepped forward, so intent with new hope and excitement that she did not try to hide her swollen appearance. "You can save the baby?"

"If we get you back to the base. We have medical equipment there. Nothing specifically for babies—who ever expected this? But, yes, we can do it." Inside the helmet, she nodded with encouragement.

"This is indeed good news, Boris!" Stroganov said. "We thought your baby would certainly die."

Boris released his hold on Dr. Dycek's arm and turned to face his companions in the cave. "Yes, save the child! And then what? Then everything will be perfect? Then all our problems will be solved? No! Then the humans will know where we are. They will come here and watch us die off, one by one. They will make a documentary program about us, the great failed *adin* experiment. Like animals in a Martian zoo? Wouldn't that be marvelous?"

He moved toward the cave opening to the deepening dusk outside. It was difficult for him to stomp in anger in the low gravity. "You are all fools!"

He stalked out into the air to stare at the brightening stars, at Phobos rising again in the east and the pinprick of Deimos suspended partway up the sky, where it had been for days.

The cold snap of night felt like a slap against him, and thin steam boiled from his nostrils as he breathed. He stood alone. The king of the mountain who had just been toppled from his throne.

BORIS TIBAN

LEAVING THE VOICES BEHIND HIM, he plunged into the darkness beyond Stroganov's shadowy monuments. The faces were silent and grim, accusing him. He listened to the wind carried up over the edge of the crevasse. Against his modified *adin* ears, the air seemed to be whispering in the voices of those who had disciplined him in the past, or cursed his name.

Boris Tiban. Little man. Listen to what your superiors tell you. It is not your place to disagree. We don't want to hear your objections.

That was what the dominating people had said to him in the freezing Siberian labor camp, in the sweltering and smelly oil refineries by the Caspian Sea, in the foster homes of his childhood in Georgia and Armenia—before he truly learned how to make people notice him, before he had learned the power of brash and unexpected actions.

He clamped down on his sudden urge to hurl the titanium spear over the cliff to stab at an invisible foe—that would be seen by no one, a pointless act. So instead he jabbed his staff into the crumbling volcanic soil at his feet, as if he were finishing off a fallen enemy.

Dr. Dycek and the other *adins* remained inside the grotto, chatting with each other like old friends. A tea party. More sugar? Black bread with marmalade? No, this is a celebration! Take out the Beluga caviar from the larder and some fine Georgian brandy.

The UNSA rover vehicle sat glittering under the starlight, like an ambassador's limousine parked in front of a hotel. Had Dr. Dycek just thought to come visiting? What right did she have to intrude upon them now, after abandoning the *adins* for so many years? And why did the others welcome her with open, plastic-coated arms?

He should have killed her as soon as she emerged from the rover. Only stupidity—and cowardice?—had stopped him. He had known others like Dycek in his life, puffed-up dictators with more than their share of power, who used it recklessly. It had been the same way in the foster homes, at the oil refinery.

Tossed from place to place as a teen, Boris Tiban grew up at war against Georgian bureaucrats who canceled aid packages so that he had to steal to keep himself clothed and fed. Against Armenian nationals who placed impossible restrictions on the movements of non-ethnically pure people such as himself, so that he could not stay, nor could he go. Or against the Azerbaijani Muslims who looked on him with glee for the virtually free slave labor he and other desperate infidels offered them.

A difficult case, often disciplined and never repentant, young Boris Tiban found himself assigned to a work detail in the Baku oil fields, away from the more civilized Republics to a place where work was hard and dirty and constant, so that he should have no time to think about causing trouble.

The hot desert of Baku had roasted and sweated him into submission within the first few months. The oil fields had been known since ancient times, when Zoroastrian pilgrims had built a temple over a burning seep of crude oil. Tsar Peter the Great had conquered the area around the Caspian Sea and attempted to ship some of the oil for use in his capitol city of St. Petersburg. In the late nineteenth century, Alfred Nobel—inventor of dynamite—invested in Baku oil, built Russia's first major drilling facilities.

The city of Baku sat on the western bank of the Caspian Sea, nestled in a kink in the shoreline. Massive off-shore drilling rigs perched on cranelike legs out in the water. Insectile pumps dipped into the desert landscape inland, groaning and sighing in the heat as they pushed down to coerce more crude from the stained sands.

Boris Tiban was assigned to work in the refinery complex north of Baku city. At nighttime, looking out the open windows of his barracks quarters, he could see the colored glare, neon scrawls in Arabic, glowing street lamps, coffee shops where the Arabs sat cross-legged under the warm night air and argued in loud voices but with smiles on their faces. Towers of mosques shone under garish white spotlights to attract tourists and pilgrims. Skyscrapers looked like pincushions of illuminated apartment windows.

The refinery workers, though, were virtual prisoners in squalid and low prefab buildings, baking hot during the day, frigid on winter nights. They ate company food that was either tasteless or so heavily spiced it burned the mucus from the back of the throat.

The air stank from chemicals escaping from the refining processes. Water from the faucet tasted as if it had been strained from a waste dump, and the fundamentalist Muslim government refused to allow consumption of any form of alcohol within the Baku city limits—which had been conveniently extended to encompass the refinery complex as well—on pain of mutilation. The home-brewed vodka available within the complex itself tasted as bad as the water did.

During the day, Boris worked in a nightmare forest of towers, tanks, and pipes. Color-coded mazes of conduits led from the pumping station to rows of fractional distillation towers topped by vapor recovery units; farther down the line waited solvent extraction basins, crystallization tanks. Substations performed thermal cracking or catalytic cracking on the straight-run products from the fractionating towers. At the far end of the farm, discolored storage tanks held reservoirs of the varied final petroleum products. Overhead, in the middle of the complex, a smokestack blazed with a natural-gas flame. Everything was noisy, and smelly, and ugly; no one else seemed to notice, or else they had passed beyond caring.

Boris's job was to walk the lines, check safety

systems, keep logs of pressure gauges, gas-flow and fluid-flow rates. His work overalls were stained and filthy—only one new pair provided every month, or pay for your own new changes . . . since the company gave him no transportation into town, and since they paid him in New Rubles that few of the Azerbaijani shopkeepers would accept, buying new clothes was out of the question.

Sometimes riding a small electric cart, but most of the time walking in leather boots on the hot asphalt, Boris moved under the humming, hissing, belching morass of conduits, staring upward at the abomination of technology. It took him months to figure out what exactly all the components did. Crude oil came in from the Baku fields, pumped through furnaces into the fractionating towers, where the superhot crude was separated into light, medium, and heavy fractions.

The work was sweaty, and unpleasant, and tedious—but at least the others left him alone for the most part, and he could get drunk as often as he wanted, provided he could stomach the vodka swill made under the bunks in the barracks. Overall, Boris found it less objectionable than many of the situations in which he had been trapped in the previous five years.

As soon as he realized the tolerability of his life, of course, it had to end. Unexpectedly, he was summoned to the office of his supervisor—Veronica Pournier, a French socialist outcast who kissed up to anyone above her while lecturing her underlings on the inequities of the management class.

Boris stank of old perspiration and volatile chemicals as he went into her air-conditioned closet of an office. Concrete walls, a metal locker, a time clock, and an unattractive juggernaut of a desk made up the office, indicating just how low Pournier was in the refinery's chain of command. Nonetheless, she was higher up than Boris.

"I am transferring you, Boris Tiban," Pournier said, pouting at him as she stared down at a multicolored printout. "Next week you will report to work out on the oil fields. You'll be trained as a roughneck on the drilling rigs. We need you more there than we do here." Her French accent made the words difficult to understand, but he knew the message all too well.

Boris felt his hackles rising. "Why? What have I done wrong here?"

"You don't get along with anyone else. You come to work drunk too often. You are a safety hazard. Your attitude is reprehensible. Enough?" She held up her fingers, ticking off his transgressions as she spoke. Boris looked at her with narrowed eyes as if she were the remnants of a bug he found squashed on the bottom of his boot.

"None of those reasons is on your official record, yet," she told him, "but I can make any of them stick if you decide to cause trouble."

His head pounded with the injustice, but he squeezed out his next words. "And who is to take my place?"

"A . . . man I know. He is in some sort of trouble with the French authorities, and Azerbaijan has no extradition treaty with France. He will stay here for a while, and you, Boris Tiban, are our most expendable worker."

She smiled at him. Her lips were thin, with a waxy coating from a perfumed balm he could smell, even above the other overpowering odors. Pournier was not much older than he, but the desert and the chemicals in the air had not been kind to her. She looked used up.

"It won't be so bad out on the oil fields," she said, turning away and distracting herself by shuffling papers. "What do you care anyway? You're not going anywhere here."

Boris leaned over the bulky metal desk and snatched the transfer paper out of her hands. He tore it in half, then crumpled the pieces. Last, he grabbed the front of Veronica Pournier's work overalls and stuffed the paper down her shirt. He hoped he left a black grease stain on her breasts.

She didn't give him the satisfaction of screaming in

terror or outrage. Her voice was cold as he turned his back on her. "I have changed my mind. You are going out to the offshore drilling rigs instead. One of the Muslim ones. And I'll see that your furlough requests are permanently denied."

Boris smashed the time clock with his fist on his way out, and left the metal door swinging open so the waves of heat and yellow sunlight would steal her air-conditioned coolness.

Hours after dark, with garish sodium lights blazing down from intersections in the girders and pipe arrays, Boris left his quarters and stalked past the night crews into the heart of the facility, where the noxious fumes were densest, where automated subsystems monitored production. Crisscrossed shadows filled the place like a surreal haunted forest.

Boris's job was to check the shutoff valves, the overpressure vents, the shunt joints to holding tanks, as well as their associated safety systems. With very little thought he figured out how to disable them all.

Boris didn't bother to hide what he was doing. Part of him instinctively tried to cover his tracks, but another part wanted everyone to know who had done this. Otherwise, what would be the point?

He closed down the shutoff valves leading to the second fractionation tower, which stood like a huge silo in the middle of the refinery. He yanked out the wires controlling the fire-suppression systems. It was all so simple.

He would show Veronica Pournier, all right.

Only one of the feed lines still led into the tower, and he cranked down the flow content so that the pipe was half full of air and volatiles from the crude. This line carried the lighter fractions that needed no heating before they bubbled through the distillation levels.

Boris withdrew a wrinkled brown cigarette from his overall pocket. With an irony he enjoyed immensely, Boris had bummed the cigarette from one of the refinery guards just before retiring to the barracks.

Loosening the top access port on the feed pipe, he lit the cigarette and took a single puff. The tobacco tasted like asphalt and benzene.

He struck his lighter again and shielded the flickering flame as he lifted the access lid. He tossed the lighter down into the pipe, then leaped away. Blue-orange flames jetted from the opening, but most of the fire spurted down the length of the pipe, the path of least resistance toward the fractionation tower.

Boris Tiban ran without looking back, his boots clomping on the hard pavement as the thin whine of devouring flames whooshed into the air. He hadn't the slightest idea how much damage the fire would cause—it might explode the entire facility in a gigantic fireball, or it might simply burn away the crude being pumped into the tower.

The *whump* knocked him to his face on the oil-soaked ground. He scrambled to his feet and kept fleeing. Something erupted far behind him. An alarm went off, then another. Boris laughed as he ran. . . .

The explosion and the resulting fire ruined part of fractionation tower number two, taking it off-line for three months of repairs and refurbishing. Several days worth of production was lost directly to the fire. Two people died.

Not surprisingly, Boris had promptly been blamed. The guard remembered giving him a cigarette and remembered later that Boris did not smoke; several people had seen Boris leave the barracks after lights-out; and Veronica Pournier had explained his motive. Boris did not deny the charges. That was, after all, the purpose behind making such a spectacle. If the disaster were deemed a mere accident, then the point would be lost, wouldn't it?

The Muslim fundamentalists had screamed for blood, proposing various slow deaths for him, the most appropriate of which seemed to be boiling Boris in oil—Baku oil, of course. But the Azerbaijani Republic and the Georgian Republic had been in the middle of a diplomatic spat at the time, and the Georgians demanded extradition for their "precious countryman." Barely rescuing him from execution, the Georgians immediately turned Boris over to the Russians, who transferred him to one of the most brutal work camps in Siberia—where he worked, and seethed in anger, and kept working. And survived.

In Neryungri, Boris Tiban had grown strong in the hellish winter wasteland, hardened by the harsh labor. And then the people behind the scenes had snatched him away, put him through rigorous selection procedures, made him sign forms written in English, a language he could not read, and then worked their black surgical magic on him.

The Sovereign Republics had sent him to Mars as an *adin*, no longer completely human but still expected to follow orders as if they believed him to be a patriotic hero with nothing else on his mind. Now he was one of the last *adins*—and Dr. Dycek had come to disrupt everything again.

How could Boris meekly let her do whatever she wished? How could he let her take control so easily? Without a fight?

Perhaps it was time for another grand gesture.

RACHEL DYCEK

NOT EVEN BORIS'S childish tantrum could break Rachel's concentration as she stared at the rounded abdomen of the *adin* woman, the protective, polymerized skin stretched tight. Cora wore a too-large overall, which had probably been fitted for one of the burly *adin* men, but it could not obscure her pregnancy.

A baby on Mars! The thought sent Rachel's perspective reeling, and she felt her emotions warring with each other over how to react. Should she be delighted, or horrified?

Cora Marisovna's hooded eyes were shadowed, masked by protective lashes. In the back of her memories Rachel remembered a frightened young Siberian girl with glistening black hair and Mongolian features, ushered into the testing labs under the combined coercion of mother and grandmother. Rachel had focused on the test results, on the *adin* modifications, averting her eyes whenever she began to think of the candidates as people. Despite what she had insisted during the UN hearings, Rachel frequently refused to think of the human aspects of the *adin* program—but now it had reared up and struck her across the face.

In the facility at Neryungri, young, dark-haired Cora had done everything asked of her. She never complained; she seemed so *trusting*. Rachel had felt uneasy after seeing this innocent test subject, but she had driven it from her mind. Cora Marisovna had passed every one of the rigid physical requirements for *adin* surgeries, and the project had too few female volunteers to choose from. The selection had to be made, and Rachel had no regrets. But the lovely Siberian girl now looked as if she had been molded by a blind sculptor, nose and ears smeared away.

Behind the whitish cast of her polymerized skin Cora showed a slight discoloration from central cyanosis due to polycythemia and reduced oxygen saturation, despite the genetically modified hemoglobin-Y and the enhanced lung capacity. As she spoke, her tongue and the inner lining of her mouth showed a ruddy, blue-tinged appearance, as had Boris and the other *adins*.

Rachel viewed all this with a distracted, clinical focus, until she realized again where she was—sitting among the *adins* who had miraculously survived years of exile in a bleak grotto high on Pavonis Mons. This *adin* woman was no longer young, about thirty-six Earth years, and had lived most of that time under extreme hardship. Cora Marisovna had endured it all, as if she had no other choice. She had stayed with Boris Tiban and his petty revolution, which had no lasting effect but to make the surviving *adins* miserable when they could have been working side by side with the *dvas* and the humans on Mars.

Her hands sweaty inside the thin-film gloves, Rachel reached forward to touch Cora. In the shadows at the rear of the grotto, Stroganov stood to watch, but he did not speak. It seemed a magic moment to her. New life springing forth on a dead planet—even Jesús Keefer's grandiose terraforming plans could not compete with that.

Cora looked embarrassed and confused by Rachel's touch, but she carried a semblance of hope she had not shown at first. Rachel held her breath, listening to the burbling oxygen regenerator on her back, feeling the faint breeze of new air wafting into her suit. Lightly, she laid the palms of her gloves over the curve of Cora's abdomen.

Though she had been involved in every step of their development, Rachel was still impressed by the survival capabilities of these augmented humans. But the simple miracle of this pregnancy—a pregnancy that should never have happened—amazed her more. She felt as if years' worth of cobwebs had been cleared from her head.

She knew, of course, that sterilization procedures were not one hundred percent reliable—but the chances were so minimal that the medical warnings were little more than legal disclaimers. With all of the other *adin* surgeries and the extreme rigors of their life on hostile Mars, Rachel and her team had deemed an unsuccessful vasectomy to be an acceptable risk. Unfortunately, medicine in the Sovereign Republics had a long-standing reputation for somewhat low standards in their "acceptable risks."

Not feeling the deep cold, Cora Marisovna unfastened the lower part of her overall to expose the tight skin stretched over her belly. Rachel pressed down with a gloved hand to touch the bulge, but she could feel little through the slick protective gloves.

She glanced up, turning her helmeted head to see where Boris had gone, but she found only the black opening of the lava tube and the darkness outside. What did Boris think about this baby? Had his frustration and helplessness at the doomed child driven him to break his years of hiding to strike out at the *dva* pumping station? But if that were true, why did he not grasp at his only chance for saving the baby? She wondered if Boris considered his anger to be more important.

Beside her, Stroganov seemed preoccupied with excusing Boris's temper. "He is not always like this, Dr. Dycek. Boris is strong and has kept us alive for fifteen years now, but everything is slipping through his fingers. You can see how many of us are left." He gestured around the desolate cave and continued in a voice that implied how much he enjoyed telling stories.

"Most of the *adins* died within four years after Boris led us away from the UNSA activities. We have a large graveyard of frozen bodies buried up in the Pavonis caldera, unless the algae and lichen have eaten them by now. Two nights ago our companion Nikolas was lost in a raid. We are all in mourning."

Rachel scowled, seeing in her mind the *dva* family who would now have to bury their own dead in the Martian dust, fix the pumping station, and take shelter from the approaching storm. "Yes, and I saw the two *dvas* he murdered." She met Stroganov's steely gaze. "So it is rather difficult for me to sympathize with your loss."

Rachel looked at Cora, then turned around in her bulky suit to survey Stroganov. Her oxygen regenerators hissed; the air tasted musty and dry. "Why don't you come down and join in the work yourselves? You no longer have to hide. We could provide you with the tools you need, some supplies. Even Commissioner Keefer would not turn down extra help, especially from people adapted to the Martian environment."

"The *dvas* are making it impossible for us to live!" Cora sat up, as if repeating what Boris had told her over and over again. Her words carried a rich Siberian accent that evoked thoughts of wild lands and simple people. "And so are the humans. The terraforming work is stealing our homes from us. Soon we will all die when the air gets too thick."

Stroganov leaned closer, as if scrutinizing Rachel. "Boris says we cannot go down to the low altitudes. The air is too dense, the temperature too warm. We would die."

Frustrated, Rachel stood up again, taking a step away. The other female *adin*, Nastasia, flitted across the grotto, stared at Rachel in her silvery environment suit as if noticing her for the first time, then disappeared up the passage that led out to the caldera rim, humming.

"But if you came down gradually, adapting as you descended," Rachel said, "it would be all right."

Cora shook her head, and Stroganov joined her, as if they had convinced themselves beyond any possibility of doubt. "We are adapted for the thinnest air and the coldest temperatures. We cannot live in conditions like those below."

Rachel crossed her arms over her chest. "You already have! You lived with all of your modifications in Siberia, on Earth, where conditions are a thousand times better for normal humans than even the low-lands below. The fact that you have adaptations to survive rugged conditions does not mean you *require* rugged conditions."

Stroganov sat down heavily with a shocked and embarrassed expression on his face. He appeared thunderstruck, as if he had maintained a fragile hold on his dignity for years, and now had finally given up. "I think Boris wanted us to live like enduring heroes, escapees from authority, bandits hiding out in the uncharted hills. And we were stupid enough to believe him."

"Not stupid," Cora said defensively. She drew a deep breath, and suddenly her mouth clamped shut. Her eyelids crammed together, and she let out a hiss. The skin on her abdomen tightened until it had a waxy texture as hard as the rind of a melon.

Rachel froze, at a loss for what to do. She had plenty of biomedical training, theory, and dissections behind her. But she had never had training as a general practioner or a midwife. She knew—theoretically—everything about how babies were born, but she had never delivered one herself. It had not seemed the remotest of possibilities.

During her contraction, Cora's hands groped for something to grab on to, finally seizing a lump of lava welded to the floor. She squeezed the sharp edges until blood oozed from shallow cuts in her palms, freezing into a sparkling smear on the rock.

Nastasia reappeared from above, bending low and showing her deep concern. "Is she mortally wounded?" Nastasia asked dramatically. "Struck down while fighting to defend the tsar?"

Cora gasped out her next words after the spasm passed. "It is all right. That has been happening for days. I can bear the pain."

"You must not have the child here," Rachel insisted. She stood up and paced, ready to take charge. "We will get you back to Lowell Base. How frequent are the contractions?"

"How should I know?" Cora's voice was filled more with pain and weariness than anger.

Stroganov explained. "We don't exactly have a chronometer here, Dr. Dycek. Boris left those things behind when we came to the highlands. We have a few survival supplies stowed in the lava tubes, but timekeeping devices were not a high priority."

Rachel knelt again, feeling Cora's abdomen. Even with Cora's modified hemoglobin, she didn't know if the baby would be getting enough oxygen through the mother's bloodstream. The baby might be dead already inside the uterus. In fact, how could she expect it to be anything other than stillborn?

"Have you felt the baby kick at all?"

"Oh, yes!" Cora said. Her eyes glistened, either in an afterwash of pain or with a sudden rush of wonder.

"When was the last time?"

"Just this morning."

Stroganov's hard hand gripped Rachel's shoulder. "You must get her away from here, Dr. Dycek. Give her whatever help you can offer at your human base. Boris may be too proud to ask, but the rest of us are not."

Rachel would do what she could to save the baby, but she realized also that Cora offered her a chance to accomplish something meaningful at the end of her work on Mars. The infant would focus Earth's attention once again on Rachel's own efforts. The return of the four surviving *adins* would raise many questions all over again. The simple fact that they had survived on their own resources and abilities for *sixteen years* justified her original vision.

Rachel might even get a reprieve, be allowed to stay on Mars to study the altered humans and how they adapted to their changing planet. They had managed to live in the worst of conditions, in the thinnest air—

how would they survive the transition back to relative comfort in the lowlands? Could they handle it? Much would depend on the cooperation of Boris Tiban.

Rachel pondered that for a moment. No, this was not Boris's decision alone. It was Cora Marisovna's. It was Stroganov's and Nastasia's.

"Let us go and save your child, Cora. My rover is right outside. We can perhaps put together a special chamber back at the base, keep the pressure low and comfortable for you as you adapt so you can see your little one after it is born."

Cora worked her way to her feet, holding out her arms to let Stroganov and Rachel help her up. Though Cora was Boris's woman, Stroganov treated her with a tenderness and care that Boris himself had not evidenced.

Cora looked around the grotto, but didn't seem to find anything too dear to leave behind. The two women shuffled to the door opening into the Martian dusk.

"I will stay here and wait for Boris," Stroganov said. "Perhaps I can speak to him."

Outside, Boris Tiban was nowhere to be seen. The sky's green had turned a muddy ochre. The upthrust rocks were stark against the slope of Pavonis Mons. Far below at the horizon, nearly a day's journey at the rover's top speed, lay the *dva* pumping station, other scattered *dva* encampments, and then Lowell Base.

"You will be all right," Rachel said to Cora. Gradually, her eyes adapted to the dimness outside.

The rover was gone.

Leaving Cora to stand against a rock, Rachel ran to where she had parked the vehicle. High-altitude breezes ran groping fingers over her suit as panic jangled her nerves. Her rapid breathing echoed in her helmet.

Had Boris somehow driven away with it? Impossible! Rachel clearly remembered engaging the lock mechanisms, and the AI pilot would not respond to an unrecognized voice signature.

Percival's tracks were already beginning to blur in the wind. She came to a sloughed-off portion of the chasm wall where a large object had been toppled over the edge. Fulcrum boulders and pry marks in the lava soil showed how Boris had used his metal staff. His footprints lay all around, as if he had danced for joy after his effort.

With dread surging inside her Rachel went to the brink of the gorge. A hundred meters down, more lava rock lay strewn about.

In the gathering shadows, she could make out the squared-off form of her vehicle, out of reach far below.

JESÚS KEEFER

THE SECOND LONG-DISTANCE ROVER rolled out of the protective overhang beside the Spine, leaving only the putt-putt for the personnel of Lowell Base. Keefer sat up-front next to Bruce Vickery, who instructed *Schiaparelli*'s AI pilot where to go.

The small white sun rose abruptly, with little fanfare of dawn. Raising a cloud of red dust in its wake, *Schiaparelli* passed out of the shadow of the peaks, heading toward Noctis Labyrinthus.

Looking out the windowport, Keefer watched the activity around the outpost as they drove off. Suited figures bustled outside in slow motion with a self-absorbed frenzy as they prepared for rough weather. Amelia Steinberg had commandeered the short-range buggy for her team, setting up a bank of pitted wind deflectors in the exact direction of the storm's approach, while other workers added an extra layer of deep-freeze caulk around the seams of the modules.

Keefer looked back at the interconnected base components dwindling in the distance and hoped he had made the right decision. Rachel Dycek had not returned during the night, nor had she made any contact with the base. The storm was fading faster than expected—Evrani and al-Somak argued as to the cause—and two *dva* mining stations in the north and Viking Base had already reestablished contact to note clearing skies. But still the satellites showed high winds and scouring dust were due to strike before the end of the day.

"We've only got a few hours to find her," Vickery said through the speakerpatch. "I'm not going to lose both of us—and our only other rover—because of somebody else's stupidity."

"I'm not asking you to," Keefer said. "But we have to make our best attempt. United we stand, right?"

"Yeah," Vickery said. "But that doesn't mean I can't bitch about it." He paused, as if contemplating revealing his thoughts to Keefer.

"Hey, don't get the impression that nobody likes Rachel. She's damned good when she's got her heart in something—in fact, when we first landed here she was hell on wheels, getting the *dvas* and the humans to erect Lowell Base and installing the new prepackaged modules. We got the sucker done in one third the time of any other base on Mars. But the last half a year she's really gotten on everyone's nerves with her doom-and-gloom attitude. It gets old, you know?" He settled back into the chair and let the AI drive.

Vickery double-checked the monitors, then sighed with relief. "Cabin's fully pressurized. Shirtsleeve weather." He popped open his faceplate and removed his helmet, scratching his thick beard. "Might as well be comfortable. It'll be a few hours drive to the Labyrinth, and there isn't a hell of a lot to see until the edge of the badlands. Flat hardpan, rust, and a lot of little boulders."

Keefer cracked his knuckles through his thin gloves and stared out at the grim scenery.

After studying Dycek's movements for the past several days and discussing her personality with the other members of the base, Vickery and Keefer had decided that there could be only one logical place for her to go. It was the anniversary of the avalanche that had wiped out the group of *dva* intelligentsia, and Rachel had just spent much of an entire day brooding at the site. She must have taken *Percival* back to Noctis Labyrinthus for . . . something. Vickery insisted that she had exhibited increasing symptoms of severe depression—listlessness, insomnia, loss of appetite—and Keefer's own arrival might have forced the issue in her mind. Keefer detected an undertone of concern in Vickery's voice that the big man tried to cover up.

After removing his own suit, Keefer shuffled back to the chemical-recovery toilet cubicle. He had gulped two cups of coffee that morning, then hurriedly eaten a microwaved tray of what the label called a "Mexican-style breakfast" that included wet and rubbery *huevos rancheros*, soggy tortillas, and salsa that tasted like ketchup with Tabasco sauce and pickle relish mixed into it.

His stomach churned with acidic dread, knowing they were not going to find anything Keefer *wanted* to find, realizing they had little time before the storm. What did he expect to see—Rachel Dycek sitting beside her rover, sticking her thumb out for some passerby to help change a flat tire? No, she had run off on purpose and disabled her locator beacon. They might never locate her if she did not want to be found.

In silence, he complained to himself about the unfairness of the situation. He had come to Mars full of exuberance, expecting to find a group of people as dedicated as he was, intent on making themselves into a hardworking team to claim a world as their prize. Instead, he had found a big dysfunctional family.

Rubbing his arms in the chill of the rover's cabin, Keefer returned to his seat beside the heater, but the landscape soon became boring even to him. He hunched forward in his seat, looking at his companion. Vickery hummed to himself as he watched the autopilot negotiate the monotonous terrain.

"So, Bruce, I need to know the people I'll be working with." He flashed a bright smile, the one the newsnet cameras always loved. "Tell me about yourself. You married? Any kids?"

Vickery turned to him a little too quickly, his eyebrows raised. Keefer thought he saw a flush creep in behind the man's ruddy complexion. "Commissioner Keefer, we're millions of miles from Earth and stationed here for years. Do you think *any* of us would be here if we were happily married, with a wife and kids and a dog and a home in the suburbs?"

"I guess you're right," Keefer said, frowning at his

faux pas. "I thought I was the only one without much at home."

"Let me give you a tip," Vickery said. "You set yourself up in a no-win situation with a question like that. Most answers will be either a) 'my marriage was a failure and I'm divorced,' or b) 'no I never found anyone in my whole life that I could get along with, so I'm here.' The best you could hope for is 'I miss my wife and kids terribly and I won't be able to see them for ages, and you've just reminded me of them all over again.'" Vickery kept his eyes ahead, but he had a roguish grin on his face. "So, we don't ask those kinds of questions. Period."

"I take it you aren't going to answer, even after I've already embarrassed myself?"

"Not on your life."

Keefer laughed, wondering which of the three possible answers seemed likeliest for this man. "Okay, so tell me about Rachel Dycek then. Gossip doesn't have to bow to the same restrictions, does it?"

Vickery shrugged, then grinned. "Now there's somebody we could talk about for hours and still not get closer to understanding."

Keefer encouraged him. "You were on the original flight with her, weren't you? I seem to remember that from your dossier."

"Yeah, but I'm not being rotated home yet. That's another slap in Rachel's face, because that means UNSA thinks I'm needed here and she's not." He sighed, and his eyes got a distant look. "Four months in interplanetary space, cooped up in a little ship with that woman. You can imagine what it was like!" He drummed his fingertips on the steering controls and stared ahead. His eyes got a far-off look, and his lips curved upward in a more personal smile than the amiable grins he had displayed earlier.

"Actually, she wasn't too bad. Not then, at least. Those UN hearings hurt her bad, I think, but she's a strong lady. She really wanted to come here to be with her *dvas*."

Vickery looked at Keefer as if to make sure he was listening.

"Sending her to Mars was a tiny bone UNSA threw to her, but she treasured it. She was going to atone for everything in the past by making the *dvas* into show-pieces. Everything seemed to be going so well—but then the avalanche in the Labyrinth knocked her flat again. That woman's been through a lot of shit, Commissioner."

He grabbed the steering controls and diverted the rover around a rough boulder field, though the AI probably would have done so automatically. Keefer sat back and listened, letting the other man tell what he wanted. Vickery didn't seem to mind chatting, once he got started.

"Actually, Rachel and I had a bit of a thing going for a while—it gets mighty lonely and boring on that ship on the way over." He raised his eyebrows at Keefer. "Haven't I seen some body language between you and that Tam Smith?"

Keefer felt his cheeks burning. "Now it's your turn not to ask questions like that. What happened between you and Rachel Dycek?"

"Well, she's not bad looking. A little intense, a little hurt, tries to make everyone think she's not vulnerable to anything. Don't go imagining some sort of whirlwind relationship or anything. Just occasional sex and not even much of that. She spent the whole time on the trip over fidgeting, waiting. We were all anxious to get to Mars, of course, but Rachel *lived* for the day we would arrive.

"When we landed she forgot routine duties for a while, scrapped the mission plan—which was a frivolous bunch of crud anyway. The *dvas* were her pets, her darling little children, and she had to catch up on everything they were doing. They had been all alone on Mars for a handful of years, remember. Sure, they had put the core of Lowell Base together, set up the power reactor, started getting the water out of Pavonis Mons and drilling ice out of the Labyrinth—they also managed to lose a whole bunch of the spare parts we had sent them. We kept thinking they were hoarding amenities like electrical connections, heaters, lighting setups out in their own dwellings, but we never found any of it. And Commissioner Dycek wouldn't hear of starting any sort of tough investigation.

"Rachel would go out on excursions to the *dva* outposts, keeping meticulous track of their progress, giving them medical checkups, writing one technical paper after another about the work they were doing on the surface."

He opened a compartment to pull out a vacuum-wrapped container of vegetable newtons. "Want a cookie?" Keefer, stomach still roiling from his "Mexican-style" breakfast, shook his head.

Vickery raised a finger in the air. "Rachel acted like a kid with a new ant farm, watching the busy little workers doing all sorts of marvelous things. Those *dvas* who died out in the Labyrinth weren't just another group of test subjects—those were educated people, talented researchers, engineers, experts. Not prison refugees like the *adins*. Rachel was counting on them."

He shook his shaggy head sadly. "We had to drag her away from the search after the avalanche. A storm was coming by the time we learned of the disaster, and we couldn't stay out any longer."

Keefer nodded, then cleared his dry throat. "So it's no surprise to you that she might have gone there yesterday when she was feeling, well, depressed?"

Vickery stuffed a cookie in his mouth and formed words around it. "Where else would she go?"

After nearly two hours of traveling, the flat red plain split open like a festering sore. Noctis Labyrinthus was the scattered western end of the vast Valles Marineris. Geological ages ago, a winding maze of canyons, spiderwebs of gorges, and sheer-walled arroyos had been etched miles deep.

"Good place for one of those scenic overlook signs, don't you think?" Vickery asked, startling Keefer.

Keefer kept his voice low. "Mars is smaller than Earth, but I'm not accustomed to the magnitude of everything! And I haven't even seen Olympus Mons yet!"

"To tell you the truth, Olympus looks a lot more impressive from orbit. The sucker is so huge and so gradual that you really can't comprehend what you're looking at from down here. Same goes for the big parts of Vallis Marineris. The canyon's so wide that the opposite rim is over the bleeping horizon. Your brain knows it's there, but your eye just sees a big cliff. Sensory overload."

Vickery turned *Schiaparelli* along the edge of one of the widest fingers of canyon, searching for the split into a smaller tributary. When he located the area where a swath of avalanche had crumbled off a few million years ago, he began to take the rover down the slope to the bottom.

"In my opinion, the Labyrinth is about the most impressive spot on Mars, right around here," Vickery said, brushing crumbs from his beard. "Big enough to be spectacular and awesome, but not so immense that it doesn't fit inside your eyeball. Know what I'm saying?"

Keefer stared through the rover's windowport to the sprawling badlands. He and Allan had hiked the Grand Canyon on Earth once, for the boy's sixteenth birthday, when his mother needed to go away to Europe for a consulting job. Carried away with the father/son thing, they had vowed to each other that they would hike to the bottom. It had been a terrific and memorable time: Keefer had showered his dreams on his son, telling him of the wonders of the future, the chances Allan would have if he dared to reach out and grab them. . . .

The rover lurched forward, keeping traction with its thousand independent telescoping legs, as Vickery drove down the slope of what had obviously been an access road some time ago. Dycek had gone this way the day before Keefer and his companions landed. As he looked across the vastness of Noctis Labyrinthus, he wondered how in the world they would ever find her out in that mess.

"The *dvas* who were killed in the accident were working in one specific arm of the Labyrinth," Vickery said. "It's got a Latin name on the maps, but don't ask me to remember it. I can find it, though. That's the important part."

The walls rose around them like towering pillars, stratified over geological ages, weathered away in jagged edges with the renewed vigor of the last half century of terraforming activities. "These canyon walls are like sponges, filled with primeval frozen water and sealed off," Vickery said. "It was an obvious bet for the *dvas* to start mining there. Unfortunately, it was geologically unstable, too."

Vickery stopped *Schiaparelli* and started to suit up. "This is the spot. I don't see the rover from here, and of course the beacon's turned off—but let's go outside and see if we can find any sign."

Keefer snorted and took a last glance through the windowport to see the monumental rockfall from the avalanche that had wiped out thirty-one *dvas*. He suited up and clambered through the rover's sphincter airlock, he stood beside Vickery looking at the debris, which was already starting to be overgrown with lichens and algae that fed on the freshly exposed mineral-rich surfaces.

Vickery stretched out an arm, pointing toward a far wall that was honeycombed with pockmarks and caves. "Up there the *dvas* found a particularly large deposit of ice, and they were tunneling in with explosives. That's when the avalanche happened. Absolutely unbelievable! Half the canyon wall fell down. My bet is they either used way too much explosives, or they hit on a resonance fracture."

Then he plodded away from the rover. "Come on, let's go hunting. I know a couple other routes down here, just in case Rachel was trying to hide her tracks. Maybe we should wear coonskin caps."

Without a better suggestion, Keefer agreed, following behind the larger man. In the low gravity they could skip lightly over jumbled boulders, making good time. "We can afford about an hour here," Vickery said, "then we head back."

"I thought we had a little longer than that, according to Dr. Evrani's estimate. Did he give you a better guess of the storm's arrival?"

"Hell, no! He's a weatherman—I wouldn't believe a thing he says. That's just my personal safety factor."

Like kids on a jungle gym, they climbed over a pile of gray-brown rubble veined with orange and scarlet, then skirted tall boulders that lay in a fanned-out pattern from the avalanche. Keefer saw no indication of chewed-up loose ground from rover tracks, no sign that Commissioner Dycek had gone this way. Constant ripples of wind stirred the dust on the canyon floor, but the suit muffled the sounds. The place seemed still and brooding. Keefer's breathing boomed in his ears.

Vickery turned to look at a side canyon leading back into the cliff that had buried the *dvas*—and they both froze at a glimpse of sudden motion. "What the hell!" Vickery said.

A strange *dva* man stood there in the side canyon, wearing a padded jumpsuit and gloves and carrying an odd backpack slung over one shoulder. He turned, saw the two suited humans, and his hooded *dva* eyes seemed to bug out of his head.

"Hey!" Vickery shouted through his speakerpatch, turning up the volume. He lumbered toward the *dva* man. "What are you doing here?"

The *dva* man bolted, scrambling down the canyon floor, dodging boulders and outcroppings.

"Wait!" Vickery ran in dreamlike slow motion,

kicking up iron oxide dust as he followed the fleeing *dva*. "Keefer, come on!"

Keefer stumbled after, not nearly as graceful as his companion.

The *dva* man turned a corner in the kinked passage of the side canyon, then vanished from sight in the jumble of avalanche debris. Boulders the size of houses stood around them, fallen into fissures in the rock walls. Keefer barely managed to keep pace with Vickery, terrified of becoming lost in the maze.

The *dvas* weren't supposed to be here; none of the other mining and processing settlements were within an hour's travel. All ice extraction in this location had stopped after the avalanche, their efforts turned toward the reservoirs near Pavonis.

But Rachel Dycek must know the assigned locations of her *dvas* at any time. Were the *dvas* here for some purpose—to meet Dycek perhaps?

When they reached the kink in the canyon wall, Vickery stopped so abruptly that his boots dug into the soft ground and he nearly toppled over from his own momentum.

The pocket in the canyon ended abruptly, showing them nothing but a blank stone wall.

"This is ridiculous!" Vickery said.

The *dva* man was nowhere in sight.

NASTASIA

In DARKNESS THE *ADINS* used tough cables and harsh white spotlights to reach the bottom of the chasm. The rover lay like a wounded beast on its side, its masses of telescoping legs flailing for purchase against the toppled rocks.

Nastasia knew it was a machine, but still she felt sorry for the thing, fallen so far below. She wondered if it had hurt when it struck bottom. She wondered if she would hurt if she jumped that far. She decided not to find out.

Stroganov took the equipment from the final cache of supplies the *adins* had brought with them when they abandoned the Martian lowlands. Nastasia thought Stroganov was very smart to remember the cables. Boris had wanted to abandon everything, and only a few of the *adin* refugees had hauled the equipment piled on their broad shoulders, balanced on the humps of their secondary lungs. But in the intervening years, Boris had grown angry each time the *adins* were forced to use the old UNSA equipment. She didn't see Boris around here, though, and she wondered if he would be angry now. Nastasia knew to hide whenever Boris was angry.

She watched the cables snake down into the darkness, and visions flickered in her imagination, blurring reality again. Ropes used by assassins to scale the Kremlin walls? Were enemies of the monarchy coming to get her again, even here on Mars? She had to run!

She was at the top of a chasm, fleeing before the Bolsheviks came for them again. She and her family had been under house arrest in the country dacha—her father Tsar Nicholas, her mother Tsarina Alexandra, all her brothers and sisters. The Bolsheviks were coming to murder them all! She had to get away! So sad . . .

"Nastasia," Stroganov said in his warm, gentle voice, holding out one of the ropes to her. "I need your help. We must get down to Dr. Dycek's vehicle. It is the only way we can save Cora's baby."

Cora's baby. Oh, yes, they had to rescue the child. She had forgotten. Nastasia saw Cora waiting by the edge of the crevasse, silent in her dread as she stared down at the wounded vehicle. Cora huddled over her swollen belly, as if trying to hold the infant inside of her where it would be safe and warm. Nastasia wanted to go hug her—but she couldn't. Stroganov needed her help. Where was Boris?

The human doctor in the environment suit paced up and down the rim of the chasm, as if trying to decide what to do. She looked so strange in the muffling garment and fishbowl helmet. Nastasia and Stroganov were the only able-bodied *adins* in sight.

Boris was nowhere to be found. Had he done something? And where was Nikolas? It seemed so long since Nastasia had seen him. Maybe the two of them should come help save Cora's baby. The *adins* had to stick together, as Boris said so often. She opened her mouth to shout his name.

"Nastasia," Stroganov repeated, jarring her thoughts, "please take this rope. Brace yourself and hold tightly. You must not forget. Be strong for me here. I am going down."

Nastasia grabbed the cable Stroganov handed to her, wrapped it around her waist, and dug her tough *adin* feet into the dust. She saw he had tied the end around the base of his Stepan Razin sculpture—not one of her favorites, but the one closest to the chasm.

Nastasia was physically fit, strong and healthy. Nothing else had troubled her since the mishap that had occurred during her first days on Mars, when she had lost oxygen to a portion of her brain. It had been difficult to think since then. Stroganov had explained it to her, several times, but it still did not make sense. Old stories, old memories, imagined happenings shuffled together into one mismatched mosaic. Not knowing what was true and what she could ignore, Nastasia chose to believe everything. Just in case.

"I hope this cable reaches all the way to the bottom," Stroganov said, looking down into the darkness. "Dr. Dycek, once I am down, I will hold the rope taut for you. If you think you can make it, perhaps by walking down the rock wall, I need you to check out your vehicle."

"If it is possible to do, then I will do it." Dr. Dycek went to the precipice and peered into the depths. "We can never bring the rover back up. We'll just have to hope I can drive out along the canyon floor, if nothing blocks our way."

Stroganov nodded and, gripping the cable, backed over the edge of the cliff. The muscles in his arms coiled like snakes as he eased himself down. Nastasia watched the shadows play across his plasticized skin. She made a low hooting sound, just to listen to the echoes in the gorge below. Sometimes, when the wind was strong, she heard so many echoed voices they seemed to be chanting at her.

From her resting position Cora Marisovna called out to wish him luck. A few loose rocks pattered down. Cora had kept Boris Tiban as her lover during all the years of *adin* exile, but Nastasia played with both Stroganov and Nikolas. She knew she was one of the more attractive *adins*, considering all of the monstrous adaptations. And two lovers seemed her due, since she was the only surviving daughter of the tsar and the true heir to the Romanov throne. Or had there been more lovers? Each time she felt the intrusion into her body, the clutching arms and legs against desensitized skin, she thought she saw a different face: strong heroes, clever advisers, dangerous bandits, men from her past and men from history.

Nastasia could not remember why she had been turned into one of the *adins*, why she had been forced to endure the indignities of the transformational surgery, why she had come all the way to Mars. It had to be a disguise! What other explanation could there be? She herself must be someone important, someone in great danger of discovery. She must be here in exile.

But what about the labor camps she remembered? Neryungri, prison, vicious work in freezing Siberia . . . Part of her kept a locked-away memory that she had killed her own children a long time ago, two naughty daughters . . . she had murdered them. She recalled sitting on the rough fieldstone porch of her small house, staring at the blood on her hands, how it reflected the bright noon sunshine, how the neighbors had come running to see the cause of the shrill screams from within the cottage. Could she possibly have done that to her own children—or was it something she had read? A true happening, or just a story, a misfired memory?

Her name must be part of the disguise, too. Her real name was Anastasia, the daughter of Tsar Nicholas II. Yes, she had miraculously survived the assassinations during the 1917 revolutions. She had been hiding on her own for all these years, taking identity after identity, fleeing and running, even across space.

Now she lived on Mars, where no one would ever find her, where Lenin and the Bolsheviks could never track her down and shoot her, as they had done with the rest of the Romanov family. The Imperial bloodline must live in her, waiting for the Sovereign Republics to reunite into Mother Russia again. Nastasia had to remain alive, for that dream alone if for nothing else.

Was that why Stroganov's statue of Lenin seemed to stare at her so intently each time she looked at it?

The rope around her waist jerked, pulling her back to the cold night on Pavonis Mons, with the icicle-bright stars impaling the sky above them. She thought she heard wolves howling in the forests, far away down the slope of the volcano.

Holding on to the rope, Nastasia leaned forward to look for Stroganov, but he had vanished down into the inky shadows of the chasm. The starlight did little to illuminate the smashed rover below.

"Nastasia," came his shouted words, "send Dr. Dycek down!"

Confused, she looked around. Who was Dr. Dycek? She did not recognize the name. Where was Boris? He would know.

The human in the environment suit strode to the edge of the chasm. "I am coming!"

The doctor turned toward Cora. "Wait for me here, and we'll see what we can do. You will be all right?" She placed her hand on Cora's shoulder. "If nothing else, maybe I can find something in the medical kit. But I hope I have better facilities than that. I need to get you to the base."

Then the doctor turned to Nastasia, placing her gloved hands back on the taut cable. "Hold that steady for me. This is very important for Cora's baby. We are counting on you. Do you understand?"

Nastasia nodded solemnly. "You can depend on me. Boris always says so."

"Good. Just hold on tight." The doctor took hold of the rope, then lowered herself over the edge.

Even as the daughter of a tsar, Nastasia was very good at following orders. Life on Mars was difficult, and she wanted to contribute her share. As a girl, riding in coaches with her father through the small villages, she remembered seeing poor peasants lining the dirt roads, waving at their "little father" Tsar Nicholas. "They all work very hard for us, Anastasia," he had told her. "We must always appreciate what the peasants do for Russia."

Since that time, Nastasia always did as she was told. She followed the wishes of the tsar, without question. She felt that other *adins*, strong leaders such as Boris Tiban and Nikolas and Stroganov, must understand her secret peril better than she did herself. These men had been placed here to protect her, to keep her identity safe. The beating wings of black fear retreated just a little.

170

And part of her duties involved making love to Stroganov and Nikolas, keeping them happy, making them strong so they could resurrect the empire on the sands of Mars. The future tsarina of all Russia could do no less for her country.

Voices shouted up from below, the strong tones of Stroganov and the more muffled words of the human Dr. Dycek, spoken through her suit. "Cora! We are going to have to bring you down!"

CORA MARISOVNA

DURING THE SICKENING DESCENT down the brittle cliffside, Cora allowed Stroganov and Dr. Dycek to help her over the roughest patches. Elbows of sharp black rock scraped against her unfeeling skin. Falling pebbles made clinking sounds like broken china as they shattered on the larger boulders below.

She swayed on the polymer-strand cable, poised on the brink of falling to her death. She felt out of control, at the mercy of too many things—but she had to move, not just wait for fate to play its games. Waves of nausea and cramps assailed her. The slope was dark and treacherous, and the slippery rope gave her no feeling of security. Her whistling breath came rapid, cold.

Cora was willing to do this so that she might save her baby. She felt an intense attachment to the life inside her, the tiny human life growing in her body. Perhaps the emotions could be blamed on mere hormones and changing body chemistry. To Cora, the doomed baby was her child—but to Boris it was only a symbol. This dismayed her, but Boris would not listen. He never listened.

Running up and down the darkened chasm, Stroganov had found a spot not too far away where parts of the wall had crumbled, leaving angled talus that proved easier for Cora to scale than the sheer cliff. With Stroganov bracing her arms and whispering encouragement, Dr. Dycek just below to catch her, they scrambled down the fallen boulders. Up above, Nastasia held on to the cable like one of Stroganov's statues.

Four times during the treacherous descent, Cora had to stop while labor cramps seized her body, demanding her attention. The others braced her in place against the cold rocks as she felt her muscles clench down, unsuccessfully trying to bite back a moan. She willed the spasms to stop, but her voice was like a whisper in a hurricane; she endured until the cramps backed off and left her gasping.

Over the past two days the spasms had tugged her stomach muscles, squeezing and pushing, then gradually loosening again. At first the episodes were intermittent, giving her an opportunity to rest in frightened anticipation before they struck again. But yesterday and the day before, the pain had grown more regular, more intense. Her muscles lowered the baby, helped position it, started to open her up inside. Cora knew the birth could happen within hours—or she could have to bear it for several more days. Either way, the baby would be born before long.

And during this most frightening time, Boris had abandoned her. That hurt like a blade to the heart. By toppling Dr. Dycek's rover, he had sabotaged her only hope of keeping the baby alive. How could he do that to his own child? But Cora understood: The point he wanted so desperately to make would be most poignant if the baby died. He had made his choice out of anger. Cora did not know if she could ever forgive him for leaving her now. Was she afraid to admit that something good might happen for a change? Boris did not want good things to happen, because then he would have to forsake his anger, and that was the only thing he had left to hang on to.

She watched Stroganov jerk the thin cable as his battery-powered spotlight shone down on the rover surrounded by broken scree. The vehicle had plowed a clean path down the cliff, but its low center of mass had brought it to a rest canted against a mound of rubble. Now the telescoping legs on one side jacked themselves up like levers, whirring and straining against the big boulders and to tip the rover back upright. On its thousand legs the vehicle adjusted itself, shifting, sighing, waiting patiently. As Stroganov played the light over the dust-smeared hull, Cora looked for the disastrous damage she expected to see. Dust still hung in the air, reddening the night.

"*Percival* appears to be functional," Dr. Dycek said. She squeezed Cora's shoulder in encouragement and hopped down the last few meters to the bottom, landing with deeply bent knees to absorb the mild impact. Her voice sounded far away as she shouted through her speakerpatch. "This vehicle is tough, built to withstand Mars—as the *adins* were."

Dr. Dycek held out her hands for Stroganov to toss down the spotlight tied to his waist. The beam toppled in a dreamlike somersault in the low gravity, and Dr. Dycek caught it easily in gloved hands, cradling it against her chest.

From above, Cora tried to pay attention to the operation. She did not want to think too far ahead. What if the rover had been ruined? What if Dr. Dycek could not help her? What if the baby were stillborn, despite all their efforts? What if she gave up hope altogether?

That last thought was the only thing Cora Marisovna could control. And she would never give up hope. She would fight in any way she could. Boris had taught her how to fight.

"Can you come down, Nastasia?" Stroganov shouted upward as Dr. Dycek shone the beam of the spotlight along the cliff edge. His words echoed up and down the narrow chasm.

"Is Boris down there?" Nastasia answered back.

Cora looked around, hoping to find him, but the gorge was filled with shadows, lit by a midnight-blue gash of stars overhead. She saw no movement but their own.

"We cannot see him," Stroganov said.

Before he finished speaking, the other end of the polymer-strand cable slithered to the canyon floor with a thin hissing sound. Nastasia had untied the rope and dropped it from above.

"I will go look for him!" she called, sounding small and distant.

Stroganov held up both ends of the cable, cursing quietly. "Now I will have to climb back up the hard way."

Using the splashing glare of the spotlight, Dr. Dycek climbed around the rover, inspecting the metal plates that protected the trapezoidal windowports. She rapped on one with her gloved fist, then held her fist high in satisfaction. "I must check with the AI inside, but it appears the seals are intact. If the engine still runs, we can be on our way. We were very, very lucky."

On her own initiative Cora finished the last part of the descent over the rugged talus. Hurrying to her side, Stroganov helped her until she stood on the uneven ground. Loose boulders as big as buildings lay strewn about, blood-brown in the daylight but black in the night shadows. Cora looked up to the top of the cliff wall, a dark knife edge that blocked the stars. She saw no silhouetted figure looking down at them, neither Nastasia nor Boris.

Unseen far above, Nastasia called into the darkness for Boris to come help them, but he remained silent and hidden. No doubt brooding somewhere. Cora felt hot tears of anger and disappointment, but her shielded *adin* eyes would not let her waste water in such a way.

Dr. Dycek trudged back over to them. "The door-lock mechanism is still functioning. The communications antenna is smashed, though. We will not be able to let anyone at Lowell Base know we are coming. That means they can't prep for you." She gestured for them to follow her. "Come and look."

The white hull looked bluish in the glare of the light. The sides of the rover were smeared with dust and scrapes from its sliding descent into the chasm. Deliberate silvery blazes surrounded the antenna base like flower petals.

"That is not a random scar from falling over a cliff. It looks to me as if Boris smashed it off with his staff.

He doesn't want us getting back. He will not let us radio for help. Not even for you, Cora. Does he want his baby to die?" Dr. Dycek's voice seemed oddly distant.

Stroganov said nothing, but Cora nodded to herself. Yes, that was the way Boris would do it. He was so predictable. She and the baby would be sacrifices to his tragic message. She bit back a reply.

Then, shuddering with horror, her knees buckled as a new labor spasm squeezed her like a fist and crushed thoughts of the outside world. Stroganov caught her and held her upright.

Dr. Dycek grabbed one of Cora's arms and began to stumble-walk her toward the rover. "Come on. We have at least a day's journey before we get back to the base. Even at that, I cannot be certain this chasm will lead us anywhere but a blind end. But there is no other way. The rover is down here, and we have no choice of roads. I just have to hope it can negotiate the terrain."

"No time to waste," Stroganov said, too close to Cora's ear.

Dr. Dycek hauled Cora to the scuffed and flexible opening of the rover's airlock. Stroganov helped, squeezing Cora's numb hand in a silent gesture of farewell.

"The storm is coming," he said, sniffing the air. "Be careful."

"Will you come with us? You and Nastasia?" Dr. Dycek asked. "There's nothing left for you here. Come back into the world. You are no longer in a prison camp."

Stroganov stood up straighter, as if startled by her question. "No, I should stay here. Nastasia needs my help, and Boris will be back. Perhaps we will come down together, soon. It is time for us to stop hiding up here. Boris believes he is the king of the mountain, but that game has been over for a long time. He is the only one who does not realize it."

In a surprising gentlemanly gesture, he shook Dr. Dycek's gloved hand. "I will talk to him, though.

Thank you, Dr. Dycek. Watch out for yourselves."

Dr. Dycek turned to face Cora. "I think the air inside the rover has been dumped since the fall, so you should be able to breathe just fine. I'll have to wear my suit the whole time. After we get you strapped in, I can begin the slow pressurization of the interior." She touched Cora's belly again, feeling the tight muscles. "We have to make the atmosphere thick enough so the baby can breathe, in case it is born along the way. This is going to be tricky."

Cora recalled all the frightening stories Boris had told them of the hellish air down in the lowlands. She dreaded the thought of air as thick as soup and heavy as bricks on her chest, making an ordeal out of every breath—especially during the most exhausting hours of her entire life. But she was like a piece of flotsam in this storm, and she could not fight free.

The way the spasms had been increasing in intensity, she doubted the baby would wait until they reached the humans' base.

Stroganov waved as Dr. Dycek helped Cora to squeeze through the flexible sphincter airlock, leaving her in claustrophobic darkness. Tasting the metallic air inside, Cora already longed for one last breath of the cold breeze on top of Pavonis Mons.

JESÚS KEEFER

THE FOOTPRINTS OF THE unexpected *dva* man made indentations in the dust on the canyon floor. The gentle winds would erase them in only a few days—but not fast enough.

"Where the hell did he go?" Vickery said, his booming voice diluted through the helmet. He looked around, windmilling his suited arms in front of him as if trying to discover some optical illusion. "And what was all that junk he had in his pack?"

As he stooped, Keefer could make out clear details. The *dva* was barefoot. The prints were widely spaced and showed only the balls of his feet and the circular indentations of toes as he ran away from the spacesuited humans.

Then the tracks ended abruptly at a stone wall, where the *dva* had vanished into thin air.

Keefer knelt, brushing the dust around the marks of the *dva* man's squarish toes with his gloves. He wondered what it would feel like to have the powdered rust of Mars between his toes, clinging to his skin. And what in the hell was the *dva* man doing out here? The avalanche had occurred in this very side canyon a year ago, but he couldn't imagine why some lone *dva* might have come to pay his respects.

Keefer's heart pounded, and his oxygen-regenerator system chugged double time. Something here didn't make sense. Did the *dva* man have something to do with the disappearance of Dr. Dycek? He appeared to have been carrying a hodgepodge of equipment, possibly stolen.

Moving slowly, as Vickery blustered around in confusion, Keefer followed the line of tracks. They scuffed together at the edge of the rock wall. He peered upward past the curved edge of his faceplate. The towering ochre cliffs looked sheer and smooth, sand-blasted by powerful and rapid erosion. He didn't think the *dva* man could have scrambled up the rock into one of the shadowed crannies. The man had been out of sight for only a minute or so.

Vickery inspected the rock face, tapping with his gloved fingertips. A scratchy gasp suddenly came out of his speakerpatch. "Oh, Jesus!"

Keefer glared at him, but saw the other man was not making a joke on his name. Vickery began pressing with his gloved fingers on the rock wall. A crack showed, an incongruous straight edge on the rugged surface. "Look at this—it's a door! A goddamned door! Those wily bastards!"

Keefer felt the skin crawl between his shoulder blades, a cold drizzle of sweat leaping from his pores. Indeed, the rock section was only a thin slab of ruddy granite a few centimeters thick, sheared off from the cliff and mounted on metal tracks that led into the rock. Once nudged open, the door moved easily on the tracks.

"A secret *dva* hideout?" Keefer said. "You've got to be kidding!"

Vickery grunted as he shoved the false rock aside. The black opening widened, shedding light inside to a small chamber. At the opposite end stood a second metal door, undisguised this time. It was the type of hatch used to seal off the habitation modules for Lowell Base. Exactly the same type. Even the serial numbers were plainly etched in the bottom of the panel.

The *dvas*, who had assembled the core of Lowell Base without humans present, must have somehow doctored the inventory records, "misplaced" spare parts to stash them away for their own purposes. Keefer had heard about the unexplained losses, the too-frequent requests for replacement components—but he had never imagined something of this magnitude.

"This is impossible!" Keefer said, then clamped his lips together to prevent himself from making another similarly brilliant comment.

"It's right in front of your eyes," Vickery answered.

The renegade *dva* man was nowhere in sight. He must have gone through the second doorway.

"Inside," Vickery said. "I wish we had some weapons back in the rover, but we are going to get to the bottom of this, Commissioner. No telling what the *dvas* are trying to put over on us."

He closed the first door, then the two of them turned to the inner door. Vickery rotated the central crank and yanked it open, breaking a seal against the jamb. Just inside, they found yet another stolen door only a few meters farther down the tunnel.

"It's like one of those crazy Russian dolls! You know, you open it up and there's a smaller one inside, and then a smaller one?" Vickery closed the hatch behind them, then worked on opening the next one.

"Do you think Commissioner Dycek had something to do with all this?" Keefer asked, more to himself than to Vickery. "This seems too extravagant to be done without some kind of high-level help. Did she set up someplace for the *dvas* to hide? Did she decide to disappear and go live with them rather than return willingly to Earth?"

Vickery paused while turning the crank on the third door. Before he tugged the hatch open, he fixed Keefer with a hard glance, squinting in the helmet lights that illuminated his ice-blue eyes. "That sounds like Rachel, all right," he said. "Now that you mention it, this place makes a whole hell of a lot of sense. But how could she have planned so far ahead? She was so preoccupied she walked into walls half the time...." He thumped his gloved fist into the rough tunnel wall. "Unless it was all an act. I didn't think she could put one over on me, of all people."

Vickery jerked the door open. Inside, a smooth-bored tunnel extended upward and curved to the left out of sight, deeper into the rock. Keefer stared in amazement.

Faint lights had been strung on the walls, wired to each other and up, perhaps, to hidden solar collectors in Noctis Labyrinthus. "I get the impression we haven't seen the half of it yet," Vickery said.

The corridor had been worn smooth by the slow carving of ancient ice, the slope steep and variable. The walls looked as if they had been melted into a lump of wax and then polished by a thousand steel-wool pads. Keefer ran his gloves along the slick surface. "The whole Labyrinth could be honeycombed with stuff like this, inclusions of water ice that volatilized out. That's what made the place so unstable when Pchanskii's *dvas* were blasting here."

The string of dim lights beckoned them onward. Keefer and Vickery began making their way down the tunnel, their boots clomping on the floor with the din of a marching army. They saw no sign of the *dva* man who had fled from them, nor of anyone else.

"Maybe nobody's home," Vickery said.

The illumination grew brighter up ahead where the clusters of lights had been spread more thickly on the walls. The two men turned through another steep, sharp turn and a roller-coaster dip to emerge into a side alcove as big as an entire module of Lowell Base.

Brilliant light shone down from heat lamps, gushing warmth and illumination onto rows of sparkling green plants. Listening through his suit speakers, Keefer could hear trickling water from basins overhead, the humming of circulation fans. Inside the alcove he saw trays full of tiny vegetable seedlings: tomatoes, corn, wheat, even rice in flat waterlogged containers. Under harsh lights fully grown plants flourished. The same types of plants grew back in the Lowell Base greenhouse dome from seeds brought over on various flights to Mars.

More stolen items. And here the plants were growing under artificial light, taking nutrients from desalinated Martian soil, from water drained out of reservoirs frozen into the rock.

They stared for long moments, until Keefer tugged on Vickery's arm. "Come on," he said. "I want to find out what all this means." They continued to trudge cautiously along the corridor, looking from side to side. Keefer kept expecting someone to lunge out at them from the shadows.

In another alcove water poured down the wall from a spring bubbling through the ceiling. Below, a basin had been carved in the rock, and a hole drilled for drainage underneath. Lush strands of algae bloomed under the moisture and artificial light, spreading outward like a sunburst. The patterns of lichen and algae seemed to have been trimmed or nudged into specific geometric lines. It seemed to serve no purpose but aesthetics.

Vickery suddenly began swearing, whirling toward Keefer. "I get it now. The whole bleeping avalanche must have been a ruse!" Keefer stopped, feeling his mouth grow dry, as if a trapdoor of realizations had just dropped out from under him.

"The *dvas* did it to throw us off the track," Vickery said. "Blasted the whole wall down, knowing that a big storm was coming, knowing that we wouldn't suspect something was wrong until after they didn't report in for a few days. No wonder we never found any bodies." Behind the dim faceplate Vickery looked incredulous. "Bunch of clever *dva* bastards!"

As if tired of skulking about, Vickery turned up the volume on his speakerpatch. "Hello!" he yelled. "Is anyone here? Dammit, Rachel, stop playing hide-and-seek!"

In the returning silence, Keefer also called out. "Commissioner Dycek, we need to speak with you. Please."

Suddenly a gash of light sliced out from the corridors in front of them, blinding Keefer. Vickery put his arm over his transparent faceplate.

Up ahead they saw silhouetted forms, humanoid bodies moving toward them—many of them, like a mob.

In a gesture that felt more like bravado than calmly taking responsibility, Keefer took a step forward and stood motionless in the center of the tunnel, placing himself in front of Vickery. He held his hands up in a gesture of peace or surrender. He felt his breakfast churning in his stomach, mixed with the acid of fear.

Vickery panted right beside him. "We're pretty helpless here, Commissioner," he whispered next to the voice pickup. "You don't happen to have a bazooka in your pocket, do you?"

Keefer shrugged inside his suit, feeling numb. "Looks like this is our big chance to find out what's going on around here."

"What are you going to say to them?" Vickery snorted. " 'Take me to your leader'?"

The silhouettes came forward, and Keefer could discern *dvas* wearing utilitarian overalls, burly people with exaggerated features from the adaptive surgery, but not quite as monstrous as the *adins*. Among them, he recognized the *dva* man who had been wandering out in the canyon. Moving his eyes quickly over the group, Keefer estimated between twenty-five and thirty of them all together.

About the same number of *dvas* that had been lost in the avalanche a year ago. . . .

One of the central figures stepped away from the others, like an emissary coming to meet Keefer. Black and silver hair covered his face, bushy eyebrows and a heavy beard. His lips were full and generous, his eyes close-set, his cheekbones wide under a high forehead, which seemed distorted by the surgically flattened nose, the fused ears. He held his hands out to show he was unarmed. The rigid, alien look to his features made it impossible for Keefer to read any sort of expression on the *dva* face.

"I recognize him!" Vickery burst out. "Rachel was always showing off his picture during our first few months here. That's Dr. Pchanskii!"

Keefer whirled to glance at his companion.

"Pchanskii?" Then he too recognized the man from the newsnet footage he had seen of the disastrous avalanche that had supposedly wiped out an entire *dva* team. Yes, it all made sense.

Dr. Pchanskii stepped forward and fixed them with the fiery gaze of his hooded *dva* eyes. He put both hands on his hips and stared for a moment. The other *dvas* remained silent behind him.

"I wish you had given me more time to finish everything up here," Pchanskii said. "More time. I hate to be rushed."

BORIS TIBAN

BORIS TIBAN HUNCHED on a spire of rock, like a gargoyle on some ancient European cathedral. He sat motionless, watching, as darkness fell to smother the land. The wind picked up, smelling dry and crackling from the coming storm. But even a gale could not dislodge him, if he did not wish to move.

Boris brooded and waited, eager to watch the reactions of the others when they discovered the crashed rover vehicle. What would Dr. Dycek do, once shown how weak and helpless she really was? Would she fall to her knees and wail in defeat? Would she cry out in despair? He wanted to see that.

Boris had scrambled up a weathered pinnacle that had broken away from the lower cliffside, clinging with his powerful but insensitive *adin* fingers. He hauled his body to a strategic spot out of sight, where he perched high and silent. The climb had not even left him out of breath. With only a third of the gravity that his body had been born to, Mars had made him into a superman.

His biceps still tingled with exhilarating exertion from rocking the rover under the leverage of his titanium staff. It had been so satisfying to see the precious vehicle tip, flailing uselessly with its automatic stabilizing legs until it slid, then finally toppled over the edge. Red dust gushed into the air, and loose rock chased it down the slope, hissing and clattering. *Percival*'s fall had been magnificent, careening into the chasm with a slow pirouette in the air.

Now, seeing the tiny figures illuminated by winking portable lights far below, Boris sat unmoving, uneasy. Watching. After the rebellion he had wanted to abandon all of the technology along with the UNSA landing site when they departed, but Stroganov and a few others had insisted on hauling along equipment, luxuries, and amenities. He himself had felt free, striding ahead of the group up the slopes of Pavonis, unburdened with useless items, while the others had looked ridiculous carrying so many useless items they refused to leave behind. Often over the years, Boris wished he had just smashed everything where it lay in the caves.

Watching the *adins* below, using the hoarded equipment to help the human doctor—their enemy!—made coals of anger and betrayal blaze within him.

They were helping Dr. Dycek take Cora away. All of them! Stroganov had been the first to clamber down to the vehicle; Nastasia held the cable willingly, though she could not be held accountable for her actions. Even Cora herself seemed ready to abandon him. She understood nothing of passions or sacrifice.

Did the *adins* forget so easily that they had survived because of *his* wits? That *he* had freed them from Vice Commander Dozintsev's tyranny and given them a life of their own on Mars?

His entire body clenched and rigid, Boris remembered Cora telling him over and over again how much she loved him, vowing to follow wherever he might lead. Boris had never asked for those assurances, but Cora had given them freely. Now, just as freely, she took them away.

It seemed an act of cowardice, running to the empty promises of the one person who had caused all of the *adin* misery. For the sake of a baby that was doomed anyway? The doctor probably wanted the infant only so she could dissect it.

In the twilight silence he heard a high voice calling from the rim of the gorge: Nastasia searching for him. "Boris!" she called. "Boris, where are you?"

He ignored her.

In the depths of the chasm, Cora and Dr. Dycek entered the airlock of the rover and closed themselves inside.

With a tight fist, Boris struck the rough edge of the rock pinnacle, lashing out in his anger. Apparently the rover had not been destroyed by the fall. They were trying to fix it.

He let out an audible curse when the rover's front spotlights burst on with a shower of light. One of them had been smashed, another skewed at an awkward angle so that the spear of illumination tilted up into the sky like a beacon, but the other two lights burned ahead of the rover's path. The methane engine started up, hissing and rumbling. The sea-urchin legs telescoped up and out, raising the vehicle up, as if testing themselves or just stretching.

Boris's throat tightened. His heart thudded in his chest. He wanted to jump up and down on the rock pinnacle, screaming *No!* at the top of his lungs. But they would see him, and that would ruin everything. He couldn't afford to be spotted, if he was ever to straighten things out again. The cost grew higher each minute he delayed, but he would pay the price.

From the moment he had learned of Cora's pregnancy, Boris sensed that their way of life was ended. An unstoppable force had begun rolling downhill toward the *adins*, picking up speed. The attack on the *dva* pumping station, the death of Nikolas. The arrival of Dr. Dycek.

Their quiet, self-imposed exile on the mountain had come to a close. The *adins* would no longer have the luxury of collecting algae from their skimmer screens, tending to their own desires in a sheltered, self-contained utopia on Pavonis Mons. Stroganov could no longer scratch his philosophical thoughts on the walls or build up his statues of historical figures. Nastasia could no longer flit along the caldera floor, hunting for mythical flowers.

And Boris could not content himself with bilious grumbling about their fate, pontificating about the way things should be and all the wrongs that had been done to them, how he would someday make the humans pay attention. Someday. For months, Boris had been anticipating his grandest gesture of all, waiting for the right moment.

Dr. Dycek had snatched the choice away from him. Now he *had* to act.

Cora should never have gotten pregnant. The *adin* surgery had been sloppy. Many of the *adins* had lost their lives because of flawed adaptations; Nastasia had lost her mind. And Cora had gotten pregnant. It was all Dr. Dycek's fault.

Both of them had always known the baby would die at birth. There had been nothing they could do about it, so Boris had adapted to the situation, drawing strength from what he would do, his terrible plan of retribution. When the helpless baby—his own child— died gasping and frozen in the catacombs, he would have all the reason he needed to strike back. It would be a catalyst, a fine excuse to bring about an apocalypse that would wipe out every last human at Lowell Base and to attack the *dvas* in their homes, leaving Mars empty and free for the *adins*. As it had once been.

Everything was perfectly justified. Those were the rules by which he played. Boris had never dreamed Rachel Dycek would come, especially now.

With a chug and a groan, the rover accelerated, building power. So soon! The vehicle rattled and strained against the loose debris around it. More dislodged rocks fell, jamming against the vehicle. On the outside, Stroganov scurried about to push boulders out of the way.

As Boris watched them, a fatalistic hope burned in his mind. Maybe they wouldn't be able to leave after all, and he could watch them fail.

Stroganov worked like a fiend to toss chunks of rock aside, clearing a swath wide enough for the rover to negotiate. The telescoping legs looked like a forest of spider limbs as the vehicle scrambled ahead. Once the vehicle got up enough momentum, it could make its own way over most obstacles.

Near sunrise, the rover finally pried itself loose of the rubble. The cockeyed spotlight poured a bright beam in wobbling arcs along the sheer, mineral-stained walls. Below, he heard Stroganov cheering, high-voiced in the cold predawn air.

Once it started moving, the rover picked up speed, grabbing traction with its thousand legs and moving like a flexible metal slug in the narrowing chasm. Boris turned his head to watch.

After a long pause, Stroganov began his ascent back to the caves and his statues. He would probably sculpt the face of Dr. Dycek as a great hero now. Nastasia was nowhere to be found; she had stopped calling his name.

In silence, Boris climbed down. He could no longer be passive. Striking out at an empty vehicle was not good enough. For a moment he considered rolling a boulder off the cliff face, knocking Stroganov down to his death like an insect squashed in an avalanche. But he decided against it. Even as a traitor, Stroganov was still one of the *adins*, and Boris could deal with him later, in other ways.

Boris had to reach the floor of the chasm before the rover made much progress. He felt like a lizard, sliding over the rock face, fingers and toes thrust into crannies. He slipped once when his fingers crushed a soft pad of lichen, then he dropped the remaining three meters to the ground, feeling light and full of energy.

Boris picked himself up, found the titanium staff where he had hidden it at the bottom of the rock pinnacle. Then he set off at a trot to catch up with Dr. Dycek and Cora, ducking in and out of the shelter of rocks and sunrise shadows. The chewed tracks were easy to follow, even in the darkness before dawn.

He could stalk the rover for hours.

As the southern hemisphere of the planet Mars entered its winter season, the drop in temperature caused portions of the thickening atmosphere to freeze out. Water vapor and carbon dioxide piled up in layers to form a polar ice cap.

The resulting drop in air pressure sucked wind from the northern hemisphere down toward the south. Gathering force, the wind rushed to fill the invisible hole at the bottom of the world. Airborne algae whirled together, clumping, attaching themselves to dust particles. By the time it reached Pavonis Mons on the Martian equator, the storm had become a fist as tall as the sky.

The afternoon turned into a soupy brownish-gray above the widening canyon, as precursors of the storm approached with frightening speed. Boris thrust his staff into the soft ground like a lightning rod and laughed. He could survive against the elements. His *adin* modifications gave him the strength he needed.

Back in Siberia, two of the *adin* subjects had escaped the Neryungri facility after undergoing their transformational surgeries. Oh, how frightened the scientists had been, because their precious project was supposed to be secret! Boris had chuckled at the thought of what would happen if one of the monstrously augmented prisoners suddenly showed up in a local village.

Guards had scrambled around; hunting parties ran into the snow-filled forests. The manhunt had been extraordinary. During the confusion, any number of the others could have escaped—but no one else tried.

Nikolas and Boris had watched snickering from their holding rooms in the medical center. Snow was falling heavily, obliterating all tracks. Finally, early the next morning, the security teams returned with the body of one of the *adin* escapees, shot in the thick fir forests surrounding Neryungri.

But as far as Boris knew, the second free *adin* was running wild out in the wasteland, surviving in relative comfort to this day. Even the worst Siberian winter was better than what the *adin* had been designed to withstand on Mars. Such an escape was the type of grand gesture in which Boris Tiban delighted.

But he could do better.

The wall of the dust storm approached like a missile, funneled into the chasm and picking up fine particles, grains of sand, and even small rocks. Boris stood motionless, watching it come toward him at a hundred kilometers per hour. He didn't even bother to take shelter.

Raising his staff high, he whooped as a precursor wind buffeted him, nearly jerking him off his feet. He grabbed for balance, braced himself against a rock, then felt the second hammer gust of wind smack him.

The rust sand and sharp flakes of rock tore at him, scoring his plasticized skin as he stood there. But he picked up electricity from the air, an energy that only made him stronger.

Against the elements, it was Boris Tiban versus Mars itself. He could survive. No other human in the solar system would attempt to face such a challenge. And Boris reveled in it. He lived for *this*. This would be better than executing the vice commander in front of international newsnets, better than blowing up the Baku oil refinery.

His battle cry was lost in the ravenous wind.

Staff in hand, he fought his way down toward the lumbering rover. The time had come.

Now he could strike.

RACHEL DYCEK

THE STORM HIT THE ROVER just past midday, five hours after they left the *adin* encampment.

Driving *Percival*, Rachel had made good time along the cluttered chasm that spilled down Pavonis Mons, fanning as it petered out and rose toward the level of the main slope. The shield volcano had left strata of built-up, pasty lava, like layers in a thick cake. Monolithic boulders lay in tumbled heaps, slumped in low-gravity falls from eons-old avalanches. A pale green fringe of lichen and feathers of algae now crept over the wreckage, claiming the landscape.

Rachel had no map, just a direction she wanted to go and the determination to get there. She let the AI pilot speculate on the best course. *Percival* scrambled over the uneven floor of the gorge, ignoring most obstacles.

Then the storm arrived in a brownish-green nightmare across the horizon, roaring along at hundreds of kilometers per hour. It struck like a meteor.

Cora strapped herself onto one of the passenger benches in the rear compartment, and Rachel clipped crash restraints around her own suit, clenched her teeth, and held on. The roiling murk shook *Percival* with a bone-vibrating wave of noise, a hiss like static scrubbing the outside of the rover.

She could barely see through the front windowport, but somehow the rover kept moving with confidence, though warning messages and status reports scrolled up over the recessed screens. All the iron-oxide dust thrown into the air would scramble the obstacle-avoidance radar. Without the communications antenna, the AI could not download weathersat data, nor could it transmit a distress signal to the other bases or even a *dva* mining station. The AI seemed unconcerned, but simply reported the warnings in bland, unembellished standard text.

Panic threatened to paralyze Rachel. She worried that the fragile containment could not keep her and Cora Marisovna alive against the lashing storm. But *Percival* had survived the fall into the chasm, and it could probably survive anything the winds threw at it.

The rover jounced along with a muffled clatter of legs. *Percival*'s high beams revealed only an opaque haze concealing the landscape; the low beams illuminated no more than a puddle of ground directly in front of her. Another slap of wind rattled the vehicle.

Rachel squinted through the dust, afraid she would see large rocks or gaping sinkholes the AI could not spot in time. The walls of the crevasse sheltered them from the worst gusts, but vicious crosscurrents forced the rover to overcompensate.

Not long ago, Rachel had briefly considered letting herself die in this storm. Had she not met the *adins*, she might have gone to stand on the caldera rim. The first gust of battering-ram force would have swept her over the edge. And she would have died a meaningless death. . . .

That decision seemed very far away from her now. She had been looking for some excuse to change her mind. Cora and the *adins* offered Rachel another possibility—a good choice instead of the poor ones she had previously had. Rachel would make it somehow. She no longer wanted to surrender. If she could just bring Cora back, deliver the baby alive, maybe she could regain the self-esteem she lost when Dmitri Pchanskii and his *dvas* had been buried under Noctis Labyrinthus.

As *Percival* worked its way farther down the gorge, Rachel had no idea where the narrow canyon would take them. The rover had online maps, but Rachel did not know where the nearest *dva* settlement was, or if she would have a better chance heading straight for the base. Any *dva* group would have a functioning transmitter, though it would be hampered by the static generated from suspended dust particles. On the other hand, only Lowell Base had the necessary medical facilities.

As they continued, Rachel remained in her environment suit and increased the air pressure in the rover bit by bit, gradually acclimating Cora. Muffled sounds of the scouring gale came through as distant whispers with an occasional *whump* as a gust hit them broadside. Rachel's suit worked overtime to absorb perspiration as she rode, teeth grinding together, hands gripping the controls in case she had to snatch *Percival* away with a manual override.

Lying on her side on the padded bench, Cora Marisovna gasped as another labor spasm hit. Rachel used the vehicle's chronometer to time them. The contractions occurred about every four and a half minutes. Cora seemed oblivious to the storm outside.

"I think . . ." Cora said from behind her, choking words that Rachel heard muffled through her helmet, "you had better find a place to shelter the rover. I need you now."

Rachel risked a glance backward. Cora had unclipped herself from the restraints and stripped off her worn, oversize jumpsuit, which lay in a cloth puddle on the floor. She lay on the floor, her back propped against the metal wall and her legs spread as far apart as she could manage. Between Cora's legs a gush of liquid spilled out, steaming as it cooled in the icy air.

Her water has broken!

Rachel scrambled out of her seat, unfastening the restraints as she shouted to the rover's AI. *"Percival!* Find us a place to stop, now! Anchor yourself against the storm."

The rover acknowledged and lurched over to the canyon wall under a barely visible overhang. Rachel stumbled back to the rear compartment. Now what would she do? She was trained as a doctor, so this should be no problem. No problem!

She had studied environmental adaptation, worked with surgical enhancements for the *adins* and *dvas*. The closest she had come to witnessing birth was staring at cells dividing under a microscope. It had been a long time since her basic training, and she had used none of it in practical situations.

But she had no choice now. This would be another new challenge for her. She bent over Cora's panting form. The *adin* woman rolled her eyes and looked up at her; Rachel hoped the faceplate hid her own uncertainty. The rover jolted, then settled to the ground with muted thuds as stabilizer legs braced the vehicle against the rock walls and the hardened ground.

"I may be able to help you myself, at least a little," Cora said, panting in the already thickening air, "but when the final part of labor comes, you must be in charge. I will not be able to hold your hand through this."

The thought of Cora assisting *her* in a medical emergency made Rachel stifle a raw-edged giggle, but Cora continued. "I helped my grandmother deliver two babies when I was a girl. Midwives still do much of that work in Siberia. In Neryungri, before you built your *adin* facility, we had very little medical help."

Rachel pushed aside her scattered emotions and stared into Cora's dark, slanted eyes. Deep breath. Slow exhale. "All right. Should I check to see how far you are dilated? I must do that first, isn't that true?"

"Yes. Reach . . . inside me. Then we can judge how much time I have left." She sighed. "Part of me wants this over right now, but another part never wants it to come. We aren't in a place where we can save the baby yet, are we?"

Rachel spoke through her teeth. "We will do our damnedest!"

She looked down at her clumsy gloved hand and checked the external air-pressure monitor on her chest pack. The oxygen regenerator on her back hissed and bled fresh air into her helmet. Though the environment suit seemed more flexible now that the pressure differential was not so great, Rachel still could not survive unprotected in the rover cabin. "I dare not remove my suit yet. There is not enough air for me. And the glove is too big as it is. I would not be able to feel properly, and I would hurt you inside."

Cora's eyes winced shut, and her body shook. Rachel watched her body straining, the augmented muscles stretched to a point where they seemed to hum from the tension beneath the milky neutral coating of plastic skin. Cora's fingers scrabbled on the smooth metal floor, looking for something to grasp. After a minute or two, the spasm passed.

Cora took five deep breaths, then brought her attention back to the problem. "We must learn how long it should be before the birth. Even though my water has broken, if I am not fully dilated, we might still have enough time to reach your base. If I am dilated, though, the baby could come in as little as an hour. It makes all the difference in the world. We must know."

Rachel tried to dredge up alternatives from the thin air. How could she probe inside the woman? Cora certainly couldn't do it herself. Rachel looked down at her suit, casting about in her mind for new alternatives, unexpected choices.

"I could slice off my glove, seal the sleeve around my arm." She stared down at the fabric as she flexed her fingers. The idea appalled her, going against the grain of her decade of training and experience on Mars—but she thought it would work. "That way I could feel inside you with my bare hand. There are small cutting tools in the repair box, and some metallized tape."

Cora looked at her through hooded *adin* eyes, saying nothing as Rachel continued. "My hand would get numb in this cold, but I can raise the internal temperature here as much as you can stand. The heaters are already on."

Cora pushed her palms against the rover's metal

floor, pushing herself up into a half-sitting position. "But if you damage your suit, you will never be able to go outside until we reach your base." Cora closed her eyes in anticipation of another labor pain. "Keep driving. We may find help within another hour or so."

"Look at the storm outside. I have no intention of going outside."

Rachel went to the tool locker. Her heart pounded, but she felt wide awake, more aware and focused than she had been in a long time. In this storm, and with the distance yet to travel, they would never get to a safe haven, not even to a small *dva* shelter, within any reasonable time. Better to prepare here. And wait. It was the best she could do, and she could devote her full attention to her patient.

First, Rachel wrapped the tape around her forearm as tightly as she could, fashioning a crude tourniquet. It made ripping, stretching noises as she yanked it out of the dispenser and circled her arm. She let the tape roll dangle, because she would have to seal the cut quickly. Next step. She didn't allow herself to think too far ahead. Gripping with the slick gloved fingers, she pulled the tough fabric close around her wrist and removed one of the small cutting tools from the locker. The tough suit material could resist most abrasions, but not intentional sawing. Wincing, she pulled in a deep lungful of air and sliced across the fabric.

Rachel's ears popped as the residual air inside the suit gushed out. She could feel the wind and the cold pushing along her skin. The tourniquet could not make a perfect seal. The air squealed out of the slice at the suit's wrist.

She cut the gash longer, enough that she could jerk her fingers out of the glove and thrust her hand through the ragged opening. With her protected hand Rachel wrapped more metal tape around her wrist where the suit material met the skin. She bound back the flopping, empty glove, then sealed the seam over and over. Sergei had always claimed she was obsessive in her thoroughness. She did not want to think what it would be like to take the suit off again.

Already the skin on her exposed hand felt brittle and crackling, as if each tiny hair follicle were covered with frost. Rachel tried to catch her breath as the suit reinflated. The chemical oxygen regenerator on her back popped and fizzed, adding to the ringing in her ears. Her head pounded, but her thoughts cleared moment by moment. Her hand was so cold it ached. She bent her hand into a fist and held it that way until the skin turned an angry red.

Cora squirmed on the floor in her own ordeal with another labor spasm. Rachel knelt in front of her. She looked at her whitening hand and flexed her fingers. "Cora? I am ready."

She touched the *adin* woman's waxy skin. Rachel's fingers felt thick and clumsy, like frozen cuts of meat. Sensitivity faded as her exposed skin grew numb. "Remind me what I should expect to feel inside you. You seem to remember better than I do."

Cora blinked and nodded. "Feel the opening deep inside. It is surrounded by a ridge," she said, biting off each word as she said it. "Tell me how wide the opening is."

The placental water on the rover floor had sheeted over with a film of ice, clinging in gummy knots to Cora's naked inner thighs. Rachel slowly felt the folds of skin between Cora's legs, dipped her fingers into them, then slid her cold hand inside. At first the temperature felt too hot on her numb skin, like melted butter, in startling contrast to the frigid air inside the rover. She forced herself not to withdraw. Her hand burned.

Rachel moved her fingers, trying to get a better estimate. She found the ridge Cora described. "It is a little wider than my hand and thumb."

Cora bit her lip and closed her eyes as she eased her shoulders back against the wall.

Rachel withdrew and grabbed the other woman's

arm. "This wide," she said, indicating the distance once again to be sure Cora understood. The biting cold of the air felt like acid on her wet hand as the dampness froze into a fragmenting glove. She leaned close. "Is that good or bad?"

"Bad. No—good," Cora said. "It means this should be over fairly soon. A few hours, perhaps."

"Should I try to move the rover again?" Rachel turned toward the front windowport. "We can get closer to the base, if nothing else. We might be in a race against the baby."

Cora shook her head. "I don't think we can win your race. We are as safe here as we will be in a few hours. This way we have more time to prepare."

Rachel adjusted *Percival*'s air compressors to increase the pressure and temperature inside the rover more rapidly, as much as Cora could stand, and more. Then she hunkered down on the floor next to Cora and looked out the trapezoidal windowport that showed the storm that held them captive, a burnt-sienna soup that blurred the rest of the world. She sat without speaking for a long time. Cora rested, and waited.

The muffled sound of the weak but angry wind outside changed in quality, suddenly turning into a monster's roar: a grinding, crunching sound that pounded through the walls of the rover.

The rock outcropping above them broke and came crashing down in sharp pieces, tossing boulders and sheets of dirt at *Percival*. The floor of the rover bucked and lurched. A sound like a truckload of cast-iron frying pans falling onto concrete clanged through the metal-walled vehicle. The avalanche tossed them from side to side, hammering the protective walls, the roof, trying to breach the hull with massive blocks of lava.

Rachel fell on her side as *Percival* shook. She grabbed at the air for balance. Cora rolled over and curled into a ball to protect her abdomen.

Rocks pummeled the top of the rover, bouncing and thudding with the separate bass notes of boulders and thin treble chimes of pebbles. Reddish wisps of dust clogged the view from the front windowports, blowing away in patches as gusts smeared it free of the glass. The sound of cascading rock faded. By comparison, the crescendo of the storm sounded like relative silence.

On the metal floor, Rachel got to her knees and gratefully breathed the regenerated air in her suit. She felt herself shaking in the afterwash of terror. The palm of her bare hand burned against the frigid metal of the deck, and she jerked it away.

"Are you all right?" she asked Cora, tapping her helmet to make sure the speakerpatch still worked. The *adin* woman nodded.

Then another, softer thump landed on top of the rover, like a footfall. Cora froze and listened. Her eyes widened.

Rachel stood up and moved toward the rover's control panel. Luckily, none of the falling rocks had smashed through the armored glass of the front windowports. Dust blocked part of the transparent screen, but there was little to see outside in the storm anyway.

Then a face and shoulders appeared from above like a gunshot in the stillness, hands thrusting down from the roof of the rover, brushing the dust aside. The upside-down face pressed against the glass, peering inside at them and grinning.

An *adin*. Boris Tiban.

In shock, Rachel stopped herself from crying out. She smacked her hands on the emergency controls for the protective plates. The last thing she saw was Boris Tiban leaping aside in angry surprise, jumping free of the rover and vanishing into the tangled murk of the storm as the plates slammed down over *Percival*'s windowports. Then the heavy metal plates clanged into place, leaving the rover in dimness. The cabin's central illumination automatically stepped up, bathing the interior in blue-white light, while the resistance heaters shed a warm orange glow.

Cora hauled herself into a sitting position again

and stared wide-eyed at the sealed windowport. "Boris!" she muttered, her voice laden with a complex mixture of terror and longing. She seemed to have forgotten about her labor pains. "He must have caused the avalanche. He has probably been working at it ever since we stopped." She sighed. "Yes, that is how he would do it."

"Out in the storm?" Rachel could hardly believe what she had seen. "How could he survive without shelter? In this wind? Even an *adin* shouldn't be that strong!"

Cora shook her head, and Rachel saw a distant smile on her lips. "He likes to do that, pit himself against the elements. He is proud of how he can cope with anything Mars throws at him. A tamer of worlds— that is what he wants to be called. He does not like to see humans domesticating this planet. You are taking away his private kingdom."

Rachel couldn't believe what she was hearing. "But if Boris kills me, he will also destroy you, and his baby. What will that accomplish? Doesn't he realize he will murder his own unborn child?"

Cora hung her head, then shuddered with another labor spasm—the contractions were not as far apart as they had been earlier. When she recovered, she looked Rachel in the eye and kept her voice flat. "Boris needs the baby to die, for his own purposes. He has always planned on that."

Rachel opened and closed her mouth without words; behind the faceplate she must look like a fish whose water has suddenly drained from its bowl. "I don't understand."

Cora let her slanted eyes fall shut beneath the thick lashes. "With the baby dead, Boris will have another vendetta against the humans who have worked to terraform this world. Especially you, Dr. Dycek." She shook her head. "It is difficult to understand. Perhaps it makes sense only to him, but he has been searching for such an excuse for a long time, wanting it desperately and afraid to act until he had an appropriate focus. If the baby does not die, he will lose that focus for his anger—and he has finally been pushed past his limits. If the baby does die, I think he'll be glad—and relieved.

"Boris plans to go to your base and destroy it. With his titanium staff, he can tear holes right through the sides of your module walls. He can run from one inflated cylinder to the next, striking and moving faster than you lumbering humans. You will never stop him." Cora looked very afraid.

She continued, "The people inside will be trapped, and he can pick them off one room at a time. The humans might be able to repair some of the walls, but Boris would just strike again. They could not possibly keep up. He can wait longer than any of them."

"But what about *you*, Cora? He's trying to kill you, too!"

Cora's voice held a winter of grief. "He loves me in his own way. I know that. For years I have known it. But he sees his cause as more important. Just like a great revolutionary, he knows the sacrifices he must make. He's fallen in love with too many of Stroganov's stories."

Rachel felt anger doubling inside her. She patted Cora's bulging stomach with her bare, numb hand and turned to look at the heavy metal plates covering the windowports, walling them off from the outside. "Then I must make sure he has no excuse to attack the base. We will take away his reason for revenge." She knelt beside Cora and smiled hopefully through the protective faceplate of her helmet.

"Your baby must live."

JESÚS KEEFER

"I HAVE NEVER SET foot in the human base we *dvas* erected for you," Dr. Dmitri Pchanskii said in a gruff and booming voice, "but then, I have never been invited. Never invited. Not even Dr. Dycek asked me inside, back in the beginning. I wonder if she thought I couldn't adapt to the high pressure. . . ." He gestured toward the tunnels behind them, lit by strings of white lights. "Allow me to be a more gracious host, though, and show you what we *dvas* have done for ourselves."

He clapped his wide, flat hands, then turned to the other *dvas*. "Leave me with them. They will require a few explanations." Pchanskii had a domineering but paternal manner that made him seem powerful but accessible at the same time.

The *dva* man they had encountered outside peered over Pchanskii's shoulder. He looked frightened, thin, and old. "But, Dmitri, we can't let them know everything! I was just coming back from my delivery from the pumping station—"

Pchanskii drew in a deep breath, expanding his huge *dva* chest that held double-capacity lungs. He did not take his gaze from Keefer. "And you led them right here in your panic. It is too late to do anything else, so we must make the best of the situation. Calm yourself—we were making ready to announce our presence soon. This will force us to be a bit faster on our feet, but perhaps it will work out better, now that we have established a direct liaison."

He leaned forward, smiling with his pale *dva* mouth. "We are like rabbits that have been flushed from hiding. These are the wolves, standing before us. They have already caught us. Now we must convince them not to eat us."

Keefer found the analogy ridiculous when he and Vickery stood outnumbered fifteen to one, and the *dvas* were generally more muscular than humans anyway—even the women, who hung back in the shadows behind Pchanskii.

"And do these wolves have names?" Pchanskii asked, raising his bushy eyebrows and waiting.

Keefer nervously cleared his throat, which sounded like a gruff explosion through the speakerpatch. "I am Commissioner Jesús Keefer from Lowell Base, and this is Operations Manager Bruce Vickery."

"Ah," Pchanskii said, stepping forward and placing a huge hand on both of their shoulders. He looked inhuman and enormous, even beside Vickery's burly frame. "So what are we going to do with you two, Commissioner Jesús Keefer of Lowell Base and Operations Manager Bruce Vickery?"

Vickery sounded indignant and shrugged off the gripping hand on his shoulder. "Why not tell us what the hell you're doing out here, Pchanskii? You've got stolen UNSA equipment all over the place. You're supposed to be dead, you and your team."

"Dead?" Pchanskii said, raising his thick eyebrows and grinning. "You found no bodies after the avalanche. No destroyed equipment. You might have *assumed* we perished—but your assumption was not valid. Jumping to conclusions. The *dva* are quite versatile. Quite versatile. And it was in our best interests to continue our work in isolation."

"Just what are your best interests, Dr. Pchanskii?" Keefer asked, forcing himself not to fidget under the heavy weight of the *dva* man's hand. "I should remind you that—regardless of your secret hideout—you agreed to come to Mars to work on the UNSA terraforming activities. You have shirked those duties for over a year now. When I think of what you could have done for Mars in that time, I find it a little galling."

Pchanskii gave a full-throated laugh. "It seems we have a small misunderstanding. Small misunderstanding. Perhaps you should reread the legal documents regarding the *dvas*." His broad smile made him look like a razor blade trying to be reasonable.

"The *dvas* agreed to undergo adaptive surgery and to live the rest of our lives on Mars. Our contract says nothing more than that. We hammered it out very vigorously with our lawyer Mannfred Rotlein. We *dvas* never agreed to do UNSA work, nor anything else. As far as we are concerned, once we arrived on Mars, our obligations to Earth ended."

Keefer's head spun. Why would anyone on Mars *not* want to work on the terraforming activities? They benefited everyone. "But then what—"

Pchanskii held up a hand for him to wait and turned to the *dva* crowd around him. "Go on," he said to them. "Just because we have unexpected visitors does not mean you may stop your work. Mars awaits. Back to your duties!"

Silently and quickly, the *dva* refugees evaporated back into the tunnels, hurrying on the polished stone floors with a scuffle and squeak of bare feet. In a few moments Keefer and Vickery found themselves alone with the *dva* doctor.

Pchanskii turned Keefer and Vickery around and nudged them along the corridor until they reached an unlit side passage. "Step in here, and let me explain." He rubbed his hands together like a fanatical preacher trying to sell salvation with a well-practiced sermon. "Who knows, by the time I am finished with our story, it might even make sense to you! Might even make sense."

He ran his hand along the rock wall and found a recessed switch. Rows of lights winked on, shining into a cluttered chamber that had been walled off at one end. It looked like a museum.

Maps and photographs had been laminated to the smooth rock walls. Enormous topographical closeups of the various Sovereign Republics, wrinkled mountain ranges, satellite images of rivers, the Black Sea and Crimea, postcards from tourist spots and exotic cities: Samarkand, Bukhara, Vladivostok, Yerevan, Minsk, Kazan, Gorky, Arkhangelsk, even Moscow. Keefer saw newsnet hardcopies, chips of the sort encoded with music and literature, a computer screen with built-in reference ROMs. A very impressive setup.

"So what is all this?" Keefer asked as Vickery stood beside him, staring. They were both afraid to touch anything, but Pchanskii urged them forward. Keefer had a weird, out-of-place vision, wondering if young Allan collected all the items his father gathered for him and displayed them with as much pride as these *dvas* did.

"Personal items," Pchanskii said. "We were each given a specified allotment when we came aboard the transport ships. We worked with each other in secret beforehand to maximize the diversity of what we would bring along, to make sure we had no duplication in our efforts. No duplication." Pchanskii took a long look at the items, as if paying them silent respect. "This way we could leave the best possible legacy for our descendants here on Mars."

Vickery bellowed through his speakerpatch, "What the hell are you talking about?"

"What descendants?" Keefer said at the same time. He knew as well as everyone else that the *dvas* had been sterilized.

"Patience, patience!" Pchanskii said. His face filled with delight, like a Father Christmas who had somehow been transformed into this rubber-faced gremlin. "Now sit down and pay attention. This is story time. Sit! That's the only way I'm going to tell you everything. Story time."

Pchanskii strode around in the museum grotto like a schoolmaster until Keefer and Vickery both seated themselves on carved stone benches.

"This had better be good," Vickery said. "There's a dust storm on its way. We didn't come here for a social visit."

Keefer looked at the *dva* man. "We must leave soon, Dr. Pchanskii. We have to get back to the base before the storm makes travel impossible."

"You will leave when I say you can leave! When I say. If you have only some of the information about us, it will be worse than if you had none at all. Besides, these caves are the safest places you'll find right now."

"Where is Dr. Dycek?" Keefer asked. "Why isn't she the one explaining all this?"

"Yeah," Vickery said. "I would think she'd want to gloat."

The question took Pchanskii off guard. "What does this have to do with Dr. Dycek?"

"Isn't she with the *dvas* here?" Vickery asked. "She was going to vanish, presumed dead—just like your group did last year! This was all her idea, wasn't it? Where is her rover? You can't just steal *Percival* like you walked off with this other surplus equipment."

"Enough!" Pchanskii leaned closer to Vickery, glaring at him. "Enough. I assure you that none of this was Dr. Dycek's idea, and I will not have her—or anyone else!—take credit for what we *dvas* alone have accomplished here. I have not seen Dr. Dycek in the past year, since the avalanche."

"Then where is she?" Keefer asked.

Pchanskii looked flustered. "How in the world should I know? She has nothing to do with us. Nothing."

Vickery leaned back against the chamber wall. "Oh, damn it all to hell! And a bunch of other expletives I haven't even thought of yet."

Keefer tried to digest the information Pchanskii was giving them. If Dycek was not here, if she had nothing to do with this secret *dva* encampment, then where had she gone with her rover? And if she really had nothing to do with these people, then—

"Perhaps you had better tell us what it is you are trying to accomplish in this hideout of yours, Dr. Pchanskii," Keefer said.

"That is precisely what I've been trying to do." Pchanskii pursed his lips, but they did not interrupt him further. Finally, he began his story.

"You should have heard Dr. Dycek treating me as her prize student, telling me the great burden I had to bear for her, that I must show the United Nations Space Agency how fruitful her *dva* colonists could be. She smiled at me and patted me on the back as if I were her favorite pet. Her pet. But we *dvas* had our own agenda; we always did. We gave up everything for our own dream here on Mars. And now we have been getting ready to show UNSA that we have accomplished it."

He lapsed into silence for a too-long dramatic pause.

Vickery sighed. "All right, what was your dream here on Mars? Tell us, please."

Pchanskii began by taking a seat beside the information-retrieval terminal. "Back in my younger days, at the height of my career, I was a prominent obstetrician in Samarkand, before the Reorganization when Uzbekistan withdrew from the Sovereign Republics. A prominent obstetrician. You might have seen on the newsnets what it was like during that time—most of the reporters gave conflicting stories, with doctored video footage, but a few managed to portray the chaos, the violence, until the new government clamped down and kicked all of us hated foreigners across the border. I had lived in Samarkand for fifteen years, but I lost my home and my land and all of my possessions, booted out without even a thank you. Fuck you, more like it."

Pchanskii grimaced as if he had just swallowed something rotten. "I happened to be Belorussian by descent, but because the nationalistic Uzbeks decreed that no outside ethnic groups could hold land in their independent and unsullied country, I found myself without a home.

"When I returned to Minsk in the Belorussian Republic, I had no problem setting up my practice again to make a living. I was, after all, a well-qualified

208

and well-experienced obstetrician. But I became very outspoken and angry, a political figure, you might say. A political figure." He lifted his head to look at them with a feigned offhand expression that did not completely mask a fire of hatred. "Oh, did I not mention that my wife was killed during the Uzbek uprisings? It must have slipped my mind."

Keefer saw that Pchanskii's hands were clenched, as if kneading a mass of well-leavened grief.

"I felt violated, like a rape victim. My integrity had been stolen from me by governmental buffoons and their sweeping pronouncements. And how does one go about getting it back? The Uzbeks had taken over the country where I had grown up, telling me I no longer belonged there . . . and I wasn't sure I really wanted to go back anyway. But how could I be comforted in Minsk, a foreign city to me? What if the Belorussians had a revolt of their own and decided to toss out anyone who wasn't born there? It was all so arbitrary.

"You see, no place on Earth is actually safe. *Every* square meter of the planet could be construed as having belonged to someone else at some time in the past. The Native Americans could demand the United States back, the Saxons could demand England back from the Normans. Siberia goes back to the Mongols. Kiev goes back to the Varangian Vikings. It goes on and on."

Finally, Pchanskii gave one of his broad grins, as if he were about to divulge a huge secret. "But not on Mars! Here, there is no such precedent. No such precedent. We would be the first. The cornerstone, the foundation of a new society."

His eyes gleamed in the light of the chamber. The pictures of Russian mountains and rivers and cities on the walls seemed insignificant to Pchanskii's scheme. The photographs were of Earth, but the reality was Mars.

"After the *adin* landings caused such a stir, and after the UN hearings opened the *dva* project to the public, I saw it as a sudden opportunity to regain my strength and my honor, to make a difference. Working with a few underground connections, I gathered a pool of volunteers, telling them about my plan to form a new country, a homeland to outwit the politicians and the nationalists. A homeland. I found a good many dissatisfied intelligentsia, talented professionals, people who wanted to be like the Thomas Jeffersons and Benjamin Franklins of the old United States. But we needed it clearly established before any of us would take such a risk."

"Rotlein," Keefer said, suddenly remembering.

"Yes! I got the best lawyer in the world—at least in my opinion. A Volga German named Mannfred Rotlein who delighted in tying up the bureaucrats with their own laws. When I and all my intelligent, professional protégés volunteered for *dva* testing, the Sovereign Republics and Dr. Dycek nearly wet themselves."

Pchanskii patted himself in the center of the chest. "We were exactly the type of people they wanted to recruit for the Mars project: educated, good workers, true thinkers, the best kind of colonists. Excellent public relations. And all we wanted was a mere paperwork concession, a simple nod from them admitting—in a legally binding way, of course—that the *dvas* would own their property in the areas they settled, not just be transplanted laborers. We had to get some rights."

Vickery gestured skeptically to indicate the dim *dva* tunnels. "Looks like you might have done better just staying outside."

"It was the principle of the thing," Pchanskii said. "The principle—and we *dvas* place great emphasis on our principles. Arguments ensued in UNSA, in front of the cameras and behind closed doors, but Rotlein was having the time of his life. He was like a piranha, relentless. I am glad he was on our side.

"In the end the bureaucrats nodded, smiling for the newsnets. They signed the right papers. After all,

Mars was not theirs to give in the first place. They agreed to let the *dvas* keep it, for as long as we remained here. Rotlein told them the *dvas* would work harder if it was for something we believed in, if we knew the land was ours. Whatever land the *dvas* established would be our own, our very own.

"The bureaucrats thought they had made a minimal concession to maximal gain. The *dvas*, like the *adins*, would be sterilized and they would be long dead before the planet's environment became amenable to real humans anyway. The agreement specifically stated that 'no heirs from Earth' would be allowed to claim rights to anything the *dvas* left behind. The negotiators believed they had everything covered. But bureaucrats are incapable of thinking in the long-term."

Inside his helmet, Keefer pursed his lips, trying to second-guess Pchanskii. "It seems to me you just emphasized the words *from Earth* when you talked about your heirs?"

Pchanskii hopped to his feet again. "Come with me. You must see this for yourselves."

Striding along in the low gravity, Pchanskii led them beyond where the *dva* had first formed their barricade. Keefer tried to look at everything on both sides of him, filled with renewed wonder despite himself as they hurried deeper into the tunnels. Though the *dva* hideout was a complete surprise to him, his mind reeled with the implications. Now, more than ever, he needed to have Dr. Dycek help him understand how to deal with the new situation—but she had vanished.

Several *dvas* turned to stare at them, some with apparent fear, some with distrust. "In here," Pchanskii said, leading them into a brightly lit room with polished, enameled walls, chrome fixtures, glass instruments, and flat tables. Operating tables.

Two *dva* women worked at the counters, one studying a slide under a microscanner, another inventorying supplies. Keefer's mind boggled as he lost track of all the equipment the *dvas* must have squirreled away here. The two women turned around to look at Pchanskii as he entered.

Both were obviously pregnant. One appeared to be in her last few weeks before labor, the other seemed about six months along.

"We did it two ways," Pchanskii said with sparkling eyes, before Vickery or Keefer could even mouth their questions. "The cheating method has proven most successful so far. Most successful. We were able to take personal possessions, you remember? With so many connections and a lot of money at our disposal—we could take no cash with us, so we were free to spend it all—it was not difficult to bribe a few of the right people. Several of us smuggled along vials of frozen sperm. A small thing, weighs little, and not too difficult to keep chilled in the Martian environment." He laughed. "Not too difficult.

"Bebez and Catherine here were artificially inseminated after we staged the avalanche, after we had the facility functioning at least up to minimum standards. Bebez is due next month, and Catherine in two more. Three of the other women are pregnant, too, but they are not showing yet."

"That's amazing!" Keefer said.

"It's crazy, you mean," Vickery added. But he seemed stunned. His words sounded choked. "No, I'm sorry—I don't mean to belittle it. It's just . . ." He let out a long breath of air, unable to find the words he needed.

"We still feel that way is cheating, though," Pchanskii continued. "I am a surgeon, remember. I took a long time to be certain I had all the right equipment, all the right facilities here in hiding. You never even noticed how many items we removed from Lowell Base." His wide lips formed a smug smile.

"Actually, we did," Vickery said. "We just had no idea where they were going. I never suspected anything like this, I can assure you."

Pchanskii nodded. "I have performed successful operations on five of the *dva* males already. Vasectomies are not really too difficult to reverse, if you know what you are doing and if you have the right tools. Five *dva* men are now fertile. We believe another one of the women is already pregnant, the natural way this time. This is how we hoped to establish our own country here."

Keefer gazed at the two *dva* women, at the medical room, at the walls tunneled out of the Noctis Labyrinthus cliffs. Despite the questions spinning in his head, he could not help but admire the incredible trick Pchanskii and his people had played on the entire Earth. He didn't even want to think of the howling the politicians would do across the gulf of space, once they found out.

"But to what purpose?" Vickery asked. "You were bound to be discovered sooner or later."

Pchanskii shrugged. "Once the babies were born here, what could anyone do? Governments back home could squawk all they wanted—we've got everything sealed up airtight by their own rules. Rotlein knew the whole plan from the start. He's got it completely documented. What can they say?" He crossed his thick arms over his chest.

"We've known all along that the *dva* project could only be a short-term phase. Mars is changing too rapidly for our type of people. We have to be ready for anything. Be flexible. If somebody is going to reap the benefits of what we have done to this planet, we wanted it to be our own descendants. Not other greedy hands.

"All human beings resist change—that is the way of the species. But when circumstances are altered, everything must adapt or die. The trick is to adapt enough—without killing yourself in the process. That's what we are trying to do."

Vickery shook his bearded head inside the helmet. "Well, I'm in awe of what you have accomplished, Pchanskii. No matter how much it irks me."

Pchanskii chuckled.

Keefer pointed to the two pregnant *dva* women. "But how can I condone this, Dr. Pchanskii? You might feel safe in your hidden shelter here, but what about the children? They'll have none of your augmentations. Mars will be just as deadly to them as it is to me. They're never going to survive, not even here inside your tunnels."

Pchanskii had his back turned to Keefer. His shoulders bunched up, as if his whole body had stiffened. Before Keefer could move out of the way or even shout, the *dva* doctor whirled. His massive, bony fist clenched into a battering ram. Pchanskii brought it around with crushing force.

Grinning all the while, he smashed open Keefer's faceplate.

RACHEL DYCEK

SURROUNDED BY THE WHIRLWIND of the storm, Cora Marisovna gave birth to a daughter. Healthy, and perfect—and human. Rachel stared at the newborn with an amazement and exhilaration that made her feel reborn as well, glowing with life again. It was a strange feeling.

Crouched under the rubble of the avalanche, *Percival* creaked and groaned as the wind tried to push its way in. The dust and blowing sand grains made a rasping sound against the hull plates, but the shelter remained secure. The deck rocked as Rachel knelt beside Cora, but she felt protected for the miraculous half an hour it took for Cora to give birth. . . .

Boris Tiban waited for them out in the storm, somewhere, but he did not strike again. Rachel secured the rover's sphincter airlock mechanism, then flicked glances to the closed-off front and sides of the vehicle. With the protective covers over the window plates, she could not see outside. The lights in the rover were harsh and blue-white, reflected from the sterile interior of the vehicle. The resistance heaters made the air dry—too hot in some places, freezing cold in others, comfortably warm in none.

Before the birth, they had little to do but wait. Rachel checked, but found no spare suit in the rover for Cora's baby—not that she expected one. They were limited to the resources and equipment on hand. She and Cora drank from packets of fruit juice concentrates, building their strength. They tried to rest, but the passage of time only increased their anxiety. Then Cora gasped, demanding all Rachel's attention.

When Cora's labor reached its peak, Rachel had no choice but to pressurize the rover interior as rapidly as the pumps could bring in more air. It would give the *adin* woman a painful headache, make her breathing difficult, and lower her tolerance for the strenuous work of childbirth, but Rachel saw no alternative.

Many of the rover's intake vents were clogged with dust from the storm and Boris Tiban's avalanche, but the gauges showed the cabin air density increasing. Rachel's ungloved hand felt numb and dead, too cold, swollen red in the low pressure. She felt her pulse throbbing deep inside her hand.

Cora cried out with the effort of her labor, and with the additional effort it took to breathe. "Like a metal band around my chest! My head!"

"There is nothing for it. The baby must be able to breathe when it comes." *No matter what it does to the mother*, Rachel thought. "You are strong. I made you that way."

"I . . . know!" Then the final stage of labor stole all complaints from Cora's armored lips, focusing her mind only on pushing down.

Overhead, they heard another thump of heavy feet, a long silence, then a loud banging. The rhythmic bursts of noise did not stop for several minutes. Boris had taken a rock and was pounding, pounding, pounding.

Rachel looked around, stared at the ceiling, the walls, the sealed windowports. She and Cora were trapped within a wounded vehicle, in a raging storm, with a madman outside. But she was too busy to worry about Boris right now.

The monotonous pounding stopped, and Rachel found herself on edge, distracted from Cora, just *waiting* for it to start again.

Boris was playing with them, trying to make them afraid. He could not breach the hull, and he knew it. But he could make strange noises. He could distract them from what was important.

Cora drew a deep breath, gritted her teeth, and pushed.

"Okay, that's good. Keep pushing!" Rachel said.

Boris hammered the sides of the rover now, a sharp staccato beat that stopped in just a few minutes. He was getting impatient. Rachel wondered if he had any idea what was going on inside.

Cora cried out, and pushed again. It went on like that for a very long time. . . .

When Rachel finally pulled the slick baby free, it steamed in the air, glistening with red wetness. "A daughter!" she said. "A girl! And it's perfectly healthy!"

Cora's mouth remained open, gasping to fill her lungs. The baby, too, worked the tiny dark hole of her mouth in a silent agonized cry of new life, but she could not find enough air.

Rachel moved quickly now. As she had planned, and dreaded, she popped open her faceplate, letting the blessed warm air gush out like a death rattle. The shock stunned a gasp out of her, but she forced herself to keep moving, to plow through the black specks in front of her eyes as she shucked her suit.

She grasped the loose end of the metal tape sealing the ragged cut on the fabric around her wrist. Her grip slipped twice before the numb fingers clutched it and tore it off. She let out a howl of pain, as if she had just flayed the skin of her arm.

She had to hurry. Grogginess started to claim her, but she stumbled through the motions. Bright pain flashed behind Rachel's forehead. Moments later, a warm, thick trickle of blood dripped from her nostrils.

Shivering already, Rachel stepped out of the empty suit, letting the metallic fabric fall in a rough heap on the floor. She wore only a light Lowell Base jumpsuit underneath, clammy with old sweat. The perspiration froze into icy needles against her skin. Her teeth chattered.

Rachel clamped the empty faceplate shut and grabbed up the baby. The infant girl's skin, smeared with red from the birth, took on a bluish tinge as she tried to breathe. Helpless, struggling. Rachel had to help. The umbilical cord, tied in a crude knot, still oozed blood.

Cora found the strength to reach over and touch the baby one last time before Rachel slid her inside the loose folds of the suit and sealed her whispered cries into silence. She began pressurizing the suit immediately to sustain the infant. The folds straightened themselves as air pumped inside, like an inflatable mannequin. The chemical oxygen-regenerator pack purred and coughed.

Heaving huge breaths but still starving for oxygen, Rachel grasped the limp sleeve where she had cut off the glove and knotted it. Suit-warmed air blew from the edge, squirting onto her skin.

Rachel grasped the roll of metallized tape and wrapped it around and around the end of the sleeve. She had to seal the gash, to keep the baby safe and warm, until *Percival* could support them both. After several layers of tape, the hissing noise stopped, replaced by the ringing in her ears, the thudding in her head.

Rachel crawled over to where regenerated air streamed into the chamber, but that helped only a little. She sat gasping, trying to find enough oxygen, praying that it would get better any moment now. Any moment.

As the air thickened, though, Cora grew worse. "Can't—inhale," she said. "Like stones...on my chest. Breathing soup." After her labor she was too weak to cope with the increasing respiratory difficulty.

Rachel felt her encouraging words drain away as she looked at the exhausted new mother, at the mess of blood and amniotic fluid and afterbirth tissue frozen on the rover floor. This had not been clean and quick like the make-believe births in entertainment disks. It looked like some slaughter had occurred here. But not slaughter—new life.

Somehow, Cora got to her knees, wavered as she tried, and failed, to draw a deep breath. She hovered over the closed faceplate of Rachel's inflated suit, look-ing to find her baby inside, and then she collapsed, barely keeping herself from tumbling on top of the baby.

With an agonized groan, Cora turned away from her new daughter and crawled toward the sphincter airlock. "You must let me back out. Need to breathe."

Rachel, dizzy from her own lack of air, tried to fight against the confusion in her. "Not in the storm! Not right after giving birth. You are too weak."

But she knew Cora was right. The pressure change was too fast, not slow and gentle as it should have been to allow her to adapt. It would kill her to remain inside the rover. If the *adin* woman had any chance for surviving, it had to be outside—where Boris Tiban was waiting.

Would he help Cora, or try to kill her?

Cora reached the flexible airlock and rested her head against it, panting. "Strong enough to survive out there," she said, repeating Rachel's words. "We *adins* are strong. You made us that way."

Cora looked one last time toward the sagging envi-ronment suit on the floor, focused on the squirming lump that showed the little girl's movement. Her expression fell, and she raised her deep-set eyes to meet Rachel's. With her *adin* squashed nose, hooded eyes, and fused-back ears, Cora Marisovna looked intensely inhuman, but human at the same time.

"I will tell Boris his daughter is alive. Safe." With great effort, she filled her lungs one more time. "He must face that. Adapt to new conditions. He is a father now." She raised her hand in a gesture of farewell, then pushed against the airlock.

Somehow, her words about Boris did not reassure Rachel.

The noise of the storm doubled as Cora forced her way into the enveloping membrane that eased her through to the outside. The noise of the storm was muffled again as Cora left all protection behind.

Rachel found herself alone with the newborn baby.

RACHEL DYCEK

SIGHING AND BLINKING, Rachel forced herself to keep moving, afraid she might freeze into a statue inside the rover. She had to continue her journey, to lumber back toward the base even in the storm. It felt good to have another towering goal, though. She fought harder, stretching mental and emotional muscles that had atrophied over the past few years.

During the rover's several hours of motionlessness while Cora gave birth, dust had piled up like red talcum powder around *Percival's* base. The vehicle strained on its telescoping legs, rocking back and forth and cranking the methane engines into overdrive to break free of the avalanche rubble piled around it. The rocks and dust soughed down the armored sides, crumbling beneath the strain as the great machine stirred.

Gasping, too cold to sweat and with stinging tears in her eyes, Rachel hunched over the controls, *willing* the vehicle to move ahead. She couldn't be trapped here—not now that she had Cora's beautiful, healthy baby to protect. Now that she had a reason to return to the base. She hissed into the voice pickup. "Go, dammit!"

The cabin lurched as the articulating legs grabbed at the rocks, pushed, heaved the bulk of the rover up, and finally over the obstacles. Rachel tried to shout, but she did not have enough oxygen to waste on such trivial things. The effort sent a wash of dizziness through her. Though the heaters had continued to work, her jaws chattered together in imagined cold. The back of the rover rose up at an angle over the worst of the obstacles—then they were free of the rockslide.

Thrown back against the hard edge of the seat, Rachel wished she had strapped herself in. Unsupported on the floor, the baby inside the environment suit slid over to one corner and came to rest against a passenger bench, with the baggy legs wadded up. The sound of the straining engine muffled the baby's cries inside the inflated package. Rachel couldn't see the girl within the silvery wrapping, but knowing and hearing was enough.

The pumping of the air recirculators sounded like a dis-tant roar as they sucked the thin outside atmosphere through clogged filters to make the air dense enough for her to survive, if just barely. Technicolor static fuzzed at the corners of her vision, as if her eyes suffered from chromatic aberration like a bad telescope lens.

Rachel slid the protective plates away from the front windowport so she could watch their progress, though the storm made that nearly impossible. Using less caution now, she increased *Percival*'s speed, trusting the vehicle to scramble over medium-sized rocks rather than picking a path around them.

She had to get away, had to get back to Lowell Base.

Weak from her ordeal, Cora was out there in the terrible storm, counting on her *adin* augmentations to keep her alive. Boris Tiban had survived the elements. Would he help Cora, or did he discard anything that was weak . . . like a baby? Perhaps he was still tracking Rachel, looking for his chance to strike, to kill his own child.

Cora might be able to talk to him, shout into his flattened *adin* ear and beg him not to attack. Perhaps he would listen. Probably he would not. Boris didn't seem the type to walk away from a challenge.

As the rover chugged ahead with its rocking, thumping gait, the chasm walls lowered and the floor widened. Rachel felt her confidence grow as the air inside the cabin became bearable by tiny degrees. She might reach the flat slope of Pavonis Mons within the hour, and *Percival* could take bearings, use the guidance gear to choose the most direct course back home, even in the blinding dust.

A bullwhip of wind cracked against the wide side of the rover, rattling it back and forth. *Percival* fought to keep from slewing laterally into a sharp boulder. The gust lost its power as rapidly as it had come, and the rover lurched quickly to avoid overcompensating.

Rachel turned around to glance at the baby, to make sure it had not been injured.

Then Boris Tiban sprang out in front of the vehicle and bounded onto its sloping hood, thumping with his heavy feet and grabbing for purchase with powerful *adin* hands. Red dust swirled around him, but Boris seemed to draw energy from the storm itself. He hefted his titanium staff over his head like a harpoon, looking like a savage from the wilds of Mars.

Instinctively, Rachel shrank back. She didn't have enough air to cry out, nor did she think quickly enough to slam the protective plates down over the windowports.

Boris brought the pointed rod down with a crunch in the center of the trapezoidal glass plate.

A white flower of damage burst around the tip, spreading like concentric petals. A high whine of air screamed out from the pressurized cabin as Boris jerked the staff away. He screwed up his face in a twisted caricature of monstrous anger, then jabbed the titanium tip down again even harder, producing a second, larger puncture in the thick glass.

Rachel heard the wind's roar outside and a distant howl that might have been triumph from the *adin* leader. A ribbon of stolen air squealed as it spurted through the punctures. The storm raged, whipping dust across Boris's body. As *Percival* continued to labor onward, Boris clung to the outer hull. He bent forward to stare in at her, grinning.

"Stop!" Rachel shouted, expending precious air from her lungs. She yanked on the emergency control levers, bringing the rover to a sudden halt. The lurching stop tossed Boris Tiban from his perch. The long silvery staff flew up into the air as he fell comically backward to the ground.

If Rachel had moved quickly, she could have forced *Percival* to trample Boris's body, crush him under the mass of telescoping legs. But she froze at the controls. Could she just kill him, the strongest of the *adins* she had made?

Before she could decide, Boris rolled out of sight only a few meters away. He staggered to his feet, using the recovered staff for leverage.

Rachel slapped at the control panel. Brilliant high beams on the rover stabbed out in an explosion of light. One set of beams slewed cockeyed into the sky, but the others blasted into Boris's eyes. He froze, blinded. He wrapped a forearm over his face. His old jumpsuit fluttered about him in shreds, tattered from the storm's onslaught. A second time, Rachel could have accelerated the vehicle and crushed him under the mass of legs. He was like a jackrabbit caught in headlights.

But she could not do it. She stared at Boris, listening to the scream of escaping air from the puncture holes in front of her. Her mouth felt like old, frozen leather. She could not swallow.

She had created Boris Tiban and exiled him here to Mars. She had been the source of his anger, whether or not she deserved to be its target. But Boris had survived everything Mars could throw at him; he was proof of her own skill. She could never kill him now.

Still unable to see, Boris staggered toward the rover, raising his staff to strike again.

CORA MARISOVNA

IN A TINY POCKET of shelter from the biting whirlwind, Cora slumped back against the rock of the canyon. Even in the clogged air, she could breathe again at last, and her body quivered with relief. Each dust-laden breath rubbed her lungs raw, but her chest could rise and fall again without effort. The cold wrapped around her like a blanket of freedom.

Without the baby, though, she felt empty inside, just a hollow shell. She had bled some, but not as much as she had seen before, in other births she had watched in Neryungri. Cora was exhausted and in pain, but it was a different kind of pain from the endless rounds of *adin* surgery she had suffered in Siberia. This was more of an ache, a loss, a weariness from which she would eventually recover.

Touching her baby daughter for those few moments would have to last her a lifetime. Dr. Dycek would take the little girl back to her base, keep her alive and safe inside the pressurized modules. It was a price Cora would have to pay. And Cora had already paid so much.

She watched the rover shudder and heave itself free of the avalanche debris, then crawl away toward safety. Its loud grinding sounds were insignificant in the howling wind. Cora had difficulty watching *Percival* go, perhaps because of tears washing beneath the clear membranes that covered her eyes, perhaps just because of the thick dust clogging her heavy lashes.

Then Boris attacked the rover.

She watched him emerge from the blinding chaos of blowing dust, as if he had finally grown tired of waiting in ambush. He jumped onto the sloping front of the vehicle. He struck with his staff like a dragon-slayer, trying to pierce the beast's tough hide and let all of the air—all of her baby's air—bleed out into the hungry storm.

"Boris, stop!" Cora cried, but her voice was weak, and she had no hope of being heard or seen through the storm. She would have to go to him herself. She made herself move, though her body just wanted her to huddle close to the ground, to sleep, to let it all pass.

She stumbled to her feet, lurching toward the rover. Her heart pounded, her abdomen ached with each step from the birthing ordeal she had already been through. But she must find the strength now. Her baby daughter depended on it.

"Boris . . ." she said again, with no hope of being heard. Cora staggered forward, thrown off balance by her weakness and the thundering wind.

She saw Boris only in fleeting glimpses through lashing dust plumes. He appeared a total stranger, an alien, but not only because of his *adin* adaptations. He did not look at all like the proud visages Stroganov carved in stone. Boris was no hero—not to her and not to anyone. Not if he would try to murder a baby just to find an excuse to kill someone else. *His own baby.*

The rover suddenly shuddered to a halt, hurling Boris from his slippery perch. He fell to the ground, rolled, and snatched up his staff to attack again. He took no notice of Cora making her way toward him.

Inside the rover, her baby daughter lay defenseless. Dr. Dycek could not defend the little girl against an *adin* attack if she could not survive it herself.

A protective, maternal instinct had grown in Cora throughout her pregnancy, but it had been tempered by the awful terror and paralyzing depression of knowing that the baby could never survive its first few breaths. She had drowned her joy with a sick dread of holding the frozen, suffocated body of her child only moments after its birth.

But Dr. Dycek had changed all that. Cora's daughter was not dead. The little girl remained alive, protected inside the fragile shelter of the rover vehicle.

Touching the helpless newborn infant had sent all those long-suppressed feelings gushing into her heart.

Cora would never stand by and let her baby die, no matter what she had to do to stop Boris. Already she felt stronger than when she had departed from the rover. Her lungs filled with breathable air, and the cold invigorated her. She ceased calling to him, intent only on reaching him.

As Boris charged forward, waving his titanium staff, Cora stepped closer to him. She held her back to the rover's bright lights, a silhouette in the storm.

Boris sensed her presence and turned. He blinked at her in astonishment. His face looked open and innocent for a moment, like a little boy caught being naughty. His dark mouth opened to gape at her.

Before he could react, Cora grabbed the pointed metal staff out of his hand. It felt as cold as frozen blood against her palms.

Delayed by surprise, he did not try to snatch it back immediately. He shouted something through the storm at her. She could not hear his words, nor did she care to.

As the storm whipped around them in a suspended moment, Cora thought of him sweeping her off her feet—the king of Mars, the great *adin* rebel who had led them to the top of the mountain to find freedom from oppression. She recalled making love to him in the cold red sand, thrashing as their bodies joined, delighting in the reawakening nerves inside. It had been magical. . . .

Why did he have to ruin it all by trying to kill her baby?

As Boris stared at her, then began to reach out, half-blinded by the rover's spotlights, Cora thrust the staff through his chest. The tip split open the thick *adin* skin, slid between his ribs, and plunged out through the second set of augmented lungs on his back.

He stared at her, appalled, before he even seemed to feel the pain. His hand wrapped around the spear protruding from him. Cora shoved farther, harder this time. But she said no word to him.

In the low gravity, her strength was great enough for the thrust to lift Boris completely off the ground. His eyes bugged out in shock, pain, and betrayal.

Then she tossed him away from her. Discarding him.

Cora could not look at him, but staggered to the front of the rover, waving her arms to get Dr. Dycek's attention. As best she could, Cora signaled the doctor to take *Percival* and flee, to keep moving. "Keep my baby safe," she pleaded under the howling wind. Dr. Dycek would understand, even if she could not hear the words.

As the rover trundled away, swallowed up in the dust-thick air, Cora crawled over to where Boris lay. She felt weak and completely abandoned now. She had lost her baby, and now she had lost her heart.

Boris lay motionless, bleeding into the already-red sands. His wound steamed from his escaping body heat, but the fresh blood froze quickly. Cora yanked the staff free and tossed it aside. By his cold actions, Boris had stabbed her in the heart a thousand times, but she had never wanted it to end like this.

She slumped down beside him, taking his head onto her lap. She cradled it, touched his face, his unfeeling skin. She didn't even notice his *adin* modifications anymore. Then she took his hand into her own.

"I will stay by you, Boris," she said.

RACHEL DYCEK

THE PUNCTURE HOLES IN the windowport shrieked as precious air flowed out of the rover, like *Percival*'s death rattle. With the loss of pressure, Rachel's ears ached, as if an icicle of bright pain had been thrust inside her skull.

Without thinking, she slapped the palm of her hand against the largest hole in the armored glass, like the legendary Dutch boy plugging the leaking dike with his own finger. It seemed the obvious thing to do, the fastest way to cover the opening. She realized her stupidity too late to stop herself.

Biting cold and suction tore at the flat of her hand, trying to pull it through the hole, ripping off what it could. She screamed.

Cora Marisovna had fallen to the ground next to the body of Boris Tiban, but she staggered to her feet and stood in front of the vehicle. She made frantic motions with her arms. Their meaning was clear: *Go! Now!*

Rachel tore her hand away from the windowport, leaving a chunk of meat behind that slurped as it was sucked outside. A dark viscous frost smeared the white cracks in the glass, veining them red. Behind her, muffled in the environment suit, the infant girl continued to wail. Condensation covered the inner surface of the helmet faceplate, blurring the baby's form. Frozen streaks of blood coated the back floor where Cora had given birth.

Outside in the storm Boris lay dead, killed by his own royal staff. Cora huddled beside him in shock and despair.

With blood dripping from her torn palm, Rachel found the metal tape she had used to seal the amputated arm of her environment suit. Hands shaking, she managed to cut strips of tape, which she slapped over the largest puncture in the windowport. The tape dug into the hole, pulled toward the outside. Gasping mouthfuls of frosty air, she added a second and then third strip of tape over the puncture. Finally, Rachel began to breathe easier. As fast as the laboring air regenerators could work, the atmosphere inside *Percival* would improve, minute by minute. She only had to wait, and endure. It would get better.

She closed her eyes. It would get better.

Percival drove itself away. Rachel blinked, taking a last glance at Cora Marisovna as she crouched over the body of Boris Tiban, her wailing lost in the storm, just like the baby's cries swallowed up in the suit. Red dust whipped around the two of them like a shroud.

Boris Tiban had thought himself invincible because he could withstand the rigors of such a harsh environment. But Mars had not killed him—an *adin* had. A human had.

Hours later, *Percival* continued on a straight downhill course, pausing near unusual outcroppings to scan and correlate its location with archival files from enhanced satellite and high-resolution topographical images. As the chasm opened up, the slope of the volcano offered a relatively gentle road, blasted clean. The rover's cockeyed spotlights kept trying to pierce the brown-red gloom, with little success. The wind hammered at her—such storms rarely let up in less than four days—but it no longer seemed such a difficult thing to withstand. She had put up with far worse.

The baby stopped crying with the constant rocking of the rover; when Rachel checked, the infant lay asleep at last. Rachel wished she could rest, too, but she couldn't afford that—not yet. She had no food for the baby, only water, but the little girl would survive until she could reach help.

Despite the layers of metal tape sealing the punctures in the front windowport, air still hummed out at the edges. The compressors labored to fill the rover; the heaters warmed the interior as fast as the Martian cold could suck it away. Rachel rubbed her arms and hoped she could remain conscious for as long as it took to reach her destination—any destination where she could receive help. She had bandaged her hand from the medical kit, but the pain gnawed at her, and she didn't dare risk taking heavy medication that would dull her senses. Not until she got back to the base.

Percival's indicators plotted the general direction of travel, though the storm and the iron-oxide dust in the air all but ruined the accuracy of the on-board compass. Because Boris had smashed the antenna, Rachel could not pick up the homing beacons of any nearby *dva* settlements, nor could she send out a distress signal.

If they continued down to the base of Pavonis Mons, though, *Percival* might encounter one of the *dva* materials-processing settlements that tapped into leftover volcanic heat, smelting metals for construction frameworks and unleashing water from hydrated rock.

Rachel squinted through the dust for hours, hoping. She thought her eyes had begun to swim with weariness and pain delirium when she finally saw the yellow lights of a *dva* processing encampment. The squat, curved walls made the outbuildings look like hulking giants. Steam exhaust plumes rose from stacks, scattered to ribbons by the storm winds. Much of the complex would be underground, protected from the environment.

She sat up quickly, unable to believe her eyes. Yes, this was one of the mining stations on the volcano's side. The chasm trail had taken her on a spiraling path around and to the side of Pavonis Mons, closer to Lowell Base.

Rachel let herself slump back in the driver's chair. The *dvas* would have no vehicle of their own, but she could at least rest here for a while, radio for help, inform the base that she was on her way—with a newborn baby.

This was much better than returning home in bittersweet failure. There was no use mourning the completion of a job well done. Weak people bemoaned the loss of great days. Strong people found new goals to achieve, new challenges to face.

Beside her on the rover floor, this new baby was also trying to be strong, to survive against all odds.

Adapt to the hostile environment, and defeat it, Boris Tiban would have said. Humanity, in all its forms, would never be obsolete. Rachel would not be obsolete until she surrendered to obsolescence. And she had finally learned how not to do that. For the first time in a long while, Rachel allowed herself a smile.

Ahead, the dim yellow lights of the *dva* settlement looked as welcoming as a traditional New Year's tree.

JESÚS KEEFER

KEEFER'S FACEPLATE SHATTERED, and he looked upon Mars with naked eyes for the first time.

His ears popped. The cold stabbed in as a gust of warm recirculated air puffed out. Instantly, he clamped down on his outcry and held his breath, hoarding precious oxygen for a last few moments.

Cold air slapped his face as his knees buckled in disbelief; he fell to the floor *knowing* he had only moments to live. After decades of work, after devoting his life to keep the terraforming project on schedule, he was going to be killed by Mars itself. . . .

Dr. Pchanskii withdrew his rock-hard fist in slow motion. Keefer could see shallow cuts on the knuckles that had not yet begun to bleed, smashed *dva* skin.

Startled into motionlessness for half a second, Vickery let out a yowl and launched himself at Pchanskii, taking the big *dva* doctor by surprise. In the low gravity Vickery's leap took him entirely off the ground, and he shot like a missile into Pchanskii's rib cage.

As Keefer's head buzzed and his locked lungs begged for a breath of air, Vickery pummeled Pchanskii, raising gloved hands again and again. In his heavy suit Vickery could not move fast enough to cause any real damage.

His chest strained to the limit, Keefer released his held breath in a gush of steam and heaved a deep lungful, then another. Air rushed into his lungs, cold enough to make his teeth ring, his throat burn. Thin . . . but nourishing.

The two pregnant *dva* women rushed over to assist Pchanskii, grabbing the handles on Vickery's shoulder pack and heaving him up like a piece of luggage. Vickery's booted feet kicked at the air. Pchanskii had already recovered from the surprise attack and heaved himself to his feet, shouldering Vickery aside, disregarding him and concentrating entirely on Keefer. But Vickery kept shouting through the speakerpatch and tore himself free from the *dva* women.

Keefer stole another breath, blinking in amazement. Everything seemed compressed into a much shorter time scale.

He stared out through the broken hole in the faceplate, too stunned to process the information fed to him through his senses. He should be feeling his capillaries expanding, blood running out of his ears, his internal organs swelling and tearing themselves apart in the low pressure. He recalled vividly the early NASA studies with lab animals, tests to see how well creatures could withstand sudden extreme decompression, results showing blindness, irreparable central nervous system damage, skin hemorrhaging, disrupted intestines, burst eardrums.

But though the air around him was frigid, Keefer took another cautious sip of air. It kept him alive.

Still on his knees on the floor, Keefer stared at his gloved hands, flexing them. His fingers wiggled, numb and sluggish . . . but functional. He had never paid attention to them before, but now they showed he was still alive.

Vickery continued gasping and struggling, his curses muffled through the speakerpatch. His air regenerator hissed and popped as he exerted himself.

Pchanskii braced himself against the wall of the medical center's grotto and shoved Vickery away again. The two *dva* women grabbed Vickery by the elbows, holding him this time.

"I tell you he is all right!" Pchanskii was shouting. "All right!"

"Bruce," Keefer said quietly, his voice carrying directly into the air, not filtered through the speakerpatch. "Bruce, I can breathe." With trembling knees, he levered himself to his feet, turning to look around in the *dva* tunnels. His skin tingled and felt scrubbed with the chill—but the air was merely brisk, not deadly. "I really can breathe."

Oddly enough, everything looked different without the distortion of the faceplate. He could see more clearly. The details were sharper, and harder.

Vickery stopped struggling and stared in amazement into Keefer's naked face. He jerked his arms free of the two *dva* women. "Okay, dammit. Let me go."

"Our tunnels are pressurized," Pchanskii said. "Didn't you notice the airlocks when you came in here? You passed through three of them.

"We keep the air thin enough to expedite our passage in and out, with only an hour-long prebreathe, but it will give sufficient oxygen for our human children to breathe—like an Inca village high in the Andes. We need to keep this place a safe haven for our babies. They cannot breathe Martian air with human normal lungs, but we *dvas* can breathe the thicker air. For now, we can tolerate it."

Keefer tottered on shaky legs over to the medical table and leaned against it for support. "But you smashed my faceplate. Couldn't you have just . . . told me about this?"

"A shock tactic," Pchanskii said with a shrug and a smile. "And very effective, too. I must confess that others have often called me too impulsive. But would simply telling you have made much of an impact?" He grinned wider. "Do you require a tranquilizer?" Still grinning, he turned to Vickery. "Do *you*?"

Moving uncertainly and keeping his eyes locked on Keefer's, Vickery reached up and unsealed his own faceplate with a *pop-hiss* of escaping air. He slid it up with a slow scraping sound, exposing his bearded face to the cold. He blinked. And breathed. Steam came from his nostrils, but he breathed again.

"Smells like a bog in here," Vickery said. "Rusty nails in a bucket of water."

"Iron oxide dust," Pchanskii said, "and high humidity at low temperatures."

"And quite a bit of body odor," Vickery added.

Pchanskii crossed his bulky arms over his bearlike

chest, feigning an offended manner. "We're doing everything else. Don't expect us to grow flowers, too."

Keefer thought about the impossible chances Pchanskii and the other *dvas* had taken for the most unlikely of dreams. He felt a few layers of his cynicism about Rachel Dycek's project begin to peel away.

The *dvas* were people, real human beings, not just a "phase in the project" as he had always categorized them before. These pioneers had given up everything on Earth . . . and they were not pathetic labor-camp prisoners who had nothing to lose, as the *adins* had been— these *dvas* had been doctors, teachers, researchers.

Maybe it hadn't been a useless PR stunt for Dycek to put people here, not just a trick to startle the world. She had demonstrated that humans really could live here—shown it in ways much more convincing than the most thorough studies or the prettiest charts. Some people could not understand a dream by reading about the concepts—they had to be shown in a more human, personal manner.

In a flash he wondered if that was part of his problem with Allan, whose eyes refused to sparkle with amazement no matter how many times Keefer showed him the wonders of the universe. Perhaps he had been trying to ram it down the boy's throat. . . .

With very limited resources and only their wits and their drive, these *dvas* had accomplished a triumph as great as UNSA had managed with the whole terraforming project. What good would it be to alter Mars in the first place, if not for this? Keefer looked around himself and blinked through his cracked faceplate. Mars looked different to him already.

A rush of cold went down his back again. What price would he have to pay for this realization?

"Dr. Pchanskii," he said, making his voice strong again. His voice carried a practical edge. "How am I supposed to get back to our rover without a helmet? I might be able to survive in your pressurized tunnels, but I certainly can't step outside."

"The *dvas* walked off with spares of every other piece of equipment," Vickery snorted. "Maybe they've got an extra helmet."

Pchanskii shook his massive head, then looked down at his feet, as if reluctant to answer. "I was hoping—well, we wanted to make sure you stayed long enough to understand us completely. To let the surprise wear off a bit, to guarantee you won't do anything rash. Why don't you remain here for a while?"

Keefer felt uneasy. "As a hostage? Or am I misunderstanding you?"

Vickery bristled. "What the hell are you saying!"

Pchanskii shook his head. "No, no. An exchange of representatives. An exchange." He paused long enough to heave a deep sigh in the chill air. "I, on the other hand, will volunteer to go back to Lowell Base. With Mr. Vickery. Seeing is believing, after all, and I will be there for everyone to stare at."

He held up his wide hands, ticking items off on his blunt fingers. "I will talk to the representatives, the newsnets, the United Nations Space Agency, the government of the Sovereign Republics. I must explain everything about what we *dvas* have done."

He smiled again. "I must also reestablish contact with Rotlein to keep all the legal matters tidy. He has been expecting this, but he never knew when it might occur. He's going to be quite busy. Quite busy." Pchanskii heaved a long sigh and met Keefer's eyes. His voice grew softer, more tenor. "It is time to face the music, as the saying goes."

Keefer felt the power of the *dva* doctor's words, but he also paid heed to his own whirling thoughts. No matter how heroic the dreams of the *dvas* were, Keefer could not ignore his own job.

Rachel Dycek's disappearance was an even greater mystery now that they had not found her in Noctis Labyrinthus. Keefer ought to be there while the base weathered the storm. The Earthbound orbiter was scheduled to depart from Phobos again in less than two weeks, and Keefer needed to be on hand to assure that the rotation up to Captain Rubens proceeded smoothly.

"I'm sorry, but I can't stay here," he finally said, "no matter how important your secret is. I'm the commisioner of Lowell Base, and Dr. Dycek is still missing."

Bruce Vickery looked around with a strange expression on his face, visible behind the uplifted faceplate. "Oh, hell," he said. He stared at the medical center, the two pregnant *dva* women, at Keefer, then finally he turned to Pchanskii. "It may as well be me. I'll stay for a while—if all you want is a hostage."

Both Keefer and Pchanskii turned to Vickery in surprise. Inside the environment suit, Vickery attempted to shrug, which looked more like a twitch under the oxygen-regenerator pack. "Why not? I'll just be twiddling my thumbs until the storm is over, probably getting on Steinberg's nerves.

"I won't have anything useful to accomplish until most of the dust gets cleared around the modules, then I'll go up the Spine and reconnect the power reactor, get the experimental stations up and running. If one of us has to stay behind, it might as well be me. I could use the vacation."

He unseated his helmet and pulled it off, extending it toward Keefer. "Go ahead, take this one. They're interchangeable."

Keefer hesitated, looking at the other man, who avoided his gaze. "I don't buy it, Bruce. What's the real reason?"

Pchanskii, looking bemused, leaned back against the wall in silence, just watching, letting them work it out between themselves.

Vickery rolled his eyes and sighed. "Do you think *I* want to be the one who comes marching in with Pchanskii and says, 'We've all been fooled, boy do I feel silly. Nyuk nyuk nyuk'? No, sir, Commissioner—the honor is all yours."

Keefer accepted the helmet, but stared down at the reflective faceplate in his hands. He thought of Allan, even his cool but tolerable relationship with the boy's mother. To avoid looking at Vickery's flushed, cold face, Keefer finally removed his shattered helmet, set it aside, then seated Vickery's over his head. He thought of the approaching storm, of *Schiaparelli* waiting in the Labyrinth, of the long journey back. He swallowed to clear his dry throat.

"The AI can take care of most of it, but won't I need help navigating the rover back to base?" Keefer asked.

Pchanskii held up his broad hands. "The *dvas* were trained on all the equipment necessary for the base. All the equipment. We tested the first long-distance rover and the putt-putt before any of you humans came down to stay. And I do know where the base is."

Vickery nodded. "You both better get going before the storm hits. It's a couple hours drive back."

"The storm started half an hour ago," Pchanskii said. "The driving will be rough, but I can handle it. The storm won't bother me too much. Let me start my prebreathe so I can accompany you back to the rover." He left them with the pregnant *dva* women as he went off to the pressure chamber.

Keefer and Vickery stood staring at each other in the enameled white medical lab, at a loss for words.

Wearing his durable overall, Pchanskii opened the hidden outer door, sliding the rock covering aside. A blast of wind from the storm knocked Keefer off balance. Pchanskii grabbed him.

"I'm going to hold on to you," Pchanskii shouted, heaving deep breaths in the thinner air outside. "Buddy system. Don't get lost!" He tied a utility line from Keefer's pack around his waist with quick, jerking motions of his thick fingers and clipped the end to one of the eyes on Keefer's suit. Keefer checked one last time to make sure his new helmet had sealed properly. Breath echoed in his helmet, nearly drowned out by the sounds of the wind.

Slowly feeling their way forward with each step, they trudged out into the scouring dust. Red-brown particles plastered his faceplate, like a blizzard of rust powder. He heard hissing like a hailstorm in his ears.

Pchanskii jerked him forward, pulling him across the soft ground. Keefer kept plodding, unable to see anything. Though he had spent the past hour depressurizing, the *dva* doctor had to take a moment to acclimate himself—Keefer hoped Pchanskii did not faint from the exertion. That would leave them both stranded out there, drowning in red dust. . . .

The tangled walls of Noctis Labyrinthus rose around them in indecipherable angles, barely glimpsed through the dust. Keefer could see nothing but a rusty blur in front of his eyes. He stepped with one foot, then the other, setting his boot down in the shifting soil. He had no idea how Pchanskii could tell where he was going. Keefer tried not to think, not to worry. He kept his feet moving, holding on to Pchanskii with one gloved hand, checking periodically to be sure the line connecting them remained fastened.

Somehow, they reached the rover. Finally. It appeared out of nowhere, armored white and squared off, waiting for them. Keefer stared at it.

Fine red dust had piled up around the base where the telescoping legs had lowered the vehicle to its most stable configuration. A meter-high drift climbed up the windward side. But the powerful methane engine could break free; the sea-urchin legs could crawl over the terrain. *Schiaparelli* was intact and safe.

The man and the *dva* clambered through the sphincter airlock, sealing the storm outside. As the chamber slowly pressurized, Pchanskii visibly relaxed. Keefer rubbed clinging dust away from his faceplate, but it would be a long time before the air was thick enough for him to breathe unaided. The *dva* doctor gave them both a cursory dusting with the built-in vacuums on the walls, sucking away the worst of the dust, then they entered the main cabin of the rover.

"Lousy weather, isn't it?" Pchanskii said, then seated himself behind the controls.

RACHEL DYCEK

THE SITUATION IN WHICH Rachel found herself seemed more ludicrous than frustrating.

She had reached the relative safety of the *dva* settlement after having survived the depredations of Boris Tiban, the birth of Cora Marisovna's baby, and the buffeting of the storm—but she had no way to get inside, no means to communicate with the *dva* miners. Now, just a few feet from rescue, she was stuck.

Percival waited patiently for her to decide the next course of action.

Rachel guided the rover to the clustered *dva* shelters, flashing the rover's spotlights and hoping some of the augmented people huddled inside would notice. With no suit, she could not go outside to contact them, nor did she have any other means to knock on their door, short of crashing through the walls with her rover.

But *Percival*'s AI pilot had much finer control than that, she realized. After waiting, sweating, and fidgeting for ten minutes, Rachel finally told the rover to ease forward and thump against the wall near the entrance. "Make noise," she said, "but cause no damage." It was difficult to be gentle with a huge long-distance vehicle, but the AI dutifully followed her instructions.

"Reverse by one meter or so, then thump again," she said.

The rover skittered backward, rocking with the tiptoe motion, then nudged the wall. She felt the vibration through the hull. Overkill, she thought, but effective.

In the swirling wind, a flash of light spilled from an opening door, and the shapes of two *dvas* emerged from their structure. Rachel slumped backward in relief.

The *dvas* saw the rover and its piercing spotlights, then they scrambled toward her, ducking their heads against the blast of wind.

Which led to her second problem.

Since Rachel could not go outside to communicate with them, she had to leave them some kind of message. Outside, the *dvas* were waiting for her, snooping around the rover. How long would they stand unprotected in the storm before fleeing back to shelter?

Taking one of the electronic clipboards from the sample cabinet, she switched to Cyrillic mode—since all the *dvas* could read Russian—and typed a message.

MUST USE YOUR TRANSMITTING APPARATUS. EMERGENCY!!! I HAVE NO SUIT. PLEASE PLACE TRANSMITTER INSIDE AIRLOCK.
--COMMISSIONER DYCEK.

She squeezed her hands against the clean plastic surface with a silent prayer, and then fed the clipboard through the gripping membrane of the sphincter airlock, releasing it to the outside as she waited for the *dvas* to find it. The sound of the storm redoubled.

A few moments later she heard someone moving around beside the oval of the airlock, then a heavy pounding against the hull—much like Boris Tiban had used to terrify them. But this was a signal of acknowledgment, not harassment. Rachel looked out the damaged front windowport, trying to see what was happening.

A gangly *dva* man appeared in front of the rover, his long patchy hair thrashing about in the wind. He waved the clipboard and raised his arm in the air to get her attention. She flashed the headlights at him. He disappeared into the mining shelter again, while the other *dvas* waited outside, making vaguely reassuring gestures at her through the patched front windowport.

Through all the murk Rachel could discern few details of the *dva* station: simply the door, a curved wall, scattered boulders, slag heaps from tailings and processing waste. Much of the real settlement was hidden within tunnels carved below the surface. She had not been out to visit this particular habitation in several years, but now the *dvas* had earned her thanks forever.

A short time later Rachel watched the splash of light again as the first man came back out of the shelter, carrying a bundle of equipment under his arm, wrapped in sheets of scrap plastic to protect it from the iron-oxide dust. Rachel heard noises near the airlock again, then a pounding to signal he was ready. She released the airlock membrane, and a bulge appeared in the center. A narrow split folded around the boxlike, plastic-wrapped components of the settlement's portable transmitter/receiver.

Rachel had no idea how well she could transmit through the rover walls, even with the portable unit. Boris Tiban had smashed not only *Percival*'s antenna, but the external transmitting components of her own communications system. But she had to try.

Rachel strung the whiplike antenna up against the windowport and taped it flat with strips of the metal tape. She hoped it would be good enough for her transmission to reach Lowell Base—but the metallic dust and the storm's static would make communication difficult.

She jacked the unit into *Percival*'s control panel, then transmitted on the distress frequency, tying in to the normal Lowell Base channel as well. Perhaps, due to vagaries in the storm, some of the more distant bases would hear her instead, and pass along the message.

"Hello? Hello?" In her last months of apathy and depression she herself had left the Lowell Base communications room unattended often enough. She could only pray the people remaining behind were not so lax in their duties. "Emergency. Do you read me?"

After a moment, the video flatscreen on the portable unit swirled with multicolored static that clustered into a fuzzed silhouette. The narrow features grew distinct enough for her to make out Evrani's face.

"Dr. Evrani—can you hear me?"

"Commissioner Dycek!" His words splattered and popped with discharges in the air. "Where are you? Where is our rover?"

"I am safe. I am attempting to return, but I will need assistance," she said, plunking down her words one statement at a time. "I am at a *dva* mining facility at the base of Pavonis Mons. I cannot leave the rover. My suit is damaged."

"What has happened? Is our rover still functioning?"

"Evrani, please put Commissioner Keefer on. I wish to speak to him."

"Commissioner Keefer is not here!" Evrani's sharp voice was clear through the static, as if his whining tone could puncture even the vicious Martian winds. "He went out to look for you with Mr. Vickery. They took our only other rover, and now they too are lost in the storm! They are hours overdue, and no one has heard from them. It is all your fault!"

Rachel sighed in exasperation. "Shut up, Evrani, and listen! This is important. I need—"

On the screen Evrani was pushed aside as another man took his place: Beludi al-Somak, the other meteorologist, the competent one. "Dr. Evrani and I are watching the progress of the storm, Commissioner. The other people in the base are quite secure inside. Please tell us what you need and when we should expect you back."

"The most important thing is I'll need a suit when I return, otherwise I can't do much of anything," Rachel said, "a spare suit. Mine has been . . . damaged. I will start driving *Percival* now, but it will take me most of today and this evening to return. Now, please listen very carefully. I have found some surviving *adins*. Four of them, living at the top of Pavonis Mons."

She paused just long enough to watch the surprise on al-Somak's face, but not long enough for him to interrupt her. "And I have with me a newborn baby. A human baby, born of an *adin* mother. She gave birth inside this rover. I am pressurized and safe for the time being, but I must bring the baby back to Lowell Base for medical attention. I will need another suit when I get there. Do you understand?"

"Yes, I understand . . . but can you give us more details?" al-Somak said. "Has Commissioner Keefer contacted you?"

"No!" she said. "Just be ready when I arrive back at the base. We'll need milk, a soft blanket, absorbent cloth, and some kind of a crib."

Rachel switched off the portable transmitter with a click like teeth snapping together. As she disconnected the apparatus from the rover's control panels, she realized she was grinning from ear to ear.

She wrapped the transmitter/receiver in the sheets of plastic again, though fine red-orange dust had already found its way into the folds and crannies. She returned the apparatus to the waiting *dvas* outside, who scurried back into shelter, waving her off and bidding her farewell.

Only after she had departed and gone several kilometers from the mining station did she realize that the *dvas* had not thought to return her electronic message pad.

Rachel's body felt like a mass of knotted chains. Though *Percival*'s AI did most of the work driving the rover, Rachel sat with gritted teeth and clenched fists in a strange mixture of apprehension and boredom. Hour after hour, she sat, occasionally unbuckling and going back to check on the baby. She drank some packaged juice from the food supplies, then diluted it heavily and gave a few sips to the baby just for the benefit of the calories. She dabbed a damp rag on her face and eyes. She changed the dressing on her torn hand and finally succumbed to the hurt by swallowing three painkiller tabs.

Rachel slept for several hours as if she had fallen

into a coma, until *Percival*'s insistent beeping brought her out of a groggy nondream—to stare at the waning fuel gauge. The rover had already gone farther than all design safety factors allowed, and the methane engines were nearly depleted.

Rachel could do nothing but continue, and hope she did not find herself stranded out on the plain.

Percival did its best, proceeding at half speed against the strong winds. The digital compass functioned intermittently, and used averages of the fluctuating readings to keep pointing in the right direction. Upon finding the *dva* mining camp, the AI pilot had been able to reset its perception of where it was on the planet, and had modified its guess of the best course for returning to Lowell Base.

As twilight came, turning the murk of the storm to a dark and bruised purple, the methane engine began to cough and sputter. *Percival* triggered a silent alarm, which Rachel read, white-lipped.

The rover lurched, then proceeded smoothly again with a rumbling patter of legs. Before long, the vehicle would be gasping for methane fumes. The gauge had long since registered dead empty.

Finally, when the sharp ridge of the Spine provided a shelter from the storm, chopping the winds in half like a saw blade, Rachel could get her bearings more clearly. *Percival* somehow found the will to move faster. Darkness had already fallen, and she hoped someone was still watching for her.

Rachel felt the strength and adrenaline drain out of her as she made out the lights and the rounded shapes of the modules of Lowell Base, glowing greenish-yellow through the translucent walls of the greenhouse dome and the mechanic shelters.

With eyes slitted from weariness and mental exhaustion, Rachel breathed shallowly of the cold air in the cabin. Though she had sponged it off, her hand felt as if it had petrified from the frozen blood and mucus after Cora Marisovna had given birth. Even with the bandages, her torn palm still oozed, and the blood-stained control panels looked like a murder had occurred in the driver's seat.

As she neared the grotto overhang for parking the excursion vehicles, the engine hiccoughed again. *Percival* staggered like a drunken man on its myriad legs, but toiled ahead. Brilliant perimeter lights seemed warm and welcoming.

Rachel saw a figure bound out of the parking shelter—bulky and strong, but wearing no environment suit. In a sudden burst of terror, she thought of Boris Tiban returning to kill her just as she had reached safety!

But then the shape disappeared, and she couldn't decide if she was being paranoid or merely hallucinating.

She released the sphincter airlock when somebody pounded on it, but instead of a rescuer cycling inside, only a packaged environment suit came through the airtight membrane. Was it Keefer himself, or Bruce Vickery? Surely they had returned by now; it had been another half day. Evrani and al-Somak must have passed along her message. But why did they refuse to come inside *Percival*?

She unwrapped the new suit and slipped her legs inside, drawing it up to her waist, switching on the implanted heater wires before she even got it up to her chest and slid her arms inside. She felt the warmth pounding against her, like a slow massage. Once she got back inside the base, she would see to it that the baby was tended and fed, and then she could fall into a deep, exhausted sleep in her own quarters.

Cora's baby would be safe. She would survive! Finally, Rachel could relax with a greater fulfillment than she remembered in ages.

With her helmet sealed, she placed the baby—still safely encased in Rachel's damaged environment suit—in a small airtight cargo container. But she had to haul the baby into the base.

Percival heaved itself into the garage overhang where it could recharge its batteries and fuel tanks. The legs retracted with a shuddering sigh of compressed gas and lubricant. Cautiously, moving with extreme weariness, Rachel gathered up the cargo box containing the baby, and she pushed her way through the sphincter airlock, outside.

Standing before her with heavily muscled arms crossed over his chest, the burly *dva* Dr. Pchanskii waited for her with a bemused expression on his scarred face. He looked at her in silence for a moment, delighted by her reaction.

Rachel stumbled back against the rover's hull, nearly dropping the box that contained the baby. But Pchanskii caught it and eased the container to the soft ground. Words tangled up inside Rachel's throat, then evaporated.

DMITRI PCHANSKII

THE CHAMBER IN THE communications center was called a "privacy booth," but the enclosing walls felt like a tiny coffin around Dmitri Pchanskii's bulky frame.

The echo screen in front of him seemed too small to capture anything more than his surgically distorted face, giving him no room at all to gesture and move his hands—and Pchanskii liked to emphasize his words as he spoke, with a wave here and a shaking fist there, leaning forward to address his audience on a more intimate level, or spreading his arms wide to encompass the whole world. Instead, the cramped image would make him look like a monster, a real Martian, when he broadcast back to Earth. But he could see no way to fix it, so he would have to take advantage of the shock value. He would get only one chance to use the tactic of surprise.

Well, he thought, *there's nothing for it*. He had to make his best attempt at telling everything to the newsnets, the governments of the Sovereign Republics, UNSA. And he planned to do it all at once, in a canned statement. That would give them something to talk about for a while. They might be stunned enough at his very presence that the politicians could be tricked into listening before their minds petrified again.

Now that the *dva* scheme had been found out, Pchanskii was anxious to go public. It felt as if a great weight had lifted from him. The *dvas* could go about the business of living again, without the difficult camouflage tactics. The *dvas* at the mining outposts and metal smelters and pumping stations no longer needed to pretend they knew nothing of the *dva* oasis. They no longer needed to steal equipment and smuggle it over to Noctis Labyrinthus.

But Pchanskii could ruin everything if he slipped up in this initial transmission. He would offer no excuses in his open videoletter. Editing the message would be time-consuming and tedious, but he had already decided to take as much time as necessary. Commissioner Keefer had allowed him that much at least. Pchanskii could make his best case, with no interference from the others.

He had been fascinated to watch as the dynamic changed in Lowell Base over the past day or so. Since the return of Rachel Dycek and the miraculous *adin* baby, Pchanskii had been in quarantine for the most part, cramped in an airlock with a few old books brought by the Lowell Base personnel, so he could read and wait as the air pressure was slowly increased, allowing him to adapt to the conditions inside the inflatable base.

Amelia Steinberg, the wavy-haired maintenance supervisor, grumbled about how inconvenient it was to have one of the anterior airlock chambers co-opted by a fugitive and a thief, but her attitude merely amused Pchanskii. Every chance he could, he waved at her suited team members through the viewport of the airlock, but they ignored him and continued digging out from the storm.

Pchanskii tried to read one of the books, but he could not concentrate. Instead, he made plans and notes for his announcement speech to UNSA and the world.

During the harrowing trip back from Noctis Labyrinthus, Jesús Keefer had spent much of the time detailing everything that had changed in the past year at Lowell Base, in the overall terraforming activities, even in Earth politics.

When they returned with *Schiaparelli* at the height of the storm, Pchanskii and his news had been greeted with awe and amazement—but Dr. Dycek had already stolen part of his thunder with her intriguing message that she had found *adin* survivors and was even now returning with a newborn baby. It seemed impossible to him, and Pchanskii had laughed out loud to see Keefer's utter disbelief for the second time in two days.

Could the *adins* and their crackpot revolutionary leader Boris Tiban have implemented a subversive plan as wild as his own? How could the *adins*—prison-camp refugees with limited resources, no technical facilities, and no special training—have succeeded in reproducing themselves? The first-phase humans were simple exiled criminals, yet somehow they had accomplished Pchanskii's goal even before the *dvas* did. When Dr. Dycek had told her story, though, explaining that the *adin* pregnancy had been an accident, Pchanskii could not keep himself from chuckling, partly with relief, partly because of the irony.

And yet, he had to admire the *adins* instead of resenting what they represented. The *adins* were wild cards, like the first explorers, trailblazers, and trappers to push their way into the Siberian wilderness. The *dvas*, on the other hand, were the actual pioneers, the next wave of settlers in a hostile virgin land, those hopefuls who went of their own free will and expected to stay there, to make it into a home.

The triple dose of shocking news—the secret *dva* settlement, the rediscovery of the *adin* survivors, and the first baby born on Mars—would throw the newsnets into such a frenzy that the uproar over Pchanskii would be only part of the confusion. If Dr. Dycek had indeed taken away some of his glory, she had also mitigated the controversy he would have to endure by himself. Pchanskii felt glad the Earth-Mars time delay would make it impossible for newsnet reps to inundate him with realtime questions he did not want to answer. He decided to enjoy his good humor while he could.

Mannfred Rotlein would love it. The Volga German lawyer would immediately target his audiences, select the appropriate interviewers, release the best photo images. Before the grinding wheels of governmental bureaucracy could decide what to do with their outrage at having been duped, Rotlein would already have won the case in the public's eyes. Pchanskii wished he could be there himself, but his work was still on Mars.

Pchanskii smiled in the privacy booth, still trying to formulate the best way to introduce himself and explain what he had done. Dr. Dycek insisted that she be able to add a statement of her own to the message, supporting the *dva* efforts. Commissioner Keefer himself intended to make concluding remarks—possibly supportive, if the new commissioner knew what was politically expedient. Showing solidarity on Mars would likely place him in the best light, but no one could second-guess how the bureaucrats would react.

Pchanskii heard others stirring in the control center outside the privacy booth, probably whispering about him, wondering why it was taking him so long. Pchanskii didn't mind when people talked behind his back—at least that meant he had their attention.

He could not wait much longer. No mention of the startling developments had yet been broadcast to Earth. Not even Captain Rubens in the transfer vehicle at the fueling station on Phobos knew anything had happened. But then, during a Martian dust storm, communications frequently blacked out for extended periods of time.

The storm was fading though, dissipating much more quickly than the two meteorologists had expected. Evrani and al-Somak used that as evidence that they needed to do more tests, more experiments, put up more satellites. Other people at the base claimed it was evidence that weathermen didn't know what they were doing.

Stepping on the ACTIVATE button, Pchanskii saw the red light wink on. The cameras began recording. He drew in a deep, thick breath, then spilled his entire story into the tapes.

When Dmitri Pchanskii went to see her, Rachel Dycek was alone with Cora's baby in the medical module. The *dva* doctor moved slowly in the heavy, hot air.

Commissioner Keefer had given Pchanskii free access to the base, despite a few sharp protests. Amelia Steinberg in particular seemed certain that Pchanskii would stuff his pockets with all sorts of precious equipment if he wasn't watched carefully. But with Bruce Vickery remaining behind at the *dva* hideout, and after Pchanskii had spent many hours with Keefer in the rover during the storm, the new commissioner seemed to trust the *dva* doctor. To a certain extent, at least.

Her gray-streaked hair freshly gel-washed and combed, her jumpsuit changed, her injured hand wrapped in clean white bandages, Rachel Dycek stood tending the baby. She hummed to herself as she bent over the little girl. One of Steinberg's assistants had rigged up a protective chamber so they could keep the *adin* infant under low pressure if necessary.

But the baby was healthy and normal, if a bit traumatized by the long ordeal inside an environment suit on the rover's floor. Pchanskii, with his medical knowledge, had checked the baby himself. Wistfully, he thought of the pregnant *dva* women, Bebez and Catherine, back in the tunnels. He hoped their children would be as healthy as this unlikely survivor. Three of the *dva* women had already experienced miscarriages after their attempts at insemination from the dwindling frozen sperm supplies. He frowned, but then dismissed the expression from his stiff face.

When Pchanskii stood at the threshold of the module, Dr. Dycek turned to look at him. A slide show of exaggerated human expressions played across her face.

"I have finished recording my message for Earth," Pchanskii said before she could greet him or rebuke him. "You may want to view it before you add your own comments."

He drummed his numb fingertips on the structural braces that reinforced the wall. "By the way, Doctor, thank you for the support you've shown me, your high opinion of me and my capabilities—both before our avalanche and now. I'm sorry I didn't exactly follow your expectations, but I hope you understand. Think of me as the prodigal son."

Dycek seated herself on one of the foam chairs next to a clean table. She pushed a rolling tray of surgical equipment out of the way against the module wall.

"Perhaps you don't realize what you did to me with your farce, Dr. Pchanskii," she said. She seemed to be fighting it, but a coldness continued to creep into her words. "That was the last straw in a whole sequence of last straws. After losing you and all my best *dvas* to something as stupid as a careless avalanche, what was the point? I stopped doing useful work around here, and UNSA quickly sent Keefer to replace me. My whole life dried up."

She raised her eyebrows and finally met his gaze. "Did you know that part of the reason I went out into the storm a few days ago was to kill myself? Everybody suspects that, I think, but no one is talking about it. It's likely I wouldn't have gone through with it after all, but if I hadn't found the *adins* when I did . . ." She shook her head.

"But now, all at once, so many things have changed. The *adins* are still alive. Cora Marisovna has had a baby! You *dvas* were not killed after all. You have built your new world and made it possible for your own descendants to follow you. It is like a masquerade with everyone flinging their masks aside at midnight."

She sighed. "I just don't know how to react to you." She turned her attention back to the baby, but Pchanskii had already seen the tears welling in her eyes.

"Maybe I should hate you for what you put me through in order to accomplish your purposes, but how can I fault what you have done? It surpasses everything I had planned for the *dvas*. I was always very proud of you, Dmitri Pchanskii, but now look at you—and look at this!" She gestured to Cora Marisovna's daughter. "I have been vindicated in everything. What more could I ask?"

Before Pchanskii could comment, the intercom screen flashed to life with its accompanying attention tone. The angular face of Amelia Steinberg appeared, speaking through an environment suit.

"Hey, Commissioner Dycek! You'd better get your butt down here to the main airlock. One of your monsters showed up on our doorstep. Looks hurt pretty bad, I think, so bring your kit." Steinberg turned away from the camera and signed off.

Dycek froze in confusion for just a moment, but she lurched into motion as Pchanskii headed for the door. Had one of the *dvas*, somehow injured during the storm, made it to the base? His large strides pulled him ahead of her, but she ran after. "Wait for me, dammit! You'll have to suit up, too—or else take an hour to depressurize."

Convinced the victim was a wounded *dva* messenger, Pchanskii wanted to go outside to the hurt "monster" as soon as they arrived, and damn the prebreathe! But even with his *dva* adaptations the sudden pressure drop would disorient him, maybe make him pass out or blind him temporarily. "Hurry up then, Doctor."

When they reached the suiting-up area and the equipment room inside the primary airlock, Rachel hauled out Bruce Vickery's spare suit from his cubicle and helped Pchanskii cram his big *dva* body into it. Dycek slithered into her suit with the ease of long practice and returned to finish clipping his helmet down, powering up his chemical oxygen-regenerator backpack.

"Hurry up then, Doctor," Dycek tossed his words back at him with just a trace of sarcasm and shouldered into the airlock with him.

Pchanskii breathed and listened to the echo inside the confining helmet. He felt stupid and clumsy and *human* inside the bulky wrapping, as if his *dva* adaptations had been for naught.

Outside under the pale Martian sunlight, he saw that Steinberg and her companions had dragged their discovery close to the airlock. Even now, they bent over the body like children at a museum exhibit.

Steinberg stood up as the two of them emerged from the lock. Dust puffed around her booted feet as she strode to them. "We found it tossed up against the side of the maintenance module," she said. "Jan thought he heard a pounding outside, but we didn't find anyone else. This one hasn't been conscious long enough to do anything. Do you want me to go look for footprints, or what?"

Pchanskii stared down at the monstrously distorted features, radical adaptations of the nose, ears, eyes, and face that made his own *dva* surgeries look like mere cosmetic changes. An *adin*, a woman.

"That's Cora Marisovna!" Dr. Dycek said. "What happened?"

Pchanskii looked at the bloodied bruises around her face, dark spots on her arms and swollen back, her torn and stained jumpsuit. Scratches and contusions covered her exposed skin, looking garish under the polymer coating.

"Might have been caught in a rockfall or something," Steinberg said with a shrug. "How else could it have gotten so smashed up?"

Pchanskii shook his head. No one else seemed to see the obvious. "This wasn't caused by any avalanche," he said. "She's been beaten. Badly beaten."

Barely conscious, Cora stirred. A single dry word hissed out of her mouth. "Boris. . ." she said.

STROGANOV

HE HELD OUT HIS HAND to Nastasia as they stood
in the dim sunlight of morning. Together, they watched
the last tatters of the dust storm fade toward the south
as the system followed the downhill slope of atmospheric pressure with the changing seasons.

"Beautiful, and frightening," Stroganov said, not
really expecting an answer. Nastasia merely nodded
and stared. Her eyes were bright beneath the thick
protective lashes, the sheltering brows.

The panorama of Mars spread out below them, as
vast as the future; but only the two of them stood there
to witness it. "Come, it is time to go."

When Nastasia finally took his hand, Stroganov
squeezed tightly, trying to send her a silent message
that everything would be all right, a strength and
caring that could be felt even through her deadened,
polymerized skin.

They turned their backs on the caves of Pavonis
Mons where the *adins* had lived alone and undisturbed
for years and years. Then they set off.

The stoic stone faces of historical rebels frowned, as
if disappointed with them for forsaking Boris's dream.
Stroganov was abandoning them, leaving the empty
lava tubes in search of something else.

During the enforced solitude of the storm, Stroganov
had spent hours squinting in the dim light far back in
the tunnels, staring at the words he had scratched onto
the walls, year after year in a desperate effort to
preserve the history of the *adins*. He read none of the
words again, having no desire to relive the years of
exile; he simply mourned abandoning so many of his
thoughts, his philosophies . . . his stories. Of the *adins,*
only Stroganov had bothered to keep a record of their
lives.

Someday he would return here, when the world had changed and their place in it was more secure. Dr. Dycek and others from Lowell Base would come and read everything he had written. They would photograph the scrawled diary on the smooth walls. His writings would be published and dissected by scholars, other teachers of history; his grammar would be criticized, his metaphors misunderstood. Somehow, that frightened him. He had no time to mark corrections or reword sentences. He had to be satisfied with the sloppiness he had allowed during times when he thought no one but himself would ever read the account.

But if he faltered now, hesitated long enough to rework just a few of the written passages, Stroganov knew he would continue to find excuses—because remaining up on the Pavonis caldera was the easiest thing to do, if not the wisest.

With Dr. Dycek taking Cora, with Boris disappearing during the storm, Stroganov had looked around their empty home with a sense of closure. This phase of their lives seemed over now. Remaining in the isolation decreed by Boris served no purpose.

"You no longer have to hide," Dr. Dycek had told the *adins* when she sat in their tunnels. "Just because you have adaptations to survive rugged conditions does not mean you *require* rugged conditions!"

Now that Boris had left them, Stroganov and Nastasia no longer needed to keep hiding. They would listen to no more of his constant saber rattling. It was time for Stroganov and Nastasia to reenter the world.

Nastasia, always amenable, agreed readily to Stroganov's suggestion and followed wherever he led her.

He had emerged from the tunnels with her, looking at the landscape of Pavonis remade by the storm. Fresh dust had settled into the rough edges on the caldera slope like a coat of rust. The statue faces were caked with powdery red-brown snow, which Stroganov lovingly brushed away with his fingers. Nastasia helped him, and they spent the morning restoring the sculptures. Stroganov was saddened that he would never be able to finish his new monument to Nikolas—but someday he might find the time and the energy.

Finally, he had no more excuses to delay.

The two of them had little to carry with them, only a few old packaged supplies and worn, barely functional equipment that was nearly two decades old. The *adin* caves were empty. Nikolas was dead, Cora and Boris both gone. Stroganov was confident they could scavenge food and water along the way.

"Come, Nastasia," he said. "We must leave here."

Her *adin* eyes widened with fear. "Are they still after me? Do we need to flee again?"

Stroganov shook his head. "No, we are safe together. Nobody is after you anymore. You don't have to be afraid. We are going to go back to . . . some friends."

"Are they good Russians?" she asked.

Stroganov smiled, having no idea which *dvas* or humans they might encounter. "Yes, I am sure they are."

"Good," Nastasia said, nodding, "then they will be glad to see me."

He led her down the slope. They set an easy pace, recalling Dr. Dycek's admonition to adapt gradually to the increased pressure. It might take them days to complete their descent; they would go only as fast as comfort would allow.

After a time, Nastasia began to sing an old Russian song, and Stroganov picked up the tune.

They slept twice out in the open of a deep Martian night, clinging to each other for warmth and staring up at the occasional streaks of shooting stars. On the morning of the third day, they reached the base of the massive volcano. Descending a sheared-off cliff, they set off across the Tharsis Plain, following the long silvery pipeline that extended from the core of Pavonis toward the human base hundreds of kilometers away. Stroganov and Nastasia rested in the volcano's shadow, ate feathery algae they found growing in sheltered pockets, sucked on dirty buried ice for their water and spat the sand grains from their mouths.

As they descended, Stroganov feared they would have difficulty breathing in the thick stew of air Boris had repeatedly decried. But it wasn't so bad. The *adins* were made to be resilient. Boris had exaggerated the entire problem. Stroganov chuckled, wondering at himself for being surprised, annoyed for having believed Boris so completely.

During the bright afternoon, with the small white sun gleaming through an olive-green sky, he looked across the bleak landscape to see where the pipeline intersected another, where a cluster of dwellings surrounded the pumping station. He realized that this must be the place Boris and Nikolas had attacked.

Stroganov swallowed his uneasiness. It was a time for changes, and he had to attempt a gesture as dramatic as the violent one Boris had made—but more meaningful. He could do things differently, because not all of the *adins* were like Boris.

He paused, shading his eyes as he looked toward the squalid buildings. Nastasia fidgeted beside him. "Is that where we are going? A peasant village? Will they welcome us?"

"Yes, that is our destination," he said. "They are expecting us, I think."

The two of them continued, lone *adins* marching across the windswept desert. As they neared the *dva* settlement, Stroganov saw figures working by the pipes and the pumping station. The *dvas* stopped moving, staring toward the approaching strangers. At a signal Stroganov could not hear, the three *dvas* dropped what they were doing and rushed to grab implements to protect themselves.

Stroganov felt a great sadness inside him. But he could not blame the *dvas* for their reaction. *Boris, look what you have done!* He and Nastasia continued walking until they had reached the settlement. He held his hands out in a gesture of peace.

The ground was churned where the pipe had burst, spilling water that froze the mud into cement, then sublimed into the air. A few chunks of dust-covered ice continued to waft fine tendrils of steam into the air.

Stroganov paused, gathering his courage, but Nastasia pulled him eagerly ahead.

The *dva* survivors had dismantled an entire section of the pipeline, sealing the water flow farther up-line. After the storm, the *dvas* were busy outside, hammering flat the torn metal, slathering them with steel sealant, then reassembling the repaired portions.

They had apparently been at work a long time, and had accomplished only a part of what they needed to do. One *dva* woman had given up on her labors and packaged new equipment and spare parts in a bulging carrier on her back, as if she were about to set off in another direction on a days-long hike.

A burly *dva* man stood his ground as Stroganov and Nastasia walked up to him. Behind the man another woman glared warily at the strangers. Stroganov pretended not to notice their hostility, but he no longer remembered how to smile with his altered face.

"Haven't you *adins* done enough damage already?" the *dva* man said. In his hand he held a long digging implement with a wicked curved point at the end of a plastic pole. Stroganov could see the man's body tense and prepare to strike.

He noticed the hardened mounds of two fresh graves in the lee of the main Quonset dwelling structure, where they had been protected from the storm. Shifting his gaze, he also spotted a long wrapped bundle tossed alongside a shed. Without asking, he knew it must be Nikolas.

"We come to you in peace, with sincere apologies for what our comrades have done to you."

The *dva* man shifted uneasily. "What do you want?"

Stroganov took a deep breath. "We would like to bury our brother Nikolas." He placed his hand on Nastasia's arm and turned to look at the wreckage of the pipeline. He blinked his heavily lashed *adin* eyes.

"Then, we would like to offer you our help."

RACHEL DYCEK

SEEING CORA'S RAGGED BREATHING, her wide, gasping mouth, Rachel swung out her med kit, checking over the woman's injuries as she lay on the ground outside Lowell Base. She found a great deal of moderate trauma, heavy bruising, cuts and scrapes, maybe a cracked rib or two. She would not be able to tell if there had been severe internal damage until she got Cora into the medical module. "Dr. Pchanskii, would you help me get her inside, please?"

Silent and obviously in turmoil, Pchanskii cradled the *adin* woman as gently as he could, dragging her toward the airlock chamber. "We'll have to take at least two or three hours to pressurize," Pchanskii pointed out. "Otherwise the air inside will kill her even faster than her injuries would."

Steinberg shook her head with a sour expression. "Man, don't tell me you're gonna block our main airlock half the morning! We've got work to do—"

"It can't be helped, Amelia," Rachel said, ready to punch her own fist through Steinberg's faceplate, just as Pchanskii had done to Keefer.

"Some people have really fucked up priorities," Steinberg said in disgust, then waved to her team members to follow as they trudged off to the maintenance sheds.

"Yes," Pchanskii muttered, "some people do."

From the med kit Rachel gave Cora some painkillers and a sedative to keep her calm as Pchanskii sealed the airlock—and they waited. Cora groaned at every spot they touched on her body. She had lost a great deal of blood, but they could replace it from the Lowell Base stores, once they got her inside. Despite her surgical adaptations, Cora Marisovna was still human inside.

The pressure in the chamber rose slowly, ramping up. Rachel considered just getting an environment suit for Cora so they could immediately take her to the medical module, but that would do no good, because Rachel still would not be able to check her over.

During the long wait, Rachel wondered what Boris Tiban was doing outside. He must be badly injured—she had seen the titanium staff plunge through his body. But he had survived enough to do this to Cora, and to bring her to the base, flaunting his anger. He was still out there.

She used her suit radio to contact the maintenance team outside. "Steinberg, I want you to keep your eyes open. There's still one *adin* man on the loose, who might try to cause some damage to the base."

"Let him try it, and I'll kick his butt all the way to Olympus Mons," she replied.

Rachel wasn't sure the maintenance engineer took the threat seriously enough.

After an hour Commissioner Keefer came to speak to them through the airlock, but he could not assist them in any way. Rachel found that it wasn't difficult to be civil to him, now that she understood him a little better—and she understood herself, too. Keefer had not come to Mars to grind her under his heel, to send her home in disgrace after all. He was just doing a job he enjoyed, releasing his own enthusiasm for Mars in a different way than she herself had.

By the time the pressure had risen sufficiently for Rachel and Pchanskii to remove their helmets and open the inner airlock door, a crowd of Lowell Base personnel had gathered to receive their first *adin* guest.

Inside the medical module Rachel watched the anesthesia wear off. She leaned over Cora's bedside like one of Stroganov's statues. Cora stirred and finally woke, looking groggy and uncertain of her surroundings. Blood had been pumped into her body, along with concentrated nutrient solutions. She had already endured the worst shock of pressure adaptation.

Groggy and hurting, Cora stared at Rachel with heavy, hooded eyes through the mesh of tough lashes. "You saved . . . my baby."

"Yes," Rachel said, whispering, "and now you'll be able to see her and touch her with your own hands. I'm sure she would like that. You're adapting to our normal pressure, just as I said you would."

"Boris," Cora said, choking on the word, "he is strong."

"I know," Rachel said, patting her shoulder with enough force to be sure Cora could feel it even through numb skin. "I think I must have made a mistake when I made him that way."

But Cora had already slipped back into unconsciousness.

Pchanskii came back to visit after several hours, but Rachel remained by Cora's side for the rest of the night, never allowing herself to sleep. One of the base's other doctors came in for his shift, checked everything, did the daily inventory of medical supplies, but Rachel alone tended her *adin* patient.

When Cora finally awoke early the next morning, she seemed stronger, realizing where she was, but confused as to how she had gotten there.

"When I drove off in the rover, you were beside Boris," Rachel said. "I thought you had killed him. You stabbed him with his staff."

Cora closed her eyes. "Boris moved," she said with a shudder. "I tried to help him up—but he turned on me. His anger was so strong."

Cora blinked and looked up at the ceiling, but she seemed to see something entirely different. "He hit me with his fist. He pounded me on the back of the head. I think he picked up a rock. The last thing I remember is curling up in the storm, and him kicking me and kicking me. . . ."

Rachel had seen that most of the severe bruises were clustered around Cora's abdomen.

"He was punishing me for giving birth. For not letting him kill his own baby." She stopped, and before she could ask other questions, Cora turned and noticed the little girl in her protective container, covered with standard-issue blankets from the base stores. She caught her breath and worked her elbows against the sheets to raise herself up. "My daughter. Can I touch her?"

"I'll bring her over to you," Rachel said. "Don't get up."

Cora lay back, satisfied, on her bunk. She winced as pain rippled through her. But she seemed to breathe more easily now. As Rachel rather clumsily picked the infant girl up from her blankets, the baby made mewling, crying noises. She gently deposited Cora's daughter into the waiting *adin* arms.

The mother stared down into her tiny girl's eyes, but the baby scrunched her face and began crying louder. Rachel wondered if Cora's fearsome features frightened the child, but Cora didn't appear to think of that. She kept staring at her child, making soft cooing noises until the baby quieted.

Rachel wished she had captured a video image of that. Cora and her baby would have worked a public relations miracle on Earth's newsnets in the face of the outcry Pchanskii's surprise announcement would create. She smiled.

A *thudding* noise came from outside. A sudden indentation appeared on the thin, flexible wall of the module before it vanished again.

Rachel jumped to her feet and looked around to see what had happened. The module snapped back into position.

Then a rapid series of large convex indentations bent into the wall, pressed from the outside, moving along the infirmary module's length. Someone was outside, pounding, hammering with fists.

Cora gasped out a whispered scream. "It is Boris!"

The glistening tip of the titanium staff plunged through the wall. The tough, flexible barrier stretched long and longer still, extremely resilient, until the metallic membrane finally surrendered and tore. The metal staff jabbed and pried around like a long claw trying to find some purchase. Air squealed as it fled the pressurized module.

Automatic alarms blared, deafening Rachel. Her ears popped with the sudden drop in pressure. The baby squalled uncontrollably. Cora Marisovna tried to wrestle herself into a sitting position on the infirmary bunk.

Boris's metal staff disappeared as he yanked it back out, leaving the ragged puncture to that fountained steaming air. Then fingers appeared in the hole, tough *adin* fingers poking through and *ripping*.

The screams of the baby, the roar of escaping air, and the clamor of alarms swallowed Rachel's words. "Stop it!" She lunged toward the opening, not knowing what to do but needing to stop Boris from causing further damage.

Boris Tiban pushed his distorted face close to the hole, fighting the out-rushing air so that he could gaze inside. His *adin* eyes widened as he saw Cora and the baby, then Rachel lunging toward him. He opened his mouth in a wordless snarl.

Without hesitating, Rachel pulled back her hand and struck with all her strength. She smashed him full in the face, crushing his flattened nose with the heel of her palm. She felt the satisfying impact jar her arm all the way to the shoulder.

Steaming blood spurted down his face, and Boris cried out in rage, backing away. Rachel could see him grasping his nose, then he leaped again toward the module wall.

Rachel looked about for some other weapon. Boris shoved his arm inside and snatched her wrist. She struggled, trying to yank herself free, but his blunt claws dug into her, dragging her toward the opening where she would suffocate.

With her free arm Rachel clutched at the table of medical equipment beside the wall. A box of plastic test tubes spilled and fell slowly, and the heartbeat diagnostic panel tipped over, but she was able to grab a hand-held surgical laser. With her thumb, she flicked it on.

The incision end glowed red. Rachel swung the cutting laser down, burning through the back of Boris Tiban's hand and slicing upward, ripping open half of his forearm. Smoke and the smell of burned flesh burst briefly into the air, then was sucked back out of the module as the air continued to roar out.

Boris howled and withdrew, but Rachel did not watch him run out of sight. She picked up a small can of polymer wound sealant and sprayed the stuff over the opening. Gummy material spurted across the seams, coagulating and filling the hole, hardening the instant it contacted the air.

Within a moment, Rachel had sealed the ragged opening, but the gray-pink patch began to pucker outward as the module's pressure continued to push against it. She emptied the entire can over the breach, then finally relaxed. They would have to patch it soon, but it would hold for now.

Cora was staring at her with a mixture of astonishment, horror, and pride. She held on to her baby protectively. The clamor of alarms continued.

Rachel felt tight inside, her entire body clenched. "I will not let Boris destroy my hope again," she said.

JESÚS KEEFER

WHEN THE ALARMS WENT OFF, Keefer was in the Lowell Base greenhouse dome, showing it off to Dmitri Pchanskii.

They stood next to each other, a trim, dark-haired man and a bearlike *dva*, listening to bright-eyed and self-assured Tam Smith describe the efforts of her agricultural section. Tam gave her lecture with the bubbling enthusiasm of a new arrival on Mars, someone who had not yet been jaded by the tedium of how slowly changes were wrought on a planetary scale. Keefer watched how she smiled, how her hands fluttered in birdlike movements, how she frequently looked back at the growing plants, as if they were all that mattered.

Keefer cracked his knuckles and wished he could see that kind of enthusiasm on Allan's face, at least some of the time. Perhaps he should stop expecting to see it. He realized he had never asked Allan what he himself was interested in.

As they walked along the groomed rows of plants, corn, soy beans, rice, Pchanskii compared the Lowell Base work to what the *dvas* had done. Tam glided along, nodding and listening, pointing out the various ways they had managed to compensate for the depressurization caused by the freak micrometeorite strike, which had traumatized the plants. She was confident the crops would recover. Tam had always impressed Keefer with her confidence.

Then alarm klaxons shrieked across the open intercom, and Tam looked with dismay up at the greenhouse dome, terrified of another meteor strike. Keefer whirled, disoriented and wishing he had Bruce Vickery beside him to help out in the emergency.

Steinberg's voice bellowed over the intercom. "Another breach, goddammit! We're responding. Should have it under control in a few minutes."

Keefer rushed to the wall-screen as he had seen Vickery do the time before, fumbling through tedious menus until he was finally able to track down a diagram of Lowell Base. He had to look at the key to identify the section flashing red. "Something's happened in the medical module."

"That's where the *adin* patient is," Pchanskii said.

Steinberg's voice broke back in after another moment. "Whaddya know! Looks like Dr. Dycek took care of it herself. The rupture is sealed."

Keefer toggled the intercom. "This is Commissioner Keefer. What is it? What happened?"

"She says that *adin* rebel attacked here. Boris whatsisname. Poked his spear right through the wall."

"Idiot!" Pchanskii muttered under his breath, and hunched forward to grumble at Keefer. "Tiban always made the Mars effort look like a mistake, long before the *dva* phase was launched. Because of him, everybody was suspicious of what we *dvas* might do if left to ourselves. I don't suppose the UNSA supplied you with shotguns?"

Keefer couldn't tell if the *dva* man was joking. "It conflicts with our charter," he said. "I wonder if they'd even function in the atmosphere anyway. We'd better get a couple of people suited up, though, in case we need to go outside."

Pchanskii hung his head and sighed, clenching his thick fist. "When I think of all the good people who died because of surgical failures, why did Tiban have to survive to cause so many problems? So many problems."

As if to offer an answer, a tall distorted silhouette of a man appeared on the other side of the translucent wall of the greenhouse dome.

"Look!" Tam shouted.

The pointed end of the staff poked and stretched

against the membrane of the greenhouse module with a rubbery sound until the sharp tip finally breached the containment. The staff ripped down as Boris hauled on his rod like a Cossack sword. He tore a wide swath that blew outward in a blast of instantly freezing steam from the humid pressurized air.

Boris Tiban stood in the opening, blown two steps backward from the force of the out-rushing air. He looked withered and hardened, vastly changed from the famous last transmission to Earth when he had killed the vice commander.

"You humans are so helpless and weak!" Boris shouted into the noise, then stood back to watch. "Mars does not want you here."

Keefer hammered his fist against the intercom as he lurched toward the door. "We need help in the greenhouse. Tiban's just attacked!"

Acting according to her training, Tam struggled toward the container of self-sealing patches mounted on the module door, though the rip looked far too large for simple patching. Keefer turned to help her.

Dmitri Pchanskii, however, bent low and sprinted across the dome floor, toward the ragged split. "I am not weak and helpless, Boris Tiban!" he said, shoving his head and shoulders through the tear. "And Mars *does* want me here!"

Struggling and unprotected, Pchanskii pushed his way out of the dome and onto the surface. He gasped and staggered from the extreme drop in pressure, clapped his hands to his head as if his eardrums had just ruptured, and seemed to be fighting waves of dizziness.

"Pchanskii!" Keefer shouted. The *dva* man, adapted to the high pressure inside the base, could not tolerate such a sudden and dramatic drop. But, with everything he had done, Pchanskii had shown his penchant for brash actions.

Heaving for breath in the thinning air and concentrating on his duty to protect the base itself, Keefer grabbed a stack of the patches from Tam. The two humans let the enormous gale of out-pouring air haul them toward the opening. Even in such a large confined space, the breathable atmosphere would be gone in only a few minutes unless they could patch it. He could not worry about Pchanskii now.

Outside, Boris Tiban whirled to take a look at the *dva* doctor, crouching in a defensive posture. Boris seemed startled to see someone emerge from the comfortable pressurized modules to confront him. Then, when he saw that his opponent was a *dva*, his confusion deepened.

Pchanskii hauled himself upright and strode toward Boris. "I have had enough of your stupid posturing!" he shouted, wheezing for breath and blinking his big eyes. A trickle of bright, flash-frozen blood sparkled at his surgically flattened ears.

Then Pchanskii dove into Boris, grappling with him. The two crashed to the ground in a curious slow-motion fall. A cloud of fresh iron-red dust deposited by the recent storm billowed up in the air.

Dmitri Pchanskii was larger than Boris and more muscular, but the unexpected and violent decompression had knocked him reeling and taken its toll. Boris Tiban was already injured, with an oozing puncture wound through his torso, a red splash across his face from a bloodied nose, and a burned slice through one hand and up his forearm. But Boris's *adin* surgery had given him more severe adaptations. He had lived longer and harder on Mars—and now he fought back.

With a silent grimace Pchanskii lifted Boris and slammed him down to the ground. Howling, Boris grabbed the *dva*'s leg and hauled up, toppling Pchanskii backward to the iron-oxide dirt. Still lying on the ground, he pummeled Pchanskii's rib cage with a meaty fist.

The *dva* doctor thrashed around and cracked his own skull against Boris's cheekbone. They both lurched, stunned for a moment, then Pchanskii picked himself up. He swung his fist wide to catch Boris in the jaw. The *adin*'s teeth clicked together, and Boris dropped forward onto all fours. Pchanskii came after him again.

Boris grabbed his titanium staff from the powdery dust and brought it up. The point clipped Pchanskii on his temple, which sprouted a pattern of blood that ran down his cheek. Pchanskii faltered, as if he had just remembered to feel pain, and Boris swung the staff overhead again like a club, smashing it down where the *dva*'s head met his shoulders. Pchanskii dropped to his knees with his eyes squeezed shut, as if he could no longer see. Blood poured from the wound in his temple, steaming through his black-and-silver beard.

Boris stepped closer with his staff, glaring down at his helpless victim and ready to deal the coup de grâce.

Pchanskii lunged forward with one huge fist, grabbing Boris hard in the crotch of his tattered jumpsuit and squeezing the protected indrawn testicles.

Boris shrieked and tried to pull himself free, but Pchanskii balled his other fist and slammed it into Boris's solar plexus. Again. A third time. Blinded with agony, Boris brought the titanium rod up under Pchanskii's chin, knocking him back to the dirt.

Inside the dome, Keefer and Tam held their breath as they slathered the breach with the largest self-sealing patches. In horror Keefer watched the battle turn against Pchanskii—but he could do nothing to assist the *dva*. The greenhouse dome had no weapons he could use, and if he followed Pchanskii out of the module himself, he would be dead in less than a minute.

Pchanskii lay sprawled on his back, trying to raise himself up. His expanded chest heaved for sufficient breath. But Boris did not hesitate this time. He took his long metal staff and stood over the fallen *dva* man.

Keefer watched him raise the spear. "No! Don't!" He could barely restrain himself from leaping outside.

Tam grabbed his arm. "Keef! Stop!"

Boris turned toward him, looking Keefer in the eye

for just a moment, then he jackhammered the sharp metal staff down three times, skewering Dmitri Pchanskii through the chest. Even with the clamoring noise in the greenhouse dome, Keefer clearly heard the sound of a cracking sternum. Pchanskii's blood spouted into the air.

Boris jabbed the staff in a final time for good measure, grinding it through the *dva* rib cage into the ground. The fallen doctor jerked, then lay still.

Keefer felt a sob and a scream build up within his throat. He barely noticed as he was elbowed aside. Steinberg and two assistants had arrived with armfuls of additional patches, slapping them across the breach in a crazy patchwork.

Through the last piece of the opening, Keefer watched Boris Tiban yank his staff free of Pchanskii's body and shake off red droplets before they froze into bright enamel on the titanium. He rested a moment. Then, obviously injured from the duel, he limped away, bleeding heavily from his wounds.

Only then did Keefer realize that the greenhouse had barely enough air left for him to breathe.

"Get somebody suited up right away," he gasped. "Go hunt for Tiban."

BORIS TIBAN

DRAGGING ONE LEG, Boris Tiban staggered away from the humans' base, toward the wall of crumbling cliffs they called the Spine. Like black teeth, the weathered rocks rose sheer and tall, a pile of sharp boulders like a festering geological scab.

In there Boris could find many places to hide, and heal.

His *adin* body, which had once seemed powerful enough to withstand any threat Mars or the human race could throw against him, now chanted an endless litany of pain. He tasted blood and metallic dust in his mouth.

His head pounded from the pressure of the lowlands and the thick air. His testicles and abdomen throbbed from where the *dva* madman had wounded him. Dr. Dycek herself had smashed him in the face with her bare hand, burned his forearm with the surgical laser. She was insane! His chest felt like lava where Cora Marisovna, the treacherous woman who had professed love for him, had stabbed him with his own metal staff.

As usual, the universe was trying to crush Boris Tiban. But he would not be so easily defeated. Never.

Worst of all was the ache in his proud heart with the knowledge that everyone, *everyone*, had turned against him. The humans at Lowell Base had always wanted to eradicate the superior *adins*, the true conquerors of Mars. They resented Boris's ability to walk on the surface, to face the storms, to roam free on the world they were trying to claim for their own. The *dva* bully who had come out to fight him showed how the second phase of augmented people were mere pets of UNSA.

A few days earlier, when Dr. Dycek had driven to

the top of Pavonis Mons and spoken her honeyed words, Stroganov and Cora were swept under her spell. The same thing had happened with the *adin* candidates back in Siberia. Dycek had promised them freedom and a happy life on Mars if they would first endure endless torture under her scalpel, endless deprivation on a frozen planet. Then after sixteen years of *adin* suffering, when Dycek returned to them mouthing the same empty promises, Stroganov and Cora and Nastasia had slurped up those reassurances like starving pigs at a trough.

Dr. Dycek had turned his woman away from him, stolen his child, and now she kept the baby like a specimen in a zoo.

In the shadows of morning, Boris used the bloodied staff to support himself as he staggered up the loose rocks of the Spine. His tough fingers found handholds, and he climbed, hauling himself to the next ledge. Below, he could look down and see the complex of inflatable modules, delicate as soap bubbles, that kept the helpless humans safe inside.

But not safe enough.

Boris kept climbing. Through gusts of wind from the dying storm, he could still see the motionless corpse of his *dva* attacker lying outside the greenhouse module. Let them look at that and see who was superior!

The humans would be putting on their feeble protective suits even now, coming out in a hunting party to find him—just like the security guards in Neryungri who had tried to track down the two *adin* escapees who had fled into the Siberian wilderness. But the humans would never catch Boris. He would destroy them first, one by one if need be—all at once, if possible.

He stood on a sharp outcropping of stiff, lichen-covered rock. The Spine, like many geological formations on Mars, was not completely stable. The low gravity, the climate, and the seismic silence of the planet let delicate pilings of rock stand for millennia like houses of cards.

Boris found one of the wider fissures and stopped for a moment, panting. A tacky mess of freezing blood clung to his face and flat nose. His vision blurred and refocused. Behind their protective coatings his eyes must have hemorrhaged from his exertion in the battle with the *dva* man, and he had no idea of the extent of the injuries inside his body.

Boris chose not to feel them. He chose not to think about them. Blood oozed from the reopened hole in his chest where Cora had shoved the cold titanium spear. But her betrayal burned more than the wound did.

Peering downward, Boris targeted the medical module directly below him. Long ago, Vice Commander Dozintsev had wanted the *adins* to assemble the base, like slaves preparing for their masters to arrive. Boris had refused to obey, but still he remembered about the base. He had carried Cora here, dumping her like a warning on their doorstep. In the darkness of the previous night he had come in behind the modules, staying close to the overhanging wall of rock. When he had pushed his head through the torn opening in the wall of the medical center, he had seen Cora, neatly tended and lying comfortably on a bunk, as if Lowell Base were some sort of spa. He had seen her cradling the baby in her arms. The baby!

The infant continued to live only through human beneficence—humans who did not care about the *adins*, but only wanted a charming token to show off for their newsnets. Another chapter in the poignant soap opera of the *adins* on Mars. Boris did not want to bear such a debt to his enemies—and Cora Marisovna had become a party to it! Cooperating with Dr. Dycek could only increase their misery. He could not understand why she had done it.

Boris's head pounded and throbbed, and he squeezed his heavy eyes shut, trying to untangle his thoughts. But too much hate and too much poison clouded his mind. He heard only the rushing of blood like kettle-drums in his head. He could see only that the scheming humans were to blame for everything, that Cora had abandoned him, that he could be at peace only if he destroyed them all and kept Mars for himself.

Lowell Base must be wiped out. He wanted to see the weak inhabitants gasping and choking in the open air, unable to survive on the planet they had tried to tame. He wanted to stand there and laugh down at them as they reached up with clawlike hands, begging him for help. . . .

Cora and the baby no longer mattered. He told himself they had never mattered, and he didn't want to leave any loose ends. Loose ends only came back to haunt you—just as Rachel Dycek had done up on Pavonis Mons.

Boris wedged his staff into the fissure on the edge of a wide column of rock. The outcropping jutted from the sheer side of the Spine as if barely holding on to the cliff face by its fingernails. Tiny pebbles bounced and clattered as they trickled down the path determined by gravity.

Outside the base below, four suited figures marched around the corner, emerging from one of the airlocks. Searching for him, no doubt. They would never find him.

He thrust the titanium point deeper, grinding it into the accumulated dust and getting good traction with his flat *adin* feet. His jumpsuit was stained with blood. His breaths came harsh and cold. The rocks hung poised directly over the base, over the medical module—right where he needed to strike.

His laser-burned hand was in agony, but he used his other fingers to wrap his palm around the staff, breaking the cauterized scabs, but freezing his grip in place. He shut off the pain in his mind. "An *adin* would not feel this," he said to himself. "All pain was deadened by the surgeries. I . . . feel . . . nothing!"

He gripped the staff with his other hand and began to pull, prying, working. He did not pause. Blood flowed down his arm, as the burn Dycek had made with the laser scalpel split open.

"I am not feeling this!" Boris said, closing his eyes. His voice cracked. He bit back a wail as he continued to push, hauling with all of his weight.

Dust crumbled. More pebbles broke free. He could actually feel the rock shifting. It was going to come away from the cliff! But he did not relent.

He let loose a groaning animal howl that had no purpose but to wring another burst of strength from his body. This was nothing like the playful cry he had made to frighten the *dva* as he and Nikolas stalked toward the pumping station. Boris did not care if this effort tore the very soul out of him.

The titanium staff shivered and creaked with the strain, quivering. Then the staff itself bent, twisted with the unbearable stress he forced upon it, buckling downward as he refused to let up.

Screaming at the staff in his anger, Boris twisted it and yanked—then something snapped, and the loose outcropping finally broke free, falling away from the face of the Spine, sliding sideways in a gut-sinking plunge that knocked off a succession of other boulders on its descent.

The entire ledge on which Boris stood sloughed down, grinding and picking up speed as other chunks broke away, dropping into the air. The cliffside began to pour down in a stream.

Boris tried to maintain his balance, but he dropped to his knees, holding on as he rode the avalanche down.

RACHEL DYCEK

THE BOULDERS STRUCK the side of the medical module like an out-of-control bulldozer. The reinforced structural beams snapped and caved in. The thin metallized fabric burst in a dozen places, crushed inward by the weight, exploding outward from the pressure.

The impact hurled Rachel Dycek back against the inner wall. She instinctively clamped her mouth shut to keep air inside her lungs. Cora Marisovna was thrown from her bed, but she made no sound as she landed on her knees and turned her back to the rain of rocks. She huddled with her hands over her head.

The baby, placed back inside her pressurized chamber for protection, bounced as the chamber tipped over.

The rockfall seemed to go on and on, like the grinding of monstrous teeth, until finally the boulders slid to a stop. The pressurized atmosphere fled screaming from the splits in the module wall.

Everything whirled around Rachel in a haze of mist and dust and sound. The bright lights inside the module went out, leaving them with only the dim Martian daylight in the shadow of the Spine. Dust and glittering steam spun in a cyclone around them.

Rachel crawled along the floor, but she couldn't see anything. Cold blood dribbled out of her nose. Smaller rocks had smashed and bruised her legs, but she felt no pain other than the need for air, the need to get out.

But she couldn't leave Cora or the baby. She had no more air, and her lungs felt ready to explode from the ache. She finally had to exhale in a despairing whisper. She watched the white mist of her breath wafting away like lost dreams.

Someone grabbed her roughly by the shoulder, turning her with rough *adin* hands. Rachel struggled, lashing out with her fingernails. If Boris Tiban had come to finish his work, she would claw his eyes out first if she could.

Then a mask was shoved against her face and a flow of cold oxygen trickled into her mouth. She gulped and took a deep breath, pulling in a lungful of blessed air. She clapped her own hand over the mask to hold it in place.

As the module's air continued to sweep past her, yanking her hair in all directions, Rachel blinked the spangles from her eyes, focusing enough to see Cora Marisovna bending over her with an emergency oxygen tank, the type kept in the medical module for surgery. This would keep Rachel alive for a few minutes, until she froze to death. She took another deep breath.

"You must get out of here," Cora said, shouting over the buzzing in the air. "Get help. Boris is coming!"

Still dizzy, Rachel scrambled to a sitting position, panting. Now the pain from her other injuries clamored for attention. The pressure inside her body made her feel like a swelling balloon. She thought she had broken her foot, cracked several ribs in the avalanche.

Rescuers from the base would be here any moment, Rachel knew, but they could not open the module door, not with the massive depressurization from the burst medical module. They would have to seal the corridor farther down, come to her wearing environment suits. By that time they would not expect anyone to be alive still. Rachel would have to get through the door herself if she expected to survive.

But it seemed too difficult, not worth the effort. Her body trembled as she searched for the strength to move.

"Go!" Cora said, urging her. The sudden depressurization must be just as difficult for the *adin* woman, Rachel realized, now that she had once again adapted to human conditions.

"No, you're—"

Then Boris Tiban climbed over the rubble, picking his way into the module he had destroyed. His blood-smeared body and wild, hemorrhaged eyes made him look like death incarnate.

Rachel heaved in a deep breath, drawing as much oxygen as she could from the reserve tanks. The black specks in front of her vision drew back a little, but the bone-cracking cold remained. She needed to think, but she could not stop shuddering. She had to face him. Boris.

Cora scrambled back, moving protectively to drape her arms over the pressurized chamber that held her baby.

Boris stood victorious for a full second, leaning heavily on his crooked staff as he stared down at Rachel in the rubble. But he didn't seem to know what to say. "I am here," he finally said.

"I can see that." Anger and frustration welled up inside Rachel, enough to drive away her panic, enough to quell her dismay. Boris reveled in his posturing, but she could knock the wind out of him by speaking first, by putting herself in control. With as strong a voice as she could manage, she spoke through the oxygen mask, ignoring the agony of the still-dropping pressure. "What is it you want, Boris?"

The question startled him enough that he drew back a step. He stumbled on a rock shard and regained his balance, gripping a bent support strut. His eyes flared with anger at appearing clumsy.

His moment of silence allowed Cora Marisovna to gather her own courage and speak up. "Boris, all your grand gestures are painful failures! Why won't you try talking to people for once?"

"What do you really want, Boris?" Rachel repeated, egging him on. The pain in her broken foot deadened as her lower body numbed with the penetrating cold. "Please tell me, because I can't figure it out. What do you *want?*"

Boris's mind seemed to be whirling, frustrated that

280

things had not happened as he planned. The words exploded out of his mouth, but he still looked trapped. "I don't know!"

"I can't believe it," Rachel said, sucking in another lungful of oxygen. Her body shivered uncontrollably, but she fought not to show it to Boris. "You attacked me in the rover, you tried to kill your own baby, you've destroyed Lowell Base—*and you don't even know why?*"

He came toward her again, lifting the pointed end of his bent staff, curling his lips back. He was trying to look powerful and intimidating again. "Because I want revenge. Yes, revenge. I want to kill you!"

But Rachel didn't flinch. "Why?" she asked. She could not fathom the depth of his hatred, how he had focused so much of it on her. "Why do you need to kill me so badly? Why me?"

Boris looked at her with wild *adin* eyes, thrusting with his gaze as if it were another titanium spear. "Because you did this to me! All my life I've been stepped on by people who thought they had power, and you were the worst!"

"How, Boris? How did I do this to you?" Rachel yelled over the muffling oxygen mask. She was dizzy now, on the verge of passing out. "You volunteered for the surgery. You came to me—I did not force you. It was your chance to get away from Siberia."

He shook his head vigorously, as if trying to cast loose thoughts from his skull. "I didn't know what you were going to do. I could not understand the forms filled with medical gibberish. You tricked us into becoming *adins*."

"That is ridiculous, Boris." Rachel felt her eyes freezing, her body aching with the low pressure. But she had nothing to lose anymore. The remnants of air continued to howl out of the torn walls.

"How could you not understand? Is the great Boris Tiban admitting he is stupid? We briefed you over and over again. We explained every step of the process. You knew all the risks, and you had the opportunity to back

out every step of the way. You made your own choice—
if you don't like it, stop blaming me. I'm not interested
in your excuses." She sucked in another breath. "Are
you afraid to look inside yourself for the truth?"

Crouched beside the pressure chamber holding the
wailing baby, Cora Marisovna spoke up. "Dr. Dycek
never tricked us, Boris. Even I understood it all, and
you are much smarter than I am. The *adin* surgery was
never any surprise to you—you told me that yourself."

Boris glared at her. "Who are you to talk? You were
an *adin*, and you have given birth to a human! You live
with the humans. You betrayed me to let this doctor
perform more experiments on you! The very same
doctor who caused our pain! How could you do that?"

Cora looked ready to burst with her own misery.
"To save my baby! Boris, it is your own daughter. And
you wanted to let her die. You wanted to *force* her to
die!"

Boris stood up and rapped his staff on the ground.
"If that baby is not strong enough to survive as an *adin*,
then it does not deserve to live. Mars is a harsh place,
and only the strong survive."

Inside the pressurized chamber, the baby's damp-
ened cries were still audible. Cora wrapped her arms
around the chamber, as if trying to embrace the infant.

A hairline crack appeared on the viewing window,
spreading in a spiderweb path.

"Look at your daughter, Boris," Cora said. "Please."

Boris strode over to the overturned chamber and
bent his head down, staring inside. A flicker of surprise
passed across his face, a moment of calm emotion that
seemed to frighten him. But then he stepped back as
his anger overflowed.

His *adin* face twisted into a monster's mask. Boris
whipped the titanium rod up over his head, above the
glass of the incubator chamber.

"No!" Cora wailed.

"Kill me instead, Boris!" Rachel shouted, and that
stopped him. She felt her heart pounding, tears freez-

ing in her eyes. "Go ahead and kill me, Boris, if it will make you happy." She glared at him. "I am willing to make that sacrifice *if it will heal you*. Will it? Is that all you want—all you need? Will that solve all your problems? With me dead, will you finally be at peace?"

Boris turned to her, looking trapped again. He stood like a statue, but she saw his body trembling.

"You can't fix one thing by smashing something else. It doesn't work that way." With each sentence she had to take a deeper breath. The dizziness was returning in great waves. The air was almost gone now around her, the vanishing air pressure killing her. If she didn't get out the door soon, she would never survive.

The crack in the pressure vessel's window extended another centimeter. Cora gaped down in horror, trying to cover it with the palms of her hands.

"Mars is changing, Boris," Rachel said. "Everything is forced to adapt. You must adapt, too. If you are too brittle, you'll shatter. It is better to bend."

Boris stared down at his twisted staff.

The baby cried in long, enthusiastic wails. "*Look* at her, Boris," Cora said. "She is your daughter!"

Boris turned and jumped toward Rachel, raising the staff over his head and swinging it down. She could see his muscles bunching, the curving arc of the shaft of metal. She squeezed her eyes shut as the staff whistled toward her—

With a cracking *thump*, the end of the staff struck the module floor a few inches from her head, leaving a deep indentation.

He had intentionally missed her.

Then, with an inhuman outcry that came from his own confusion and frustration, Boris Tiban scrambled away from the wreckage of the medical module. Without another word to them, he picked his way up and over the boulders, and vanished out into the blowing dust.

JESÚS KEEFER

THREE DAYS LATER Keefer himself selected the spot where Dmitri Pchanskii would be buried. The *dvas* had asked him to find the most appropriate location. It was not a duty he enjoyed as the new commissioner, not something for which his training had prepared him. But he would do his best for Pchanskii.

He wanted to find a special place where the *dva* doctor and his dreams would be remembered by the future inhabitants of Mars. If Pchanskii had indeed established a dynasty founded on the daring risks of one group of *dvas*, then there would be people on Mars for a long time to come who might make a pilgrimage to the grave site.

Keefer was accompanied by a limping but stony-faced Rachel Dycek, withdrawn Tam Smith, stunned Bruce Vickery, and subdued Amelia Steinberg. Cora Marisovna had remained back at the base, still recovering, holding her baby—whom she had named, to no one's surprise, Rachel.

Vickery drove *Percival*, which was now fully recharged and repaired, up the slope of the Spine. The AI pilot found the convoluted path and picked its way around debris stirred up by the storm, squared-off boulders disturbed by the avalanche. Morning shadows kept them in gloom on this side of the Spine; farther out, the Tharsis Plain glowed with early light, sparkling as night ice crystals volatilized into steam.

Pchanskii's wrapped body lay in *Percival*'s cargo compartment, ready for burial.

The passengers remained silent and uncomfortable, packed next to each other in environment suits, breathing the recirculated air and thinking their private thoughts. Keefer looked across the red oxide plain. Boris Tiban had vanished into the distance, leaving his footprints to be swallowed in the sea of dust. Keefer hoped they would never again see a sign of the *adin* terrorist.

After Boris's attack on Lowell Base, Steinberg and her people had been suiting up to hunt for him when the avalanche hit the medical module. The base airlocks froze up with the massive decompression. By the time her team finished donning suits and hurried outside to the scene of the wreckage, Boris had already fled.

Keefer and three others had helped a nearly unconscious Rachel Dycek push open the door to the the the main hub, dragging the oxygen tank with her as more air gushed from the intact modules. Stumbling, Cora Marisovna had dragged the pressure chamber containing her baby to the safety of the warm, humid quarters.

Amelia Steinberg had personally carried Pchanskii's body back inside the base. The *dva* doctor was nearly twice her size, but she was able to haul the large man in the low gravity. Then she and the others had toiled out in the putt-putt to chase down Boris Tiban. They had searched the rockfall up the side of the Spine, then circled the base perimeter, finally finding *adin* footprints that arrowed directly northward across the flat, rusty plain. It looked as if, moving single-mindedly, Boris did not ever intend to come back.

Now Keefer squinted out *Percival*'s front windowport as they reached the silent power reactor and its accompanying experimental stations atop the jagged crest. "This is good," he said. "Pchanskii would like it here. I meant to show it to him myself, as soon as we cleaned up from the storm."

Vickery stopped the rover on the top of the mesa. Odd-shaped lumps of battened-down meteorological stations and shielded sensitive equipment lay buried under a sheet of red dust. Vickery sighed. "It's going to be a bitch digging all this out," he said.

"We'll have plenty of time," Keefer said, feeling a difficult future open ahead of him—a challenge. By accepting it, he had already won Mars.

They squeezed through the sphincter airlock of the rover and stepped down onto the soft surface, jumping down into the blowing dust. Keefer gestured to their left. "Over there, by that outcropping. The one with all the lichen on the east face."

Inside his helmet, Bruce Vickery nodded. "That's the greenest place around here. Pchanskii would have liked that. Yeah, I think the *dvas* will come up here." Keefer looked sidelong through Vickery's faceplate and saw tears streaming down the big man's cheeks and into his beard.

Vickery had returned to Lowell Base two days before, after Keefer and Steinberg had taken *Schiaparelli* out to Noctis Labyrinthus to pick him up. Not knowing the Labyrinth well, Keefer and Steinberg had hunted through the maze. Even *Schiaparelli*'s AI had difficulty retracing its path. They searched most of the morning for the hidden *dva* doorway, since the entire landscape appeared different after the storm. Finally, it took one of the renegade *dvas* to track them down and lead them to the entrance.

Inside the tunnels, Vickery had greeted them, looking relaxed and even more amazed at the *dva* accomplishments than he had been before. Steinberg kept gaping at the lighted tunnels, the infrastructure, the stolen bits of equipment, taking an off-the-cuff inventory. But she did no more than mutter quietly to herself.

The *dvas* reacted with great sadness to the news about Pchanskii's heroic battle against Boris Tiban. The pregnant women cried out, as did many of the men, sensing that their hopes had wilted like a dying plant. Keefer insisted that he would transmit Pchanskii's message to Earth, see that the *dva* doctor's videoletter got the widest possible play on the newsnets.

The *dvas*, in turn, promised that as soon as they chose a new leader, they would work with Lowell Base to help expedite repairs.

"You'd damn well better," Steinberg growled at them. "You've got all our spare parts."

In the sunlight on top of the Spine, Vickery and Keefer removed Pchanskii's stiff body from the cargo hold. The other *dvas* had asked that he be buried there, at a high point, on the cusp of sunrise, where the terraforming could overtake him and enfold his body.

The distant sun shone through a salmon-colored sky. Tam Smith and Rachel Dycek bent down to scoop out a hollow in the loose dust, using small digging implements. Pchanskii's burial would be a mere formality; the Martian environment would quickly desiccate his tissues, leaving only an iron-hard mummy. But Keefer wanted it this way.

Pchanskii and his brash but successful actions had pointed out a harsh lesson to Keefer. The *dvas* had been given meticulous instructions about what they were expected to do, and they had been granted the equipment and support they would need. But they had refused to follow the exact orders, breaking the rules to accomplish what meant the most *to them*, not just some distant externally imposed agenda. And they had succeeded in far more than merely building another few pumping stations or metals-processing encampments.

Being told what to do, and given the proper resources to do it, meant nothing if a person's heart wasn't in the work. Sometimes, a person had to make his own decisions, regardless of the other opportunities he might be giving up. He thought of Allan.

Keefer stood motionless for a long moment, staring out at the bleakness that showed little visible mark of the decades-long terraforming activities. Then he turned to help.

They placed the *dva* doctor into the depression and scooped dust over him. Covered with the powdery iron oxide that clung to their gloves, their suits, they stood next to each other, looking down.

"We going to say anything?" Vickery asked. "Some kind of eulogy?"

Standing atop the Spine, Keefer looked out at the changing landscape of Mars. He couldn't think of words that seemed important enough.

"Up here Pchanskii can watch this planet come alive. He'll be able to watch as cities of his own descendants spring up. He'll be able to see Mars grow green." Keefer sighed. "Nothing I'd say could ever compete with that."

Steinberg and her team, Vickery, and most of the other inhabitants worked outside Lowell Base, attempting in various ways to repair the damage Boris Tiban had wrought: patching walls, repressurizing sealed rooms, laying down caulk, exhausting waste dust to the Martian air.

Inside, though, the place seemed like a tomb.

Keefer sat in the privacy booth, recording another message to his son. What would Allan think of what had happened here? Would the boy lose faith in what his father was trying to do, or would it emphasize to him just how important and how difficult the struggle for Mars could be? He thought about trying to convince Allan to keep up his studies so that he could eventually come here, too. But he had said all those words, given those pep talks too many times before. Allan had stopped hearing them.

And over the past day or so, Keefer had realized one important thing: He had never bothered to ask his son if that was what he *wanted* in the first place.

"I'm sorry if I pressured you, Allan, tried to force you to do the things I wanted you to," he said, aware of the RECORDING light out of the corner of his eye. "With the events that have occurred here, I've seen what people can do if their dreams are strong enough. With that kind of vision, you really can accomplish anything— but it must be your own dream. Not mine, not someone else's. I keep trying to make you dream my dreams."

Keefer had always seen the terraforming of Mars as a central motivation, something to be accomplished. But Keefer, with his rigid adherence to his own goal,

288

had missed the point somewhere. He didn't want the same thing to happen to his son.

"Take your own path, Allan. Dream your own dreams and choose your own destination," he said. "The future will always be there."

He smiled into the camera for perhaps a moment too long, then transmitted the videoburst.

RACHEL DYCEK

COMMISSIONER KEEFER FOLDED his hands in front of him, cracked his knuckles, then reached out to shake Rachel's hand. She gripped his paper-dry skin. He still seemed a total stranger to her, though she now wanted to open up.

While taking over her duties during the transition days, Keefer had settled in to her old office cubicle as his commissioner's desk. But Rachel no longer saw this as greedy usurpation; it was just the most appropriate place to do business. It really didn't matter to her, and she wondered if it ever had . . . or if she had just been doing her own kind of angry posturing, like Boris Tiban.

Lowell Base was Keefer's now, and she wished him the best of luck.

"Is everything ready, Dr. Dycek? Captain Rubens is establishing rendezvous times in orbit for the next window to Earth. I'm sorry you have to leave us while we're still in such turmoil."

He looked around for something on his work surface, then punched up a schedule on the embedded terminal screen. He hadn't yet had time to clutter up his new space. Rachel had left most of her paraphernalia in the desk drawers, and he was welcome to it if he could find a use for her ten years worth of odds and ends.

"Yes, I am ready to go." Rachel was certain the others in the control module were eavesdropping on the conversation. Let them have their last bit of gossip. "I am looking forward to being back on Earth."

Keefer sat straighter in his surprise and laughed once. "You *want* to go back there?" Though he was nearly her own age, he looked boyish and naïve as he blinked his dark eyes.

"Yes. Yes, I think I do."

Keefer pursed his lips. "Well, I never really got to know you here, Commissioner, but it's no secret that you fought to stay on Mars in every way you could think of." He looked down at his fingers, then straight at her. "What changed your mind?"

Rachel sat stiffly in the chair, looking across the cubicle at the new commissioner. She glanced at the walls and the curving dark support struts, at the seamed floor, at the sound-damping partition. She had removed the little touches that had made the place her own—the pictures, the arrangement of furniture— though she left the clambering vine she had grown from a cutting in the greenhouse.

"Cora Marisovna changed my mind," she said. "And Dr. Pchanskii."

Keefer raised his eyebrows, waiting for her to say more. How could she ever have seen him as a power-hungry ogre? He was merely a bright-eyed boy with a lot of new responsibility, trying to understand what was going on, but with too little time to do it.

Rachel closed her eyes. She could not explain to him that Dmitri Pchanskii's example had taught her that it was time to face the music and take responsibility— for her mistakes *and* for her triumphs. She had to take advantage of her successes and her fame, and she had to learn from her failures. That was what life was all about.

"It was something he said," she finally answered. "Rather personal."

Keefer nodded. She couldn't tell if he believed her or not.

Rachel knew she should go back to Earth to learn new tricks. *Adapt or die.* Her position had changed entirely. In only a few days, the whole situation on Mars had been thrown into chaos. On Earth she would be able to use her influence to help establish a strong future for everyone on this world.

"Let us be honest, Commissioner," she said. "I am breaking no new ground here. I am simply sitting back and watching the slow progress of the long-term mission. What good does that do?

"But," she continued, "with Dr. Pchanskii dead, the *dvas* have no spokesperson. If I return to Earth personally, I can have a much greater impact than any long-distance communication from Lowell Base. Even more than Pchanskii's last videoletter. If I accept all the speaking engagements I am offered, if I do carry the message to anyone who will hear, think of what I can accomplish. The *dvas* have a right to live their lives here, as do the few remaining *adins*. I plan to work directly with that lawyer Rotlein to make sure no one tries to take this away from them."

"If you take the *dva* side, the newsnets and the politicians will chew you up," Keefer warned.

Rachel gave him a slight smile. "I have been through all that before. They will find me hard to chew."

Keefer nodded with a smile of his own. "Yes, I suppose they will."

When Rachel had finally gone into the communications center to view the impassioned message Dr. Pchanskii had recorded only half a day before his death, she found herself profoundly moved. With tears in her gray eyes and without any preparation, she added her own persuasive speech and tagged it to the same videoburst. More people would see those few words than any other broadcast from Mars since the first surprise *adin* landing.

Then Commissioner Keefer had recorded a few concluding remarks. He had been enormously supportive, claiming solidarity with their position, even though he had nothing to gain by it. With that, any lingering resentment Rachel felt toward Keefer vanished.

"Turning Mars into a living, breathing world must not be looked on as folly," Keefer told her, looking down at his feet. "Make them understand that, Commissioner, and you will have my eternal blessing."

"You just worry about Mars," Rachel said. "Let me work with the people on Earth." People, not *subjects*. Like Cora, and her daughter, and the survivors of Rachel's efforts on the planet's surface. They had work to do on Mars, as she had her own work on Earth.

Captain Rubens had already disengaged from Phobos station and brought the transfer ship into a low orbit. The lander near Lowell Base was prepped and ready for takeoff. Rachel's allotment of personal cargo had already been stowed, along with a cargo of geological samples and sealed lichen specimens for the voracious scientific demand back on Earth.

It would be a long trip, Rachel knew, with plenty of time to plan her strategy. Four months. She felt tired already with the overwhelming responsibility, but also exhilarated.

Alive.

BORIS TIBAN

ALONE AND GLAD OF IT, Boris Tiban left Pavonis Mons behind.

Looking ahead, feeling neither the cold nor the pale sunlight on his plasticized skin, he set out across the Tharsis Plain, heading westward into unexplored territory . . . away from the taint of *human* presence.

The symmetrical cone of the volcano looked like a weather-smoothed pyramid behind him, dead and abandoned like an ancient Egyptian tomb. Equally distant to the north and south—hazy swellings at either horizon—stood two similar volcanoes: Ascraeus Mons and Arsia Mons. They held nothing for him either. They were still too close to this place.

Boris walked across the dusty plain, noting the sickening frequency of greenish lichens and algae colonies. The olive tinge on the ochre plain made the planet look like a slab of spoiled meat. Pristine Mars seemed to decay in front of his eyes. When he stooped under an outcropping of basaltic rock to rest, he found a tiny puddle of ice, naked and intact in the open air, as if the gods had spat on the world.

His footprints left a solitary path across the wasteland. Gentle winds would nudge dust particles back into place, erasing his tracks as if he had never been there. He would make no permanent mark after all.

After leaving the devastation of Lowell Base behind, Boris had hiked back to the top of Pavonis Mons, returning to his home of fifteen years. But it was empty like a haunted house.

He thought of staying there, at least until his wounds healed—but they would never heal entirely. The fire-storm of treachery had scarred and crippled him. He knew the human scientists would soon come up to study the *adin* caves with their tweezers and their magnifying glasses, their holocameras and sample collectors, to dissect exactly how the exiled rebels had lived.

The thought nauseated him.

In the deep sulfurous tunnels, Boris spent hours with bricks of rough lava clenched between his hands, scraping away the delicate words Stroganov had tediously etched onto the walls. He wanted to leave no saga for the humans to enjoy, no biased historical account for them to interpret as they argued their justifications for being on Mars. Most of all, he wanted to leave nothing behind that would allow the humans to laugh at him.

When Boris stepped out of the tunnels, aching and dust covered, he looked at the frowning faces of Stroganov's sculptures. Heroes made of clay. Lenin, Bulavin, Razin, Pugachev, Bolotnikov. They were all false.

He had no doubt that whatever stories Stroganov had told the *adins* were distorted lies, bloated retellings of mythical happenings. Boris Tiban had surpassed anything these rebels might have done in the eye blink of history. *He* had been the one to conquer a new world and make it his own—until someone else took it away from him. Would future historians ever build a statue of him, on Earth or on Mars?

He did not care. He would never see it.

With the bent titanium staff, he battered the faces of the statues, breaking off Lenin's pointed beard with one swing, cracking Bolotnikov's Cossack nose with another, splitting Pugachev's forehead and flaking away the dust-scoured eyes.

Chips of rock and mud cement flew into the air with the bright chime of metal ringing against stone. Boris kept smashing and smashing until all of Stroganov's statues were unrecognizable. Then he departed.

It took him twenty days at a forced march to reach Olympus Mons, a gigantic blister on the face of the planet. The tallest mountain in the entire solar system, it rose up at a gentle slope to the fringes of the thickening atmosphere. A glitter of what might have been frost clung to its peak, which surrounded a caldera large enough that it could have swallowed one of the smaller Sovereign Republics.

Gasping and weak, like one of her own specimens about to be dissected, Rachel Dycek had attacked him with her words. She had told him that Mars was changing and that he, too, must adapt. She wanted Boris to change himself in ways that he could not. She understood nothing.

He toiled up the side of the volcano, working his way to higher altitudes. He panted deeply, heaving to fill his four lungs with the frigid air. His wounds still caused him a constant, ripping pain, but they would heal. They would heal. He pushed onward. The pressure of the heavy lowland atmosphere made him feel sick. The headaches and labored breathing had ceased for him days before, but still he was convinced he could not live down below. He knew he could never adapt.

He needed to climb higher, where the air was thin enough, the temperature cold enough that he could live in comfort for whatever years he had left to him, where no one else would bother him. No matter how much the Martian environment altered below, he could find a place that was still comfortable to him. He would climb higher and higher, always one step above the humans.

Boris Tiban did not need to change himself inside; he would just keep scaling the heights. And Olympus Mons was very high indeed.

He stopped and turned to stare down at the plains extending around him, as far as he could see, until the foreshortened horizon swallowed the edge of the world. He could barely make out the distant lump of Pavonis Mons on the horizon. He had come very far.

The humans would continue terraforming Mars. He could never stop that. The red planet would stir with spreading signs of life, while at the same time, for him it would be dying. In a few centuries Mars would be a green world, warm and wet and bursting with new species.

Boris Tiban had no desire to live to see that day. He would reign here by himself on Mars. He would always be the king of the mountain.

For a long time, he surveyed his planet from the height, then he turned, gripped his bent staff, and climbed higher.

Red Mars
Kim Stanley Robinson

WINNER OF THE NEBULA AWARD

MARS. THE RED PLANET.
Closest to Earth in our solar system,
surely life must exist on it?

We dreamt about the builders of the canals we could see by tele-scope, about ruined cities, lost Martian civilisations, the possibil-ities of alien contact. Then the Viking and Mariner probes went up, and sent back - nothing. Mars was a barren planet: lifeless, sterile, uninhabited.

In 2019 the first man set foot on the surface of Mars: John Boone, American hero. In 2027 one hundred of the Earth's finest engineers and scientists made the first mass-landing. Their mission? To create a New World.

To terraform a planet with no atmosphere, an intensely cold climate and no magnetosphere into an Eden full of people, plants and animals. It is the greatest challange mankind has ever faced: the ultimate use of intelligence and ability: our finest dream.

'A staggering book . . . The best novel on the colonization of Mars that has ever been written'   *Arthur C. Clarke*

'First of a mighty trilogy, *Red Mars* is the ultimate in future history'   *Daily Mail*

'*Red Mars* may simply be the best novel ever written about Mars'
        Interzone

ISBN 0 586 21389 9